ALBERT FINNEY
IN CHARACTER

ALBERT FINNEY
IN CHARACTER

A Biography by **QUENTIN FALK**

Robson Books

First published in Great Britain in 1992 by
Robson Books Ltd, Bolsover House, 5–6
Clipstone Street, London W1P 7EB

British Library Cataloguing-in-Publication Data
A catalogue record for this book is available
from the British Library

ISBN 0 86051 823 X

Typeset by Columns Design & Production
Services Ltd, Reading
Printed in Great Britain by W.B.C. Print Ltd. and
W.B.C. Bookbinders Ltd., Mid-Glamorgan,
S. Wales

For Ben and Laura

Contents

Acknowledgements

Not long ago I read a review that generally accused star biographies of being 'a slavish expression of an empty consensus', going on to say that many were 'largely cannibalizations of earlier writings on the subject, avoiding serious judgement in favour of servile documentation'. It is a tough verdict but one quite difficult to refute, bearing in mind the speed and proliferation of this regularly criticized genre. Therefore, after settling on Albert Finney as subject, I was determined first of all to try to get his involvement in the project. He politely declined, indicating that the road he had travelled had a 'hard top on it' and that he wasn't interested in 'drilling it up to go over it all again'. Not for the time being, anyway. Also it seems likely that, sooner or later, he will write his own autobiography. It then became clear that Finney's non-involvement would also preclude the active participation of some other key players in the story. This has made the business of careful, original research in locations ranging from Salford and Birmingham to Los Angeles and London even more crucial in order to present what is, I hope, as full an account and judgement of Finney's life and career to date as possible.

So I'm especially grateful to the following for their

personal recall and individual contributions: Karen Allen, Lindsay Anderson, Alan Ansley, James Aubrey, Keith Ball, Trevor Bannister, Geoffrey Bayldon, Michael Blakemore, Betty Box, June Brown, Carol Burnett, Simon Callow, Charles Champlin, Terence Clegg, Anne Coates, Jennifer Collen-Smith, Michael Crompton, William Daniels, Olive Dodds, Brian Doyle, Vince Edwards, Malcolm Feuerstein, Tony Flynn, Freddie Francis, Sonia Fraser, Richard Goodwin, Robert Hardy, Nicky Henson, Bernard Hepton, Joan Hickson, Gregory Hines, Anthony Hopkins (also for permission to reproduce a section of his taped 'Nativity'), Derek Jackson, Richard Johnson, Angela Lansbury, Sidney Lumet, Ann Lynn, Gillies MacKinnon, Gillian Martell, Ferdy Mayne, Ronald Neame, Peter Nichols, Gerry O'Hara, Edward James Olmos, Jerry Pam, Alan Parker, Phil Penfold, Simon Perry, David Puttnam, John Quested, Lynn Redgrave, Karel Reisz, Jim Rose, Leslie Sands, Ridley Scott, Carolyn Seymour, Peter Shaw, Martin Sheen, Judith Stott, Felix Trott, Dave Turley, Michael Wadleigh, Peter Weller, Peter Werner, Susannah York, many more who preferred anonymity, and particularly to Michael Billington and Sheridan Morley (who also suggested the subject), both Finney-watchers since their teens.

Fulsome thanks, as always, to the many 'backroom' people who have helped me with this book: to Stephanie Billen (also for tireless library research) in London and Barbra Paskin in Hollywood for inestimable help with original interviews; Marney Wilson for transcribing tapes; Val Sillery for my index; Kevin Bourke in Manchester; Dave Price, Recording Services BBC Radio; the British Film Institute Information Department; National Film Theatre (Leslie Hardcastle); Theatre Museum (especially Barry Norman and Janet Foliett); the Shakespeare Birthplace Trust; Glasgow University Library (Elizabeth Watson); Royal Exchange Theatre Company, Manchester; Adrian Turner; Adrian Beaumont; Lee and Pauline for printing and copying; Birmingham Central Library (Steve Haste); Video

Collection International Ltd; Warner Home Video; Castle Pictures; *Albert Finney's Album* © 1977 Memo Music Ltd/ Essex Music International Ltd; and especially my agent Jane Judd and Jeremy Robson and Louise Dixon of Robson Books for their encouragement and support.

Thanks to the following writers, magazines and newspapers not already acknowledged in the text: Sue Arnold, Michael Behr, Tom Burke, Terry Coleman, Judith Cook, John Cunningham, Victor Davis, Sydney Edwards, Stephen Fay, Ronald Hayman, John Heilpern, David Lewin, Todd McCarthy, Philip Oakes, Michael Owen, Stephen Pile, Steve Pratt, Christopher Tookey, Tom Sutcliffe, Thomas Wiseman; *Cosmopolitan, Daily Express, Daily Mail, Daily Telegraph, Elle, Evening Standard, Film Comment, Good Housekeeping, Guardian, Northern Echo, Observer, Radio Times, Sunday Telegraph, Sunday Times, Times, You.* And thanks also to the books, authors and publishers listed in the Select Bibliography.

Where requested, credit has been given to photographers. Where an appropriate acknowledgement has proved impossible owing to lack of information, the publishers will rectify any omission in future printings. Otherwise, I should like to thank for the use of photographs: BBC Photographs Library (Bobbie Mitchell); Associated Newspapers Picture Library (Bob Dignum); The National Film Archive; The Sir Barry Jackson Trust and Birmingham Library Services; Birmingham Post & Mail Ltd; North West Film Archive; Dominic Photography; Sandra Lean; Lewis Morley; The Estate of Angus McBean; Woodfall Films; United Artists; Twentieth Century Fox, Universal, Columbia, Orion, Samuel Goldwyn and MGM-Pathé.

Little Marlow, London and Los Angeles, 1992

1

Masks

In any cursory overview of Albert Finney's career, one is irresistibly reminded of the story about that great Liverpool actor William Armstrong, who, when he informed his mother that he wanted to go on the stage, was told tersely, 'You'll find it cuts into your evenings'. At the turn of the sixties, Finney was the screen's incarnation of the new working-class hero. In the theatre, he was barely twenty when hailed the 'new Olivier'. Yet instead of doggedly pursuing either mantle, he became a millionaire and made love to beautiful women on several continents. Whenever routine threatened, he simply took off. To some he is still the leading actor of his generation; to others, though, he has suffered an ambition by-pass. To even severer critics, he appears to have remained cheerfully indolent, almost wilfully failing to fulfil the remarkable early promise which led to comparisons with not only Laurence Olivier but also Paul Scofield and Richard Burton, and even with James Cagney and Spencer Tracy. The truth, as this book will show, is an intriguing mixture of all three.

At fifty-six Finney has, to date, earned four Oscar nominations and won a host of awards here and in the States for his work on stage, screen and television. He has been married and divorced twice, indulged in very public affairs, owned a fortune in horseflesh, travelled to most corners of the world and become a millionaire twice over merely from profit participation in his own movies. Yet the man who, from his past and present record, would appear to be a pillar of the establishment has remained something of an outsider. Friends say that he has two distinct personalities: one moment, direct and friendly; the next, complicated and guarded. He is a Northerner.

Some commentators clearly find the lack of an 'organic' shape to his career frustrating; to others, he does what he's paid to do, he always 'delivers'. What you see is what you get. Finney himself talks about the fact there are 'no real constants' in his life: 'The pattern of my life is that there is no pattern. In work I like doing things that are different, contrasting. And I feel the same way about women. None of those that I've been involved with has been remotely alike. I'm lurching rather than pointing in any given direction.'

On- and offstage, though his close friends may be few, it's quite apparent that Finney is both admired and extremely well liked. He also appears to be at ease with himself: 'I'm perfectly rejectable. The idea I have power is a bit of an illusion. I can't, for example, make people go and see my films. Sometimes they've not seen them in large numbers.' He doesn't appear to take himself too seriously either. A journalist once wrote to him asking if he would contribute to a charity book about a provincial theatre at which Finney had appeared earlier in his career. Finney sent back an autographed photo on the back of which he'd written: 'This is me appearing as Tamburlaine the Great in the National Theatre production at the Olivier and not, as you might assume by looking at it, playing principal boy in Aladdin at the Salford Empire.'

However, the following continue, bafflingly, to be mysteries: though he is jokingly referred to by some colleagues as 'Sir Albert', he's never figured in an Honours'

List; he's among a select handful – the tiny list also includes Prince Charles, Laurence Olivier and George Bernard Shaw – who have turned down the chance to appear on *Desert Island Discs*; and, in the mid-fifties, he even managed to wriggle out of National Service.

Finney, who admits he enjoys the 'disguise' of acting, has stated enigmatically: 'I'm not sure whether the real Albert Finney has stood up – or will!'

So here are some random clues as to the 'real' Albert Finney.

August 1960 With the opening night of *Billy Liar* less than a month away, Finney was rehearsing hard when he received a call to screen-test for the role of Lawrence of Arabia in a new David Lean epic which still had the working title *Seven Pillars of Wisdom*. There had been talk of trying to get Marlon Brando to play the role, but this may well have been a ploy by the producer, Sam Spiegel, to whip up Columbia Pictures' interest in the subject (anyway, Brando was already deeply involved in MGM's remake of *Mutiny on the Bounty*). Finney arrived at Metro's studios in Borehamwood to find that this was not so much a test as a mini-movie in its own right. More than £100,000 had been spent on building quite lavish interior and exterior sets.

Lean was closely attended by his cinematographer, Geoffrey Unsworth, an assistant director, Gerry O'Hara, editor, Anne Coates, Spiegel of course and the project's adviser, Sir Anthony Nutting, an Arab expert and former Minister of State for Foreign Affairs, who'd resigned over Suez. 'Co-starring' with Finney in the test were a number of excellent 'I know the face but . . .' British actors of the period – among others Gregoire Aslan, Ferdy Mayne, Laurence Payne and Marne Maitland – playing, variously, the roles of Prince Feisal, Auda Abu Tayi and Sherif Ali.

That twenty-minute test, now residing in the National Film Archive in London on two large reels each of ten minutes' duration and marked 'Seven Pillars of Wisdom', was shot over four days and consisted of five scenes with a close-up monologue in between each dialogue sequence – in an Arab tent, a hut, around a campfire against a vivid red sunset, etc. Finney, with dyed-brown wavy hair, is first seen in a white rollneck and then, as the action progresses, in army uniform, headdress and full robes. The robes, incidentally, were being used courtesy of Sir Anthony Nutting, who'd been presented with them by a Saudi prince. They'd reappear later in Peter O'Toole's one-day test, before being relegated to cushion covers for the Nutting family's dogs.

Finney's demeanour throughout is very serious and solemn; his verbal delivery is a mixture of dialogue from Michael Wilson's draft screenplay (which preceded the final Robert Bolt version) and whole chunks of the T E Lawrence memoir; 'I was sent to these Arabs as a stranger, unable to think their thoughts or subscribe to their beliefs . . .' sounds positively sepulchral. Yet Finney, though taller and more solid than the tiny Lawrence, doesn't look unlike certain portraits of T E, and conveyed enough to suggest a curiously offbeat but undeniably charismatic quality – certainly a very different Lawrence from the one that would emerge when the lankier, more outgoing O'Toole began filming, with a different script and different cameraman, ten months later.

Finney dazzled the editor, Anne Coates, who thought him 'fabulous', and Nutting, who felt he would have been a 'marvellous' Lawrence. Lean's reaction is not publicly recorded, but Spiegel was obviously convinced, offering the twenty-four-year-old a £10,000 fee for doing the film and then a contract worth £125,000 over the next five years.

To be fair, the various inducements offered alter endlessly in the telling down the years, from a seven-, to a five-, then a four-year contract, with figures up to £250,000 bandied about. What is certain, though, was Finney's rejection of all offers. At the time, with John Osborne's play *Luther* also in the pipeline, he said that he didn't want to become just a 'property', adding that he 'didn't know where I want to be in five years' time – or tomorrow, for that matter. I hate being committed – to a girl or a film producer, or to being a certain kind of big-screen image.' He said that friends had told him: 'Nobody can force you to do something you don't want. They can lead a horse to water, but even Spiegel can't make it drink.'

More recently, Finney recalled a conversation with Spiegel during which the producer told him, 'We probably wouldn't want to change your name.' Finney thought, 'Bloody cheek. Why don't you change yours?' Added Finney 'Well he had, actually. And then he said, "You'll go to my tailor," and I thought, "I don't want any of those shiny suits." ' Lean's only reported comment on all this was Finney telling him simply that he 'wasn't interested in becoming a star.'

March 1962 Finney was just twenty-five but had already made his mark in *Saturday Night and Sunday Morning*, *Billy Liar* and *Luther* when he was invited to appear on the BBC's probing, often controversial but always popular, Sunday night interview programme *Face to Face*. Finney, the penultimate in a total of thirty-five guests throughout the show's three-year run, was one of the rare young interviewees (only Adam Faith was younger) to be given the John Freeman treatment, which had been known to reduce grown men to tears.

The lighting was harsh, the camera in relentless monochrome close-up and Freeman himself rarely seen – just a stern, disembodied voice. First came the Berlioz overture, then a series of Topolski scribbles of Finney – penned at a sitting a couple of months earlier – over the credits, and finally the introductory shot of the young actor, tousled, hands clasped and shuffling slightly, dressed in dark rollneck sweater and light suit. 'Albert Finney, would you mind telling me first of all how old you are?' By the programme's usual standards, this was a pretty gentle and relaxed affair. By about half-way through, Finney was calling Freeman 'John', and two-thirds of the way in he was puffing quite contentedly on a cigarette. The embryo fruitiness of the voice was already apparent in what seems to have been a quite carefully thought-out performance. Only in the cold light of verbatim print does Finney sound a little clumsy from time to time.

What did he spend his money on? Clothes? Horses? Women? 'Women, not tremendously, no. Horses, I don't bet.' Was his first marriage a mistake? 'No . . . I don't feel anything's a mistake, John, if you come through the other side of it.' Was there a common view of the world held by him and others from the North Country? 'Well, I don't know. In a certain sense this is a difficult thing to answer, John, because I am an interpreter. I often wondered why I am an actor. I think I am always watching and balancing, and sort of tabulating my own emotions. And the only way I can lose myself is when I'm acting. I respond to text. I am not an original artist, you know.' What, finally, was his greatest personal weakness? 'Self-indulgence, I think.'

May 1977 At Manchester's newly refurbished Royal Exchange, just across the river from his home city of Salford, Finney briefly broke into a two-play engagement to give a fund-raising concert to try and add to the £1,000 he'd already donated to the fine, 'in the round' theatre. His material wasn't the usual thespian mix of well-known prose and poetry. Instead, he used the occasion to introduce the world of Finney the sophisticated balladeer. If it wasn't for some carefully manufactured hype at the time, his only album of songs would no doubt have remained one of the music industry's better-kept secrets. *Albert Finney's Album*, as it was matter-of-factly titled, was a collection of twelve numbers, penned by the actor with music and orchestrations by an old friend, Dennis King, one-time member of the crooning King Brothers, whose biggest hit was 'Standing on the Corner (Watching All the Girls Go by)' back in 1960.

To be honest, it is a fairly turgid collection of ditties whose unmemorable rhythms range from jaunty to portentous. Not that Finney was any stranger to singing: he'd already done both a stage and a screen musical. But the contemporary reviewer who likened his delivery to a cross between Val Doonican and Frank Sinatra frankly did both those singers something of a disservice. Perhaps the most astonishing thing about the album was that it was released by Motown Records, the black soul stable better known as home of the Supremes, the Four Tops, Stevie Wonder and Marvin Gaye.

Read in isolation, the lyrics are occasionally incisive and even self-revealing. In one, Finney sings:

> What have they done to my hometown?
> They've pulled the terraced houses down
> And put the people in the sky,
> In towers twenty storeys high.

In another:

> The love we feasted on has gone and we've become
>   estranged,
> Now don't let's have another row and cause each other
>   pain.

However, if one had to settle on what appears to be closest to a personal affirmation, it must be:

> The waters of the stream of life
> Take me I know not where,
> I will ride them while I may,
> Free and easy without care,
> And I will never fear again
> The tunnel of despair.

Christmas future   Somewhere on the South Bank (with due acknowledgement to the fertile imagination and many voices of Anthony Hopkins), in a large emporium of concrete that was once a vast theatre but now houses a lunatic asylum known as the Lord Hall/Viscount Attenborough Foundation, the restless spirit of Richard Burton prowls the corridors. In this home for the waifs and strays of the performing arts and restplace for the artistically confused, Burton encounters previous denizens of the National . . .

BURTON: Wait, listen, who is there?

FINNEY: 'Allo, Richard. Still waffling on, are you, still telling those endless anecdotes?

BURTON: Hello, Albert. What are you doing here?

FINNEY: Well, I run this place as a consortium. It's a big business now. Just closing up for the night, that's all.

BURTON: Tell me, Albert, what's down there at the end of the corridor?

FINNEY: Sorry, love, you can't go down there. Even the tourists aren't allowed down there.

BURTON: But what's down there? It can't be worse than anything we've seen so far.

FINNEY: It's the Jack Tinker Ward.

BURTON: Jack Tinker . . . Wasn't he . . .?

FINNEY: That's right, love, he got too powerful in the end – Critic of the Year. After that he took over the *Mail on Sunday* and devoted the whole of the colour section to the worst performance of the month. And that was it. His power was absolute. Monolithic. He even had a column about the worst critic of the month, and after that they just started flocking here in their hundreds.

BURTON: Who?

FINNEY: No names, no pack drill. But, you know, let's say a couple of the . . . Well, not the big ones, mind you, but ones that looked like they were going to be big. You know what I mean? They had their own theatre companies, got involved in a lot of good works instead of minding their own business and making some cash and having a good time and a giggle. And if they failed their expectations, that was it – in the ear. As I said, there are one or two of the lads themselves in here as well. And Irving.

BURTON: You mean Henry Irving?

FINNEY: No, Wardle. Irving Wardle. He's down there with Mickey Billington.

BURTON: Why?

FINNEY: They'd strayed too far from the party line. Too nice, too accommodating, weren't members of the Joe Allen set.

BURTON: How shabby.

FINNEY: Yeah . . . Well, you've got to have a laugh, haven't you? That's what you should have done, Richard. Livened up a bit. You took it all too seriously, like everyone else in this place. Anyway, can't hang about, I've got to go over to the car park, make sure it's all locked up.

BURTON: Car park?

FINNEY: Yes, it used to be the Old Vic. I bought it from Honest Ed Mirvish and turned it into a multi-storey. Ed's in here as well. He's down at the Duncan Weldon Ward. Well, see you around, love. And Richard . . . have a laugh before it's too late.

2

Educating Albie

Albert Finney's birth certificate contains both a euphemism and an inaccuracy. Item 6, Occupation of father, neatly proclaims, 'Turf commission agent'. In fact, Finney Senior, third of four consecutive Alberts in the Finney line, was a bookmaker. One hesitates to add 'pure and simple', because until the 1960 Betting Act Finney often operated illegally, following in a great family tradition which dated back more than fifty years. With cards printed 'Honest Albert' and a betting board declaring, 'A Finney – Civility and Prompt Payment', Finney Sr plied, in addition to legal on-course betting, a profitable back-street trade. Bets were taken by telephone or in a yard and then transferred to bookmakers on the track. As other notorious local back-street bookies of the time – like Johnny Boden and Jimmy Downing – would doubtless confirm, it was a trade not without its fair share of adventure.

The dodge in those days was to use somebody else's house to take bets and then pay any winners out in the kitchen. The bookies would employ lookouts known as 'jockeys' or 'runners'. These would generally be unemployed men who not only kept a lookout for the police but also were prepared to go to court and be fined instead of the

bookies for illegal gambling. Naturally, it was traditional –
indeed, it was a matter of honour – that the bookmaker
would settle any fines and also pay their 'jockeys' a wage of
between five and ten shillings a day, depending on the
meeting. The rewards were clearly worth the hassle. Being a
bookmaker gave you considerable clout in the community,
not to mention an income which, particularly during the
Depression, meant you could afford the essentials and even
the fripperies that were regularly beyond your money-
strapped neighbours.

When, at the turn of the sixties, the law was eventually
tidied up, Finney Sr, like Boden and Downing, established a
proper over-the-counter business by opening one of the
new-fangled betting shops. The erstwhile turf commission
agent had officially become a turf accountant.

But just where was all this going on? Item 7 on the
certificate lists Finney's birthplace as '53 Romney Street,
Broughton'. For 'Broughton' read Pendleton. However, if
you ask Finney's aunt, who still lives in the neat little two-
up, two-down Edwardian terraced house, whether Romney
Street is in Broughton or Pendleton, she'll simply but firmly
reply, 'Salford' – period. The nearby twisting River Irwell
separates Pendleton from Broughton and also, in a more
general geographical sense, acts as the boundary between
the twin northern cities of Manchester (to the east) and
Salford, of which Pendleton is just one of a number of once
village-like communities. Finney is often mistakenly described
as a Mancunian. He is, however, like broadcaster Alistair
Cooke, composer Sir Peter Maxwell Davies, football
commentators John Motson and Kenneth Wolstenholme,
rock musician Graham Gouldman, artist Harold Riley,
union boss Brenda Dean and writer Shelagh Delaney, not to
mention the late comic actor Will Hay, musical comedy
queen Lily Elsie and playwright Walter Greenwood, a
Salfordian. They are all, of course, Lancastrians too. And
while Salford might, at first glance, seem to be totally
overshadowed by its neighbour – Manchester is, after all,

Britain's third largest city – it has collected enough references in its own right to have created a unique niche in Britain's culture; from the literary world of Harold Brighouse's *Hobson's Choice* and Greenwood's *Love on the Dole* to the alias of 'Weatherfield' in television's thrice-weekly soap opera *Coronation Street*.

Unlike most of the householders in Romney Street in the thirties, Finney Sr has no occupation listed by his name in a *Kelly's Directory* of the period. However, the Finneys' nearest neighbours down the arrow-straight street seemed to represent a wide cross-section of working folk and include a motor driver, a postman, a joiner, a plumber, a cloth dryer, an insurance agent, an iron moulder, a wire worker, a bus conductor, a cable layer, a spring axle maker, a turner, a fitter and a damper. From builder Edward Anthistle's house, at the junction of Romney Street and the main Littleton Road, which swept north to Prestwich, you could peer almost directly into the parade ring of Castle Irwell racecourse, once home of the famous Manchester November Handicap. These days, the racetrack is no more; the huge area set in a convenient curve of the river, which tops out at Kersal Dale, now houses a student village and playing fields. But in those days, for the Finneys it must have been rather like living over the shop.

Finney Sr, one of four sons, and his doughty wife, Alice (*née* Hobson), already had two daughters, Marie and Rose, respectively ten and five when their only son made his first, noisy appearance on 9 May 1936. He could soon be viewed by the neighbours in a shiny red pram.

Bookmaking wasn't the only tradition in this close-knit family. One of Finney's grandfathers was a bricklayer; a grandmother had started her working life aged eight as a 'knocker-up', ensuring that the streetful of labourers clocked in on time; and Alice, now eighty-nine and living with Marie in Davyhulme, had left school at fourteen to work in a mill. However, before quitting school, she had, it seems, appeared in school productions of *The Merchant of*

Venice and *Macbeth*, so perhaps another family tradition was quietly being forged at the time.

When Finney was just five, he and the family had to wave goodbye to Romney Street. In 1941 the Luftwaffe, once again mistaking the racecourse for the docks, caused the rafters at number 53 to buckle and the budgie to be blown out of its cage as a landmine exploded in the next street. No one was hurt but the Finneys were effectively bombed out. From the terraced house in Romney Street to their new garden semi-detached at 5 Gore Crescent, Weaste, might have been only 1¼ miles as the crow flies across Salford, but socially it represented a quantum leap for the family. Though Finney himself would later come to personify the working-class hero in several of his earliest roles, the Gore Crescent move confirmed a strictly lower middle-class status for a family, who were never really less than comfortably off.

To cross from Pendleton to Weaste also represented another kind of leap – across a stretch of depressed housing between Broad Street, Ellor Street and Hankinson Street (known notoriously as 'Hanky Park', though, as the old joke went, the only grass that grew there was between the cobbles). In these 2 solid square miles of cramped housing and seething humanity – made famous by Greenwood's *Love on the Dole* – were crammed 3,300 terraced homes, with outdoor lavatories or 'ginnells', and families frequently boasting between eight and ten children each. Despite, or perhaps because of, so much cheek-by-jowl poverty, Hanky Park promoted an amazingly close-knit community, but now, like so much of Salford, the area has changed its face or gone altogether in the course of massive – some say savage – redevelopment. Hanky Park today is no longer even cobbles but a relentless series of dreary high-rise flats, apparently matched by an equally high crime rate.

As if to prove the exception, Gore Crescent, just to the west of Hanky Park across Langworthy Road, nowadays probably looks pretty much as it did when the Finneys first moved there: a gentle, leafy curve with a pleasant stretch of green, Buile Hill Park, just a street north and, at its junction to the east with Weaste Lane, Salford Rugby League football ground. Within short walking distance too of number 5, a twenties-built, two-storey semi-detached with bow windows was Finney's first school, Tootal Drive Primary, where the stocky youngster quickly began to exhibit an ability to mimic. So when he got involved in the school's puppet theatre, he found himself playing many of the parts rather than operating the puppets. He was a shepherd in the nativity play and the mayor of Ratville in a production called *Belle the Cat*. He could imitate animals so well that at the age of ten he was taken by his mother along to the BBC in Manchester for an audition.

At a time when horse-drawn trams were just beginning to convert to electric traction, Salford Grammar School – motto '*Audendum Dextra*', or Fortune Favours the Brave – first opened its doors in 1904 at Peel Park. Ten years later, it moved across the railway line to new buildings in Leaf Square, but the timing couldn't have been more unfor- tunate, for just two weeks after the pupils had transferred, war was declared and they all had to shuffle back to Peel Park so the new school could be used as a military hospital. The reoccupation of Leaf Square in 1918 coincided with an amendment of the school agreement which meant that pupils could stay to the end of a four-year course. Three years on, with the roll up to 440, this was further altered so that pupils could attend for five years, leaving aged sixteen.

Eric G Simm, MA (Cantab), nicknamed 'Eggy', the school's fifth and perhaps most influential headmaster, arrived at Leaf Square in 1945, having been Assistant Education Officer in Hertfordshire and, before that, a senior English teacher in a number of schools. Simm, a gaunt, rather severe-looking man of medium height with hair parted high on his head, took over at a time when the school had barely recovered from yet another war, but he quickly made an impression, encouraging the growth of a sixth form – which would result in a rash of academic awards and university entrants over the next decade – and the development of a proper canteen, biology laboratory, music room and library. In 1945 there was no school stage and those plays that were performed were staged either in premises hired for the purpose or on an improvised structure put up by the Works Department. Simm, who was mad keen on the theatre, was determined to improve school drama. In February 1948 the school's first ambitious venture, *Merrie England*, was staged, although it was necessary to book the Co-Operative Hall for the performances. A year later, however, a stage of sorts had been built at the school, thanks partly to a grant from the Education Committee and partly to funds from the Parents' Association. Curtains were also generously donated. So when the school's first full-length play, Shaw's *Arms and the Man*, was staged in February 1949, it marked the beginning of a new tradition of high-quality drama, manifested in a series of increasingly ambitious shows.

In the days before the eleven-plus, entry to grammar school was by scholarship, and Finney gained his with sufficient ease to ensure a place in the top stream. However, the euphoria was short-lived when, at the end of the first term, he was relegated to the bottom stream, where he stayed for the next four years.

The main problem was that Finney seemed to regard homework, which was plentiful, as a monstrous imposition. He'd spread ink on his exercise book and later explain the blots covered up his homework. On another extraordinary occasion, the eleven-year-old seriously planned to run away to a favourite old family holiday haunt, 'Fish Mountain', part of Prestatyn Heights in North Wales, rather than face his maths master with uncompleted prep. He actually got to the station before discovering that no trains went from Salford to Prestatyn or Rhyl and so had to creep home and climb in through a lavatory window. What, he always wondered, was the point of homework when he could be playing sport, going to the pictures or shooting a few frames of snooker at the room above a nearby branch of Burton's. He even baulked at the routine of piano lessons. Each week he'd be sent off to his piano teacher clutching half-a-crown, which he'd then spend at a miniature golf course near the house. His cover was blown when the teacher finally asked Finney's parents if the boy was ill as he hadn't turned up for two months.

By all accounts, Finney was a fine young sportsman – a sturdy centre three-quarter, useful wicketkeeper-batsman, decent tennis player and reasonable swimmer, excelling with a swallow dive off the high board. The school, which introduced rugby union alongside soccer in 1947, gradually built up a formidable fixture list against schools like De La Salle, Cowley, Stockport and Wade Deacon, and early defeats soon turned into regular victories. As well as earning school colours for rugby and cricket, Finney played rugger for the local Albert Schweitzer club and cricket for the junior section of Weaste CC.

His enthusiasm for Rugby quite clearly came from his and his friends' noisy support for Salford RLFC, and in particular stars like scrum-half Tommy Harrison and the big forward, Bomber Brown, who helped Salford get to Wembley in those far-off days when the club was still in its prime.

As for the cinema, you could barely move 100 yards in Salford without bumping into a picture house. During Finney's early teens, he would go twice, maybe three times, a week to the movies. There were no fewer than twenty-four cinemas in the city and Finney claimed to have visited them all: the Alexandra, the Ambassador, the Arcadia, the Bijou, the Carlton, the Central, the Cromwell, the Dominion, the Embassy, the Empire, Trafford Road, the Empire, Great Cheetham Street, the Kings, the Langworthy, the Olympia, the Palace, the Poplar, the Prince of Wales, the Rex, the Rialto, the Royal, the Scala, the Tower, the Victoria and the

Weaste. And this excludes another eight that had closed
before 1947. The Weaste, the Langworthy and the
Ambassador, where *Hobson's Choice* enjoyed its Salford
'première', were the closest to home and so the most
regularly frequented. At the Ambassador on Langworthy
Road – for many years now a bingo hall – for one and
ninepence, you'd get Pathé News, trailers, a cartoon, a
second feature and the main film. Now there's just one
cinema left: a new-style multiplex on the redeveloped
Salford Quays.

When he wasn't playing in teams or watching films,
Finney frequented a dance hall in Eccles and also spent time
at the nearby Seedley Youth Club, off Langworthy Road,
where on Saturday mornings the youngsters could play their
records. According to schoolfriends like Derek Jackson,
Alan Ansley and Keith Ball, Finney was a confident and
optimistic youngster, not to mention a good and loyal
friend.

As well as playing and watching much sport together,
Jackson recalls holiday hiking trips to the Lake District and
camping at Edale and Hayfield in the High Peaks, south-
east of Manchester, while Ball especially remembers a two-
week school 'educational' trip to Favège in the Haute-Savoie
near Annecy. It began badly with a horrendous rail journey
disrupted by drunken Luxembourgers, but ended well with
Finney entertaining everyone on the coach. Family holidays
were much enjoyed too, with Blackpool as well as Prestatyn
a regular favourite. Ansley says that the Finneys were
always a friendly family: 'When Albert and I were school
friends, Marie was married and had left home and Rose
(who later married the playwright Richard Harris) was
working for Columbia Pictures in Manchester. Father and
son seemed to have a great rapport. Though not physically
similar, they both had the same kind of quiet smile.'

Finney, who was taken by his father to the races – to
Castle Irwell, Haydock Park, 9 miles away, and even York
– from the age of eight, later described him like this: 'He

was a wonderful man. He wasn't a big man. Emotionally, he was very inhibited. He had a father who had four sons and his father did not want the sum total of his sons' personalities to add up to his. My father was very sensitive.' That sensitivity, he suggested, didn't go too well with the business of being a bookie.

With his mother's endless encouragement, his head-master's enthusiasm and his own penchant for mimicry – a passable Robb Wilton and Al Jolson had by now been added to the usual repertoire – Finney was soon sucked into the school's Dramatic Society.

After his début in *Clipper Ships*, as a grizzled, pipe-smoking nightwatchman – though the youngest member of the cast he was playing the oldest role – there was no holding him and he notched up fifteen plays in the next fifteen terms.

Among the more memorable performances were Mrs Joe Gargery in *Great Expectations* (still sporting a black eye from cricket), the title role in O'Neill's *Emperor Jones*, with boot polish and mannerisms adopted after closely observing black seamen at the nearby docks, a wild-eyed Ali in *Hassan* and, in his last year, a heavily padded Falstaff in Shakespeare's *Henry IV*. Simm also revived the school's Declamation Shield, initially with one boy from each of the four houses – Seedley (Finney's house), Pendleton, Weaste and North – reciting passages of verse and prose at Junior, Intermediate and Senior levels. Finney, like another fellow school actor, Harold Singer, who'd later become a success-ful QC, was a dab hand in that competition, once even delivering his entry in broad Scots.

By this time, after a new burst of academic activity had swept him back into the top stream only to see him relegated again when it as quickly dwindled, the future began to beckon worryingly. His O levels were a disaster, with two complete sittings yielding just one pass – in geography. Had, Simm asked Finney, he ever thought of the Royal Academy of Dramatic Art – RADA? Finney looked blank. It was in London, he would be there two years and they'd train him properly to be an actor, the headmaster explained. Though the teenager took school acting seriously, he had never thought beyond it or even considered the implications of his obvious talent.

He was fifteen before he went to the theatre for the first time, on a school trip to the Manchester Library Theatre to see some Shakespeare, and he joined the party only because it meant he could get out of schoolwork for the afternoon. If anything, it was his love of films, particularly gangster movies, that triggered off the sketchiest thoughts of becoming an actor.

Finney told his parents what Simm had suggested. His mother, who'd read a recent newspaper story about the number of actors out of work, was slightly hesitant. His father was more sanguine: 'Well, let him go, and if he doesn't like it he can always come back into the business.' That decided Alice; she'd much prefer him to be an actor than a bookmaker, so she firmly backed the RADA move. Simm was clearly delighted by the decision, although he later refused to take any great credit for it.

I'm no Svengali . . . Anyone would have seen a great future in that boy. He's just a natural genius, a truly committed actor. He likes to pretend he was a hopeless duffer at school – he says I sent him to RADA because I knew he would keep failing his exams – but don't you believe it. In fact, with his intelligence he could have succeeded in anything he put his mind to. But thank heaven he decided to be an actor.

Any account of Finney's life to date cannot emphasize too strongly the formative influence of Salford Grammar School. But like so much else in the city, it has long gone. The school moved from Leaf Square in 1956 (the old buildings now house the Salford College of Technology) and stopped being a grammar school altogether in the mid-seventies. Memories, though, are regularly revived in meetings of the Old Salfordians, occasionally attended by Finney.

The plan was that Mrs Finney would accompany her son to London for the RADA audition, but when daughter Marie tried to book them a hotel she ran into a major obstacle. This was 1953 and coinciding with her brother's schedule there just happened to be a Coronation taking place. Every hotel in London seemed to be full.

The story then goes that father, after leafing through a guidebook, said, 'What about this one? The Dorchester. Try there.' Success. A room was reserved for 'Mrs Finney and son', and when they arrived, it turned out to be an extremely grand affair; in fact, a suite, no less, with a cot provided for 'son'. But could they actually afford it? Mrs Finney counted up her cash, which consisted of £38. The auditions were on Tuesday and Friday, so at £5 a night they could just about make it, so long as they kept their eating and drinking to a minimum.

Sporting a crew cut and an unashamed Salford accent, and being, frankly, hundreds of miles from his natural habitat, Finney needed all his natural confidence when he first passed through the portals of RADA in Bloomsbury. He still managed to land the Lawrence Scholarship, one of a number of grants offered by the Academy. At only seventeen, he was easily one of the youngest men there – many, having completed National Service, were already in their twenties – and he felt, on his own admission, 'unsophisticated, ungainly, clumsy and a bit uncouth'. After halting progress at first, things began to click in his third term. He told critic Ronald Hayman:

I'd enjoyed school plays and at RADA suddenly something you'd been uninhibited and free about became like work. And work had been something I'd not wanted to do all through my adolescence, and the craft side of acting worried me a bit.

You tended to be told how many steps to take by some of the teachers there. You'd got to control your breathing and the pitch of your voice. But then it changed. I remember almost thinking deliberately, 'I'm not going to go on at rehearsals saying the rest of the class is laughing at me. I'm going to say they're *learning* from me.' It was almost as deliberate a conceit as that. I realized that I had to make a positive step from feeling self-conscious with my classmates.

Thanks to the helpful prompting of one of the teachers, Wilfred Walter, a one-time actor who'd lost a leg through injury, and the juicy role of Sir Toby Belch in a production of *Twelfth Night*, Finney gained new confidence. At the first rehearsal they were blocking out moves and when it came to Finney's initial entrance, he checked the script and asked Walter where he should come in from. 'Come in from where you like,' was the reply. Finney's initial response was that this was an awful responsibility, 'but he gave me such freedom by doing that, by not imposing on me a way of acting, that I suddenly felt very free'.

In a vintage period at RADA, Finney's fellow students, though not all exact contemporaries, included Peter O'Toole, John Stride, Frank Finlay, Roy Kinnear, Bryan Pringle, Richard Briers, Virginia Maskell, Brian Bedford, Gary Raymond, Alan Bates, Peter Bowles, Keith Baxter and Gillian Martell. It was a great time for asserting your personality as strongly as possible, in terms of clothes and attitude. One girl even used to wander about with a boa constrictor round her neck.

Gillian Martell, who was Thea to Finney's Lovborg in a student production of *Hedda Gabler*, said that Finney reminded her of James Dean: 'He did that great moody thing and would wander around with his head down. I remember asking him about it and he explained, "I go downstage with my head down, then I look up and give the audience *my eyes!*" I thought this was wonderful.'

An aura of mystery began to develop around Finney. When, aged eighteen, he left RADA to tackle National Service only to return some weeks later, it was said that he'd managed to throw a convincing fit to get out of his two-years' hard. Then there was the name. This was still the period before *Look Back in Anger* and so actors' names tended to err towards the romantic. 'Albert Finney', redolent of football and ale, was clearly a vexation to some. The *Daily Herald* actually organized a competition to come up with some alternatives: suggestions included 'Hank Peters' and even 'Halbert Finisterre' – because it was thought that this would at least get a plug several times a day on weather forecasts. However, it was finally decided to leave the young man and his name alone.

When the students weren't quaffing coffee at nearby Olivelli's, there were classes and rehearsals. The staff at RADA included Clifford Turner, author of the influential *Voice and Speech Training in the Theatre*, Hugh Miller, master of technique, and the veteran Ernest Milton, in the great 'actor-laddie' tradition. For the women, there were Ellen Pollock, Mary Duff and Mary Phillips.

During Finney's time there was also a change of principal, with the long-serving Sir Kenneth Barnes being succeeded by the more down-to-earth John Fernald. Fernald was always very anxious to refute the suggestion that RADA was somehow a snob nursery for stage-struck Southerners, and was even more contemptuous of the notion that the Academy fostered a 'RADA accent', pointing out that the 300 or so students accurately reflected all corners of the British Isles.

Barnes was, however, still in the hot seat when, in December 1954, RADA was able to open its new private theatre, the Vanbrugh, in Malet Street, on the site of the earlier theatre which had been destroyed in 1941. The gala show, devised by Barnes, was intended to 'show the stage equipment and trace the traditions of drama through the ages'. The programme was produced by the playwright John Whiting, who was also responsible for the prologue and linking dialogue between scenes ranging from Greek tragedy to Christopher Fry.

There were ten items in all, given before a royal guest, the Queen Mother, and Finney appeared in two – most substantially as Third Neighbour in Fry's *The Boy with a Cart* and, minutely, among the Courtiers and Villeins in a section of *Adam*, an early Anglo-Norman play. Among the other highlights were Stride and Maskell in a scene from *Romeo and Juliet* and Angela Crow as Prue in a part of Congreve's *Love for Love*. Finney was also, from the wings as it were, able to observe a slice of the old Cornish mystery play, *The Three Maries*, which had been rehearsed by Ernest Milton. Years later, Finney and Alec Guinness would read the lessons at a sparsely attended memorial service for the distinguished old actor.

First royalty, then the Great British public. Finney was still only nineteen when, in January 1956, he was Mr Hardcastle to the older Kinnear's Tony Lumpkin in a production of *She Stoops to Conquer*, involving RADA's finals students. As this was also transmitted by the BBC, it could be officially designated Finney's first professional appearance. Many years on, Finney, who had almost worn away a recording of Mel Brooks's classic comedy routine 'The 2,000-year-old Man', was offered the role of Lumpkin in a mooted Brooks's retread of the Goldsmith, but the project came to naught.

Yet an event much more significant than any of this for signposting Finney's future – aside from, at eighteen, losing his virginity – occurred a month later at the Vanbrugh Theatre. This was Fernald's production of Ian Dallas's *The Face of Love*, a modern-dress version of *Troilus and Cressida*. A promising play, it seems, but with one great reservation, according to Kenneth Tynan, the *Observer*'s controversial twenty-eight-year-old theatre critic.

'Why,' wrote Tynan, 'having garbed his Trojans in modern dress and chosen as his theme the contagious faithlessness of war, does Mr Dallas drape his climaxes in verse – and bombastic, quasi-Marlovian verse at that?'

But of the young actor playing Troilus, Tynan had no qualms. Here in Albert Finney, he told his avid Sunday readers, was a 'smouldering young Spencer Tracy ... an actor who will soon disturb the dreams of Messrs Burton and Scofield'.

3

Station Streetwise

Tynan's eulogy was somehow the logical climax to a gathering storm of enthusiasm which had rapidly been growing round the apprentice actor in his last year at RADA. More obviously practical appreciation came in the form of approaches from London's omnipotent theatrical management, H M Tennent, run by the formidable 'Binkie' Beaumont, and also from the Rank Organization, always looking to add new 'faces' to its well-scrubbed stable, officially designated the Company of Youth but by then better known as the Charm School.

According to Olive Dodds, Rank's director of artists, the company's design was 'to harness as many of the confirmed star players as would fit into the spread of filmscripts waiting to be made or being discussed and developed; and, in addition, to look for new young players or personalities who could be helped to develop into a new, additional line-up of box-office, or at least well-known supporting, artists'. It was in this latter category that, on the recommendation of Mary Duff, who coached at RADA (and scouted for Rank), Finney was summoned to Organization head-quarters at 38 South Street. Mrs Dodds's memory is hazy about the actual encounter but one of the fading cards in her artists' index records that on 19 December 1955 she noted of Finney, 'Liked him very much. Would like to test.' However, bravely resisting the lure of becoming one of Binkie's boys or part of a Brylcreemed roster that included the likes of Patrick McGoohan, David McCallum, Tony Wright and Ronald Lewis, not to mention yet another offer from a rival film company, Associated British, Finney instead decided to head North and join the Birmingham Rep at £10 a week.

It should also be noted that as Finney made his way to the Midlands, he'd left RADA 25 guineas richer, having been awarded the Emile Littler prize at the end of his two-year course. The Littler was one of a number of prizes handed out after the annual public matinée, the last of its kind, featuring the final division students in a nerve-wracking show given before critics, agents, friends and families, not to mention a panel of judges. Sitting in judgement on 27 March 1956 at Her Majesty's were playwright Clemence Dane and stage stars Margaret Leighton, John Clements, Eric Portman and Laurence Naismith. Finney's showcase was Act II, scene I of *The Taming of the Shrew*, in which he was Petruchio to Liz Yeeles's flame-haired Katherina, and among the other performances that day were extracts from *As You Like It*, O'Neill's *The Long Voyage Home* and Chekhov's *The Proposal*. One of the judges' programmes from the occasion contains several revealing margin notes. Richard Briers showed 'considerable promise' in Molière's *Sganarelle*; Gillian Martell's Natalia in *The Proposal* was 'well done'; Keith Baxter gave a 'sensitive performance' in the O'Neill; while one unfortunate actress in *As You Like It*, though 'promising . . . slouches, lacks deportment'. Of Finney, the verdict was 'vigorous and competent'.

After the show the students made their way back to the Little Theatre at RADA, where they were then informed of the judges' decision. Martell won the top prize, the Bancroft Gold Medal; Briers, the silver; and Keith Baxter, the bronze. In awarding Finney his prize, the judges declared that he had shown 'outstanding talent and aptitude for the professional theatre'. The prize was all the more poignant in view of Finney's preferred destination, as a quarter of a century earlier Emile Littler had managed Birmingham Rep.

Finney's declared aim at the age of nineteen was 'repertory, Stratford and the West End'. With this kind of single-mindedness, it was really no surprise that he should opt so happily for the financial poverty of Birmingham over the potential riches of Rank, Associated British Pictures Corporation or, for that matter, Tennent's. After all, Birmingham could boast Olivier, Ralph Richardson, Felix Aylmer and Paul Scofield among its earlier alumni. And for someone who'd already been mentioned in the same breath as both Olivier and Scofield, what better than to follow a similar 'prentice path?

Founded in 1913 by a wealthy entrepreneur and theatre lover, Barry (later Sir Barry) Jackson, Birmingham Rep, even in the fifties, could still reasonably boast the best company in the land (Bristol Old Vic, who'd snared O'Toole, might possibly have demurred): adventurous in its varied material and renowned for discovering new actors, playwrights and directors. Tucked away in Station Street (just two minutes from the New Street terminus) the Rep remained a magnet for both fresh and established talent as well as enthusiastic audiences.

According to the Rep's Boswell, the late critic J C Trewin, who enthusiastically chronicled the theatre's life and times in a regular *Birmingham Post* column, Sir Barry – a tall, slightly aloof man and a chainsmoker who used a curious, long, home-made holder – saw:

> repertory theatre not as an annexe to the West End but as a revolving mirror of the British stage ... He had great courage, believed in the fresh inspiration of youth (if not its excesses) ... [and] though he thought poorly of the star system, he understood more than

anyone about the creation of stars. Jackson was both a man of the theatre and the theatre's patron; and though he was lucky enough to be rich, I am sure that, even had he been near-penniless, nothing would have kept him away from his destined course in the theatre.

He had to face jealousy and ignorance – the Repertory was sometimes called 'a rich man's toy' – but he laughed these off, even if, like Shakespeare, he could find it hard to forgive the cardinal sin of ingratitude. Through half a century of the stage his name stood for infallible taste.

Rather less than a decade after Sir Barry's death in 1961 (aged eighty-one), the company eventually moved to new custom-built headquarters in Broad Street; the Station Street hall was turned over for hire to amateur companies and became a permanent base for the city's Theatre School. The Old Rep Theatre, as it's now officially called, is presently wedged between a conventional picture palace, the Tivoli, on one side and a sex cinema (where they once used to keep the props) on the other. Enter through the stage door in Hinckley Street to the rear, and nowadays there's quite a warm, welcoming feeling, with carpet on the floor, concealed lighting and a conventional bar. In Finney's day, the atmosphere was distinctly spartan: marble floors lay uncovered and the lighting was bare. It was rather like 'a very clean but large gentlemen's lavatory', according to another alumnus, Bernard Hepton. It was said that this austerity concentrated the mind wonderfully. In the two main dressing rooms on the first floor – the chorus is another floor up – there are still traces of the old gas mantles. Down the passage was Sir Barry's old office, now a VIP room, which was bigger than both the dressing rooms combined. Through the Green Room at stage right, you can wander out on to the stage and into the auditorium, where the old, rather dingy-looking dark browns and beiges of the Rep's heyday have been more cheerfully refurbished.

The seating for around 400 is, as before, steeply, not to say quite alarmingly, raked, with a small balcony perched high up at the back. As for the stage itself, the proscenium is surprisingly small – surprisingly because one of the most regularly remarkable features of productions down the years were the sets, often huge and innovative, certainly elaborate, and nearly all making a mockery of the theoretically confined space. This stunning design was pioneered at the Rep by one Frederick William Severne North, better known as Paul Shelving, who arrived at Birmingham after demobilization in 1919 and spent the greater part of his working life there before retiring in the year Sir Barry died. As early as 1924, it had been written of this designer–management team: 'Shelving and Jackson have raised this theatre, so far as scenery is concerned, to a high place among the art theatres of the world.' Between 1919 and 1961, Shelving reckoned he had worked on at least 185 productions at the Rep. The tradition was maintained by another fine designer, Finlay James (known as Jimmy Finlay), who alternated with Shelving in the older man's later years and continued up to and beyond the Rep's eventual change of location. The design was perfectly complemented by Sid Webster's spectacular lighting, using his own Heath Robinson-style board. He had complete control through a show, so if anything went wrong – say, for instance, someone 'dried' – he was given a cue and could do something about it.

The Old Rep may, if one listens very carefully, occasionally echo with some long-ago sounds, but otherwise there is now little tangible reminder of the great days. A carpet covers the cold marble; there are no photos nor posters on the walls; and only a small blue plaque high up on the front of the building is proof that Jackson and his company were once here.

Mind you, that sort of anonymity is perhaps in keeping with the tradition of the theatre, if one is to believe Sir Barry, who, despite loyally large houses, constantly fretted that the local population for ever seemed ignorant of the thespian jewel in its midst, not to mention its actual location. The last was certainly true, according to Bernard Hepton, who together with the theatre's director Douglas Seale auditioned Finney after the young man had been recommended to Sir Barry by RADA's John Fernald: 'We thought he had something special . . . though we didn't know quite what.'

This uncertainty probably accounted for the fact that in early April 1956, some three or four months after the audition, Finney was even later arriving at the Rep than was originally intended. The arrangement was for Finney to come to the theatre to 'play as cast'. As Hepton said:

> We knew he was already going to be a week late for his first rehearsal because he had a final show at RADA. In a company, everyone clusters round the cast list to see what they're playing and much ribaldry goes on. When the list went up for *Julius Caesar* and they saw 'Albert Finney – Decius Brutus', to a man they said, 'Who the hell's that? He'll have to change his name.' During the first reading, I had to explain why he'd be late joining, which didn't go down too well either.

Geoffrey Bayldon, one of the company's leading actors at the time, added: 'When we heard that Albert was coming, heralded by the tremendous Tynan notice, we certainly were saying among ourselves that he'd better prove himself, this upstart. We were just waiting to see what was wrong with him.'

And then he arrived – at New Street Station, where, traditionally, he asked for directions to the Rep and, just as traditionally, no one appeared to know. So by the time he finally turned up at the theatre on the appointed day, it was already mid-morning and coffee-time. The day was cool and the reception even icier. According to Hepton, who was directing the production:

In those days, when he was upset, Albert used to go very white, rather puddingy and a bit sweaty. Here he was, suddenly in our midst, wearing an old, short duffle-coat, hair all over the place, his little Temple Shakespeare in his pocket, and distinctly nervous. I tried quickly to make him welcome but you could tell that everyone was sort of agin' him. Then we started and, for the rest of the morning, we were just 'blocking' him in to what had been marked out before. The duffle was round his shoulders, he was still white with cold and he gripped the Temple. At lunch we broke and, apart from Albert, who was sorting out things at the theatre, went over to the pub (the now defunct Black Lion) and, to a man again, everyone said, 'He doesn't need to change his name; he's a star.' During that morning, I was out front and, though his nose was stuck in the book, I couldn't take my eyes off him. What makes that happen? It must be something to do with concentration. A deep confidence that conveyed that this was *the* place to be. Albert was totally his own man from the very start.

The local paper acknowledged the newcomer – auburn-haired, good-looking with a quality of toughness' – while Trewin, in his review of Julius Caesar, noted briefly but presciently: 'He is a young actor to observe.'

Compared with fortnightly or even, God forbid, weekly rep, the monthly regimen at Birmingham was luxury; three to three and a half weeks of rehearsals, changeover on the Sunday, dress rehearsal Monday and then open Tuesday. Normal productions would run from three to four weeks, with the annual Christmas show usually lasting seven or eight weeks. Following that icy introduction, Finney, embarking on the first of no fewer than nineteen plays during his two years with the Rep, was quickly drawn in to what was a very happy and close-knit company. It was a fine, distinctly unstarry, ensemble, led by actors like Ronald

Hines, Geoffrey Bayldon, Kenneth Mackintosh, Geoffrey Taylor, Colin George, Doreen Aris and Nancie Jackson (no relation to Sir Barry), not to mention Bernard Hepton, who as well as regularly appearing in plays was also serving as second-string to the internationally renowned Douglas Seale. When Seale left Birmingham in 1957, Hepton officially took over as Director of Productions for the next four years. Sir Barry, still vigorous in his late seventies, would pop into the theatre a couple of times a week to talk to his faithful administrator, Nancy Burnham, or consult over coffee with the director. He rarely spoke to the rest of the company.

After doubling as Decius and Strato in *Julius Caesar*, Finney, now just twenty, played in quick succession George Boleyn in – 'for the first time on any stage' – Peter Albery's historical drama *Anne Boleyn*, Belzanor in Shaw's *Caesar and Cleopatra* and Cleante in a BBC Birmingham production of Molière's *The Miser*, directed for television by Barrie Edgar, formerly of the Rep himself. Philip Hope-Wallace wrote of Finney in the *Listener*: 'He has a most amusing face and looked like a younger edition of Quinn (as Hogarth painted him) . . .'

Caesar and Cleopatra, intended to mark the centenary of GBS's birth, must have been quite a summer adventure for all concerned since, after the requisite month in Station Street, it was off to Paris following an invitation to the Rep from the prestigious International Theatre Festival. Sir Barry was regularly asked to lend his company to various festivals and, just as regularly, he would refuse. According to Hepton: 'He was very singular in his attempt to put Birmingham on the map as *the* place for the arts, so anything else seemed to him a diversion. In this case, he gave way, but permission was only grudgingly given.'

At the splendid Théâtre Sarah Bernhardt, all reds and golds, in the Place du Châtelet, they encountered a proscenium more than twice the width of their own. However, according to the critics, they rose – perhaps it should be 'widened' – to the occasion, in their final performance even managing to compete favourably with the fireworks outside on Bastille Night. The next day they flew home, and it was off briefly to the Malvern Festival for a few days before bringing the Shaw caravan finally to a halt – for a full fortnight – at the Old Vic in London. By this time, wrote Trewin, 'it was with the nonchalant command of a cast that, almost at the drop of a dagger, would have skated through *Caesar on Ice* at Wembley'. Offstage, Finney and his fellow actor Michael Robbins were also gainfully employed playing, respectively, ocarina and drum 'to suggest the mystery of the Nile at night'.

As a schoolboy in nearby Leamington Spa, Michael Billington, now theatre critic of the *Guardian*, was, from the mid-fifties, a regular and enthusiastic visitor to the Rep. Seated high up, 'staring precipitously down, with the smell of coffee coming up from the bar in the foyer, it was a fantastic place to be because you could see the whole of world drama there season by season,' he recalled. 'It was the Oxford or Cambridge of repertory theatre, so any actor who wanted to earn his spurs usually went to Birmingham, which was why people like Tynan would go up there regularly to see the productions.'

On an autumn afternoon in 1956, young Billington dropped into the theatre to see a:

prankish, whimsical Irish melodrama ('an Eire-faery midnight,' Trewin described it) called *Happy as Larry* by someone called Donagh McDonagh, whom I've never heard of before or since. The only thing I remember of the play is that there was a chorus of six dancing tailors who all came on in sober black with measuring tapes around their necks and danced across the stage in formation, like a Tiller Girls' chorus line. In the midst of them was this extraordinary figure who had very square shoulders, a bullet-like head and thick-set body. With his round moon-calf face, shoulders protectively hunched and centre-parted hair, ironed flat across his head, he looked as if he had bounced straight out of some sepia photographs of Irish village life. You simply couldn't take your eyes off him. I must then have seen Finney in at least half a dozen other things he did at the theatre after that and what always astonished me was his combination of enormous physical power, weight and muscularity, combined with an extraordinary impishness, humour and sense of mischief on the stage.

Billington also recalls once walking past Finney as the actor was making his way from New Street Station to the theatre: 'What struck me was the confidence with which he held himself. It was that certain set of the shoulders. He didn't so much walk as swagger in a curious kind of way – call it, perhaps, saunter aggressively – as if he knew exactly who he was and was very, very sure of himself.' Then there was, Billington went on, the occasion – a Sunday night talk given by Trewin at the theatre – when Finney got up and made 'this extraordinary vocal attack on one of the neighbouring theatres, the Alexandra (just across the other side of Hill Street). Again, it was done with a sort of working-class swagger and ebullience as he slammed the Alexandra as middle-aged, musty and middle-class.'

There were two (three, if you count his cheerful toy soldier in the yuletide *Emperor's New Clothes*) more highlights for Finney that first year: playing Richard, the orphaned clerk, in *The Lady's Not for Burning*, the role in which Burton had made astonishing West End and New York débuts some six years earlier, and as Tullus in *Coriolanus*, which would presage later events. The Fry opens with the young clerk on his hands and knees, scrubbing the floor, with his face to the audience; all the other actors are upstage setting the plot. Billington remembered: 'There was Finney, chuckling quietly to himself at everything that was going on, and again the eye was drawn to this boy when maybe it shouldn't really have been.'

As for *Coriolanus*, Hepton said: 'If I had had a little more courage, I would have given Albert the title role, but bearing in mind his age and comparative inexperience, I think it might have upset the company. So he did with Tullus what he does beautifully: that's listen. He played him as a very still, dangerous man.'

While Hepton was preparing *Coriolanus*, he was summoned by Sir Barry and asked whether he would look at the play's first few scenes to see if he could cut out some of the battles.

According to Hepton:

When, in something like *Macbeth*, the battle comes at the end, the audience knows full well who's fighting whom and why. In *Coriolanus*, it's early on and no one really knows and it's all fairly confusing, particularly as, anyway, it's reported through speeches. I looked carefully at the text and, of course, the old bugger was absolutely right. So that's what we did.

As an ironic aside, Hepton was acquiring quite a reputation as a director of fight scenes and two years on was invited to do the *Coriolanus* battles in the 1959 centenary season at Stratford.

Glen Byam Shaw asked me to come across to the theatre and meet the director, Peter Hall. In those days, they used to have large models and move them about in the course of preparing a new production. Hall was talking most eruditely about everything when, remembering what Sir Barry had suggested to me, I chipped in with that thought about cutting some of the battle scenes. Hall looked at me as if I'd crawled out from under a stone and has never spoken to me since.

Trewin described Finney's Tullus as 'watchful as a cat'. Rosemary Anne Sisson, then an aspiring playwright who earned bread-and-butter money as critic for a local paper, the *Stratford Herald*, was also impressed: 'As Aufidius, Albert Finney is outstanding. Particularly effective is the moment when he wipes Coriolanus' handshake off his hand, leaving it free for treachery and, his energy matching that of Coriolanus [played by Geoffrey Taylor], the death scene becomes not a bland but a worthy scene.' Yet another, more general, testimonial was provided before the year's end by Gwen Ffrangcon-Davies, who, a quarter of a century after she'd first played at the theatre, returned to hand on some personal pearls to the Playgoers' Society.

Of the current company, she picked out Finney, saying, 'He has a great future.'

That future, in the short-term anyway, appeared sealed when, the following February, Seale selected Finney for his Henry V. The director wanted plain statement and humour too, which Finney used in his playing of the early scenes, when he's dealing with the archbishops who are trying to persuade him to war. Billington recalled: 'There was a kind of wry mischief about his face, as if he saw through those guys, as if he knew that they were self-promoting ecclesiasts.'

Michael Blakemore, playing Henry's uncle Exeter, thinks it was the first time he ever saw an actor not wearing stage make-up; Finney became increasingly battle-besmirched at Agincourt, but remained white-faced underneath.

Hepton, as Chorus, believes that Finney probably came up with the idea himself after chatting with the director about how lack of make-up could only help to emphasize Hal's youth and early insecurity. His was a low-key approach, 'a warrior for the working day, one of the band of brothers but also its leader unchallenged, conscious of the weight of his crown, the task of his dedicated office'. Much of the Crispin oration was delivered as he sat on the ground among his nobles, while, at the gates of Harfleur, he addressed his soldiers (who were assembled in the orchestra well), half crouching and in a near-whisper.

This deliberate muting of a famously explosive exhortation didn't much please Trewin, who wrote:

> He failed in the Harfleur speech, a passage that demands the fullest drive. Looking down on his army as it began to make its assault from the coffee bar along the front row of the stalls, Henry had to declaim in a hoarse whisper, half crouching, as if on the order, 'Knees bend!' There we did want the blaze: as a character says elsewhere, 'You must allow *vox*!'

That aside, though, the critic was delighted:

> Often in the theatre, a Henry has been arrogant, self-righteous, the star of England shining like a gas jet. But Finney could remind us of a cricket captain able to keep our spirits up on a tricky third day. He might not have been a greyhound in the slips; he would have been an uncommonly safe cover-point. This Henry knew his people, and he had enough of the old Hal in him to turn to rough jesting in that moment of relief, the battle over.

This *Henry V* enjoyed huge box-office success, raking up a remarkable 99 per cent capacity, easily a Shakespearean record at the theatre. One particular fan was so overwhelmed by Finney's recent achievements that the gift of a volume of Shakespeare, published in 1859 and with a preface by Dr Johnson, was left at the stage door with the following anonymous note attached to it: 'I saw you in *Coriolanus* and then as Henry V. You greatly impressed me in both characters. The book is very old and has been in our family for years. I am in my middle seventies and only an old-age pensioner and I thought I would like to give it to you as a token of my appreciation for the pleasure you have given me.' Despite an appeal through the local paper, Finney was unable to trace the generous donor.

With barely time to draw breath, Finney's next move was out of the limelight and into an ensemble double bill of Miles Malleson's Molière adaptations, comprising the one-act farce *Sganarelle* and a two-acter, *The Slave of Truth*, from *Le Misanthrope*. The highlight of that particular month, though, was undoubtedly his twenty-first birthday, celebrated in great style, recalls Geoffrey Bayldon, at the young man's digs in Pakenham Road. When Finney had first moved to Birmingham, he was billeted in the distinctly insalubrious area of Balsall Heath, but with Bernard Hepton's help he had relocated to higher-class Edgbaston, where in Pakenham Road the formidable Mrs Copley ran her famous theatrical digs. When Mrs Copley died, she left the house to Winnie Banks, her downtrodden companion and housekeeper of many years. Winnie's accession to this suburban throne was the making of her. The one-time chrysalis became a butterfly; she actually started wearing lipstick. Finney and Winnie became close friends and she even became a sort of confidante to him.

Winnie was probably among the first to know about the pretty actress with topaz-blue eyes Finney had met in March at a river party in Stratford-upon-Avon. At twenty-seven, Jane Wenham was already quite a long-established performer, having joined the Old Vic aged seventeen. She had starred in a West End hit, *Grab Me a Gondola*, and was now playing three juicy roles at the Memorial Theatre: Celia in *As You Like It*, Calpurnia in *Julius Caesar* and Iris in *The Tempest*. By July 1957 Finney had moved out of Edgbaston and into a small flat in West Street, Stratford.

Meanwhile, the work went inexorably on with little regard for any new emotional entanglements. In *Be Good, Sweet Maid*, a study of bewildered adolescence by C E Webber, commissioned by the Arts Council through the

Repertory, Finney was Harry Hicks, 'a ruthlessly clever fellow with a brain like the clicking of a safe-deposit box'. His Archer in *The Beaux' Stratagem* was, thought director Hepton:

> a bravura performance; a sort of dummy run for what he'd do later as Tom Jones. My wife, Nancie Jackson [they'd been married in the January], who was playing Mrs Sullen, adored working with him. They had to have a love scene on a bed and I remember Nancie being very delighted, and rather flushed, after one particular rehearsal because Albert had been the steaming male as only he could. After his rather contained Henry V this was an altogether much broader performance.

Then, at the height of that summer, came a rather strange new play, with a suitably enigmatic title and Eliot-like pretensions, called *The Lizard on the Rock*, by John Hall.

Set in Western Australia, it was, according to Trewin, 'about a man of big business, a too confident senator (called Rockhart), who is back suddenly in the desert' with his three sons, an adulterous daughter-in-law and even a ghost. Finney played one of the sons, Malcolm, who ends up being shot in the stomach at point-blank range. Said Billington: 'I can recall even now the image of his being suddenly rooted to the spot and emitting a strange sound of mewing pain, like a dog caught in some kind of trap — a quiet, almost internal noise. Then, after about five seconds, he did a straight fall forward, hitting the floor with an enormous thud. That look of shock, horror and pain on Finney's face still stays with me.' Where did the title come from? Trewin explained: 'The senator's daughter-in-law asks, "How does one live in the desert?" and Rockhart answers, "I saw a lizard, lying on a rock, where no one marked it, motionless, wise and terrible. The lizard looked upon peace." ' It was that kind of play!

Still keeping careful tabs on him, Tynan, a regular and eagerly anticipated visitor to Birmingham, hailed Finney yet again, this time comparing him to Feuillière in the brilliant execution of a death fall. Less specifically, he noted in his *Observer* piece: 'Birmingham is perhaps the only city on earth that has a population of more than a million and only two legitimate theatres. It may therefore be the right place for a potentially great actor to learn his craft unobserved, and that is what Albert Finney is doing.'

Tynan was not the only person in London earmarking such exciting, if provincial, goings-on, but clearly he was the signpost.

Caryl Brahms, writing in the August 1957 issue of *Plays and Players*, noted of Finney:

> In looks he comes somewhere between Sir Donald Wolfit and Paul Scofield. He is raw, for this is his first season of professional playing. But he has a fine sense of timing, attack and dramatic urgency. I saw him in *The Beaux' Stratagem* at a matinée – both circumstances might be thought to tell against his performance. But it was well spoken, full of fun, with pace and a certain rough and ready grace and an immediate response to action. Finney may still lack elegance but he does not lack eloquence. I am sure he will give us many memorable performances and much magic. It is a privilege to introduce to the interest and regard of readers an actor in the raw – it is only fair to emphasize this, and I daresay the young actor will be the first to agree, that he has much to learn – and fallible, but of flesh, blood and generosity.

Another magazine, *Encore* – 'The Voice of Vital Theatre' – was also sufficiently enthused to have a front cover featuring O'Toole and Finney just one issue after it had featured two faces of Olivier. In 'A View from the Gods', 'Groundling' wrote loftily of O'Toole's Bristol success with, among other things, Alfred Doolittle, Jimmy Porter and an elegant Molière fop, while Finney had 'already startled audiences' with his Tullus Aufidius and Henry V.

What have these young actors in common? Above all, the magic touch of personal magnetism. Love them or leave them, you can't ignore them when they make an entrance, move across a stage, run, leap, clown, cry, die, reject or exit.

Alive to all life around them, all the life within the plays in which they are acting, they never relax that special actor's tension which is always in the eyes, in the voice and in the moves. With worlds of technique and experience still before them, they are fortunate to have the quiet apprentice worlds of Bristol and Birmingham in which to learn.

Just after the Lizard's run was completed, Finney and Nancie Jackson were invited from the Rep to BBC Birmingham to join the cast of *The Claverdon Road Job*, an efficient, taut (just forty-five minutes) detective drama written by Willis Hall. Finney was playing a young police constable opposite the seasoned Leslie Sands. The schedule was short so the actors had little time to mix socially, but Sands recalled Finney as 'hard-working, dedicated and a very private and reserved person. Our director, Peter Dews [who would much later become director of the Rep], no mean judge of character, described him to me as "the new Olivier". He never became quite that, but my firm belief is that he could have done if he had wanted to. Albie chose other paths to greatness, and perhaps his decisions were wise.'

Sands and Finney have met just once again since then, in 1970, when the older man was appearing with Frank Finlay in David Mercer's *After Haggerty* at the Criterion in London. As Sands was leaving the theatre, he spotted Finney at the head of the line of admirers waiting in the corridor to congratulate Finlay, who at that moment was closeted in his dressing room with Olivier:

> Albie greeted me warmly and we chatted about the early days. Then he asked me a question about my make-up. 'You're playing Mercer's father, a man of seventy, and you're what – touching fifty? Do you use much?' I had the advantage of silvering hair, but my eyebrows were in those days still jet-black. 'Nothing at all, Albie,' I told him truthfully. 'Except a bit of whitening on the eyebrows.' He considered this. 'You certainly look seventy, from the front. How do you do it?' Now it was my turn to consider. Finally I told him, 'I feel it. Think the lines . . . and feel it.' 'I'll remember that,' said Albie, seriously. Since then I've watched him playing older men in many productions, and always excellently.

That autumn, Finney resumed at the Rep, playing a blind soldier-visionary, O'Riordan, in Joseph O'Conor's *The Iron Harp*, about the IRA, and then went even further back into period, playing a mischievous Face in *The Alchemist*, Jonson's Restoration satire, which was given a distinctly eighteenth-century look by Hepton. Was it too convoluted for its audiences, as Trewin had suggested? The play certainly appeared to worry most of the actors, according to Sonia Fraser, playing Dame Pliant. Fraser, a young actress whose first job had been at the Bristol Old Vic with O'Toole before she arrived at Birmingham at almost the same time as Finney, had since then virtually matched him play for play, most notably as Katherine to his Hal in *Henry V*, as a bewildered Brenda to his Harry in *Be Good, Sweet Maid*, as Celimene in *The Slave of Truth* and as a most convincing Australian heroine in *The Lizard on the Rock*. Referring to *The Alchemist*, she said:

> I don't think that any of us thought it was the greatest

piece of British theatre ever to hit the stage, with the result that many of us became a bit screwed up and neurotic about it. Just before going on that opening night, I remember saying to Albie, 'Are you all right, love?' because everyone else was worrying, the way actors often do. He said, quite calmly, 'Oh, I've just decided to go on and be wonderful.' It wasn't said conceitedly but quite seriously, conveying an awareness that he could do just that, take the stage and make it all work.

Billington said Finney earned a huge laugh when Face had to come on and say, 'I've just been in the laboratory'; with his still-strong Northern accent, it sounded more like 'lavatory'.

Fraser, a year younger than Finney, found him a breath of fresh air. He was an instinctive performer, no slave to Stanislavsky and more in the rollicking actor-laddie tradition, with lots of energy and a lack of pomposity. 'I don't think he was particularly aware of being good-looking, though he was in a way aware of being special as an actor. He had a real sense of his own value. I thought he was gorgeous, quite the most magical thing I'd ever met. Lots of girlfriends? Every three minutes I should think; he was devastatingly charming.'

Clearly Jane Wenham thought so too, for after a mere six-month courtship she and Finney, six years her junior, were married on 1 November 1957 at Holy Trinity Church in Stratford. The bride, who wore a white suit with brown accessories – as we learned from a *Birmingham Post* report imaginatively headlined 'Actor Marries Actress' – was given away by Peter Dews and the wedding was purposely quiet, with just family and very close friends in attendance. Any honeymoon plans were postponed, for that night Finney was back on stage in *The Alchemist*, while his new wife prepared to resume in *As You Like It* on the Monday.

The last two Rep productions of the year gave the new

couple a chance to act together: first, in a new musical (just piano and percussion) version of T W Robertson's pleasant if sentimental slice of Victoriana, *School*, composed by a local man, Christopher Whelen, with lyrics by the Rep's own Redmond Phillips; and then in the Christmas show, *The Imperial Nightingale*, adapted from Hans Christian Andersen by Nicholas Stuart Gray, which featured Finney as a fisherman called Bamboo and Wenham as the White Princess.

When Finney began rehearsals for *Macbeth* towards the end of the following January, his wife was just pregnant with their first child.

Hepton, now the fully-fledged director of the Repertory, had a very clear idea about how he wanted to stage the Scottish Play: the emphasis was to be on the supernatural and it was built up on the concept of evil.

> I took the witches to be the embodiment of that influence, so when they say to Macbeth, 'You will be king', it starts a process of evil. The witches totally control him and are, in a sense, almost the leading characters, so I wanted to have them hovering all the time. I even used one of the witches as Third Murderer too [another would appear as a gentlewoman attending Lady Macbeth]. When Macbeth and Banquo first meet these hags, I wanted to make their eyes so riveting that Macbeth simply couldn't take his own eyes off them.

The question of who was going to play Macbeth then arose. There was talk briefly of inviting someone outside the company, but that was quickly dismissed. Hepton said: 'Because Albert was still so young, I suppose we took a great gamble with him. But Sir Barry and I agreed it was a perfectly good gamble. Albert took my idea of the importance of the supernatural and translated it into everything he did. "Is this a dagger . . ." came deep from inside his gut and subconscious.'

June Brown, in her first foray at Birmingham (and her only season there, for she too became pregnant, with the first of five children), was to play Lady Macbeth. She had known Finney half socially, as it were, for she was with Jane Wenham at Stratford and had met him at various cricket matches the previous summer. On the opening night, Brown was laughing and joking one moment and then, about to go on, was suddenly seized with panic, feeling that they hadn't had enough rehearsal. As she explained:

There are hot nerves and cold nerves. Hot nerves are all right; they're the excited, worried nerves. These were cold nerves and made you feel as if you were paralysed. Did Albie notice? God knows. I think the nerves probably came in that first scene when I'm on my own, reading the letter. Anyway, it didn't make me very happy, not in that first week. Later, I'd ask people whether they'd seen the play early or late in the run. If it was early on, I'd be dreadfully embarrassed. If it was later when I had a dreadful cold but was suddenly rather good in the role, that was OK. Incidentally, I remember seeing Albie much later on doing Macbeth at the National [in 1978] and thinking to myself, 'Well, I don't know, Albie. Parts of it I liked better when you were twenty-one. He was a very good, powerful young actor and quite unaffected.

I didn't actually meet him again until the end of the sixties, when I was doing a play at the Royal Court called *Life Price*. One night there was a knock on my dressing-room door, which I shared with two other people, and a head popped round, saying, 'Hello, do you remember me? I'm Albie.' And I said, 'As if I wouldn't know you. Don't be ridiculous.' He looked round the dressing room and said, 'Oh, it's so long ago.' I replied, 'It's not that long, Albie, it's only twelve years.' But to him it was a long time, for when you think about it, his whole life had changed during that period.

On a stark Shelving set – several squared pillars, a few steps arranged at varying angles, an occasional piece of furniture and the odd prop like a cauldron – Brown's nerves seem to have been undetected by the critics, unless Alan Dent's suggestion in the *News Chronicle* that her early attack appeared to be 'perfunctory' is to be interpreted in that light. Most column inches were, though, saved for Finney. According to Dent once more: 'He now proves that his Henry V last season was no mere flash-in-the-pan. His Macbeth has an authority truly astonishing in an actor of only twenty-one . . . the young actor may take it as a high and true compliment if I rate his Macbeth as being already half as good as the Olivier Macbeth in voice, bearing, pathos, poetry and sheer resource.' In truth, Finney may have been a little shorter on poetry than Dent suggests and rather longer and more effective on bragging exultations of power and moments of terror – like his shriek at seeing the royal blood dripping from those hands after he'd committed murder. Hepton's feeling was that Finney would be a 'great Macbeth in about ten years' time'.

As far as Charles Laughton was concerned, Finney was either 'really awful' or 'bloody terrible, but what can you expect at your age?' depending on the version of events you believe following the grand old man's visit to Birmingham on a scouting mission. Apart from Lean's film of *Hobson's Choice* four years earlier and a less-than-triumphant provincial tour of Shaw's *Don Juan in Hell* in Festival of Britain year, it had been more than thirty years since Laughton had seriously theatre-acted in England. Now he was recruiting for *The Party*, a new play by the young writer Jane Arden, Wales-born, RADA-trained but New York resident.

According to Simon Callow in his biography of Laughton:

It was widely felt at the time that he wanted to associate himself, rather in the manner a couple of years earlier of Olivier's appearance in *The Entertainer*, with the new wave of English writing, and it may be so ... there were all kinds of new waves going on: socially, theatrically, in painting, in writing.

Class seemed to be breaking down, and it was no longer comic or pathetic to come from the provinces: perhaps it was even an advantage. He was excited to discover a painter like Alan Lowndes in Manchester, and an actor like Albert Finney in Birmingham. No doubt he thought *The Party* was another manifestation of the same movement; if he did, he was wrong.

None of that would worry Finney, who must have been quite overwhelmed when, after a knock on his dressing-room door – number 7, way up on the second floor – in came Laughton, accompanied by a chum, James Stevenson, also an actor and a one-time Grenadier Guard. 'My boy,' said Laughton, 'after Macbeth an actor needs a drink. I know. I've done it [indeed he had, at the Old Vic in 1934, and it had flopped].' So off went the trio to the nearby Queen's Hotel, where Laughton called for a steak – 'after Macbeth an actor needs food too' – and whisky. A steak, three double whiskies and an hour or so later, the audience was over and Finney was on his way back to his Edgbaston flat. Ten days before the run of *Macbeth* was due to end, Finney was officially informed that Laughton and his impresario, Oscar Lewenstein (who'd also seen the *Macbeth*), would like him to join the cast of *The Party*, which was due to start rehearsing soon in London.

The last word here is rightly left to Trewin, who had so carefully, regularly and sympathetically charted the Birmingham progress of

the friendly, self-contained 'Albie', thoroughly sure of himself and his future ... [who] had gained a local reputation hardly below Paul Scofield's ... I am sure that Finney is a little tired of being called promising, much as a novelist begins to fret and foam when he is told – even affectionately – that he is readable.

Such praise as this appears to be guarded. The artist is hearing, in effect, that he will be better by and by. And we know, on good authority, that by and by is easily said ... Before I know it, I am suggesting that Finney's performance, already confidently true in its development (or, if you will, crumbling) of character, promises grandly for the future. Ever the old promissory note – in the sense that we expect our praise to be paid back in achievement.

4

In Period

Despite Laughton's unswerving support for *The Party*, it became quite quickly apparent that Jane Arden was no distaff John Osborne and that her first play was no great entertainer either. As directed by Laughton, it was less a look back in anger and more the portrait of some maddening suburban never-never land devised by a great star who, noted Tynan, had not appeared in London for twenty-two years and as director was now 'here to prove it'. The party, itself, is to celebrate Ettie's seventeenth birthday, but lurking behind this impending celebration is a gloomier family drama. Her father, a Kilburn solicitor (Laughton, sporting a curious, olde worlde, Cockney accent), has been away in a 'home' trying to overcome his alcoholism, which may have arisen out of incestuous feelings he nursed for his daughter. Will he return home in time to wreck the party of the child who despises him?

The action, wrote Tynan:

> seems to unfold in a timeless nowhere. The hero has a wife (Joyce Redman) who speaks perfect Schools Programme English and is his junior by about twenty-five years, yet the disparities in age and accent are

never even explained, let alone mentioned. They are broke, yet manage, with one lodger, to run the kind of mansion, all bookcases and pale beaming, that you would expect a visiting film-star to take near Henley for the summer.

Add a garrulous neighbour (Elsa Lanchester, Laughton's wife), who runs a 'nylon shop', and a potential boyfriend for Ettie with the unlikely Christian name of Soya (Finney), and it becomes even clearer that we are partying more on whimsy than on white-hot wrath.

Nevertheless, Laughton's enthusiasm for Arden's youthful vision remained admirably unwavering throughout rehearsals and during the six-month run at the New Theatre – publicly, at least. To Ann Lynn, closely related to the legendary Whitehall farceur Ralph Lynn, Laughton was palpably 'frightened', what with the combined pressures of being star-director and of facing a London theatre audience after such a long absence and in such unfamiliar material. Lynn, who had earned her 'big break' as Ettie over other early twenty-somethingish actresses like Maggie Smith, called the experience 'ghastly'. As she said: 'Instead of being reassured by Laughton, I found his intensity nerve-wracking. We had hell during rehearsals. It was quite a difficult play to understand; the language was non-realistic and the intricacies of the relationships between the various people were confusing. Yet Albie just seemed to get on with it, while the rest of us had suicide pacts about it.'

Lynn met her young co-star at the first rehearsal after a big build-up by Laughton, who then made Finney do some *Henry V* as a kind of party piece for the rest of the small cast. Rehearsal was so intense that there was little time for people to get to know one another. Lynn had only one scene with Finney anyway; most of her work was with Laughton and Redman. Then the play went on a pre-West End tour – Scotland, Liverpool, Birmingham and Manchester – during which there was more of a chance to make friends. Lynn found Finney 'extraordinarily mature' for his age, possessed of 'a nice sense of humour and . . . not easily ruffled. Perhaps his part was slightly easier in the sense that it was straight while the rest of us were fairly nutty, with endless problems. He was quietly self-assured, but I don't remember feeling he had any great vanity.'

Most other critics seemed to agree with Tynan, who had concluded, wittily, that it was 'too late now for anyone to come to the aid of *The Party*'. However, all of them, including Tynan and Trewin (perhaps predictably), were prepared to save some words of comfort for the West End débutant. Finney and Laughton shared one long scene together. In it, the boy Soya has a chance encounter with the boozy but, in this scene at least, briefly subdued, ex-lawyer without realizing he is Ettie's notorious father. At this point, wrote J W Lambert in the *Sunday Times*, the play:

> swung up out of competent manufacture and into art. Here, too, Mr Laughton is at his best, without bravura, gruff, giving the reassurance this poor man himself desperately needs, while the young man first steadies, then rallies, then — when he realizes the tainted source of all this comfort — collapses into bitterness. Here two acting generations meet and blend: a heartening sight.

Laughton, added Tynan, rose 'like a salmon to the occasion: few young actors have ever got a better performance out of their director'. They were, enthused Laughton's personal assistant, Ann Rogers, 'like Falstaff and Hal together'.

Sheridan Morley, though only seventeen at the time, still retains a very strong impression of the play and, in addition, feels that a more subliminal performance was taking place:

> Laughton clearly sensed in Albert a sort of much

younger, though kindred spirit; that here, like him, was another Northerner, outside his own class and generation, unacademic, not afraid of being theatrical, with an almost sensual enjoyment of the theatre. Look at Finney now and you have something of the Laughton – not the gay private life, of course, but chubby, though, a bit sinister and with almost a feline quality.

During *The Party*, you got the sense that Finney was shadowing Laughton, rather in the same way that, much, much later, Edward Fox did when playing with the by-then octogenarian Rex Harrison in *The Admirable Crichton*. You saw Rex handing on the torch to Fox – literally, there on stage. With the extraordinary affinity between Laughton and Finney, something then was clearly being handed on too.

While the rest of the cast somehow resisted their suicidal urges during the remainder of the run, Finney, now living in Bayswater, had plenty of enjoyable diversions. There was a radio play, Willis Hall's *The Larford Lad*, which also featured his wife, and '. . . *View Friendship and Marriage*' (as in a lonely-hearts advertisement), a ninety-minute *Sunday Night Theatre* play for BBC Television, in which Finney, well down the cast list, played a flat-capped motorcar fanatic called Arnold. Then, on 16 September at St Mary's Hospital, Paddington, Wenham gave birth to a son, Simon.

Lindsay Anderson saw *The Party* and thought that:

Albert acted in it like I would expect a young actor to act. I didn't know enough about the theatre to know that young actors didn't necessarily act like that; there was a kind of truthfulness and directness about the way Albert played which, in fact, was not in the least typical of the people of his generation. I guess class came into it, of course.

Aged fifteen months with his mother. (*Associated Newspapers*)

Pictured centre with Form IIIC at Salford Grammar School. (*Associated Newspapers*)

In 1977 outside his father's old betting shop. (*Daily Mail*)

As a padded Falstaff in *Henry IV*. (*Associated Newspapers*)

(*Below left*) With Sonia Fraser in *Henry V*. (*Lisel Haas/Theatre Museum*)

As Francis Archer, with Jacqueline Wilson in *The Beaux Stratagem*. (*Lisel Haas/Theatre Museum*)

As Malcolm, with Rosamunde Woodward in *The Lizard on the Rock*. (*Lisel Haas/Theatre Museum*)

With June Brown in *Macbeth*. (*Lisel Haas/Theatre Museum*)

With Charles Laughton in *The Party*. (*Zoë Dominic*)

As Cassio, with Zoë Caldwell in *Othello* at Stratford-upon-Avon. (*Birmingham Post and Mail*)

As Lysander (*right*), with Edward de Souza, Priscilla Morgan and Vanessa Redgrave in *A Midsummer Night's Dream*. (*Birmingham Post and Mail*)

As First Citizen (*right*), with Julian Glover, Roy Dotrice and Laurence Olivier in *Coriolanus*. (*Estate of Angus McBean*)

As Edgar, with Robert Hardy in *King Lear*. (*Birmingham Post and Mail*)

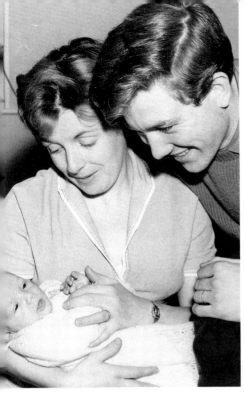

With Jane Wenham and three-week-old baby, Simon. (*Associated Newspapers*)

As Arthur Seaton in *Saturday Night and Sunday Morning*. (*Woodfall Films/National Film Archive*)

With Rachel Roberts in *Saturday Night and Sunday Morning*. (*Woodfall Films/National Film Archive*)

As Billy Liar with George A Cooper. (*Lewis Morley*)

As El Aurens in a screen test for *Lawrence of Arabia*. (*Columbia/National Film Archive*)

As Luther. (*Keystone*)

With Susannah York in *Tom Jones*. (*Woodfall Films/National Film Archive*)

Directing Graham Crowden and Anne Kristen in *The Birthday Party* at the Glasgow Citizen's Theatre. (*Associated Newspapers*)

As John Armstrong in *Armstrong's Last Goodnight*. (*Estate of Angus McBean*)

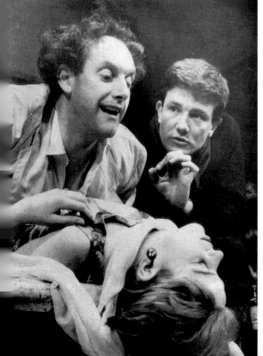

As Chandebise and Poche in *A Flea in her Ear*. (Zoë Dominic)

With Audrey Hepburn in *Two for the Road*. (Twentieth Century-Fox/National Film Archive)

At this point, Anderson had been an Oscar-winning documentarist and film critic. His only theatre work had been one Sunday night production at the Royal Court, courtesy of his friend and colleague Tony Richardson.

Out of the blue, Oscar Lewenstein asked him to direct a Willis Hall play, *The Disciplines of War*, at the Court, after it had already been presented at the Edinburgh Festival. This moving play about a trapped British patrol and its Japanese prisoner in Second World War Malaya had an especially strong central character: loud-mouthed Private Bamforth, who is determined not to let his fellow soldiers shoot the hapless prisoner. Anderson asked Hall if he could change the title of the play to *The Long and the Short and the Tall*, because he'd always liked the song. Hall replied, typically, that he could call it anything he wanted as Anderson was 'the bloody director'.

By then, Lewenstein had with Finney the closest thing to a long-term contract the actor has ever signed. When Finney agreed to play in *The Party*, all Equity standard contracts had an optional clause whereby, if mutually agreed, the manager and the artiste entered into an agreement. This gave the manager the option to present the artiste in two additional plays within a specified time of the run of the earlier play finishing – and at an agreed increased salary. As Lewenstein points out, and as Finney would then also have been made aware, there was no question of his playing a part that he didn't want to play. But the option at least enabled the management to do some forward planning that would not otherwise have been possible.

Anderson met Finney (who was to play Bamforth), liked him and remembers being invited along with the rest of the cast to Bayswater, where Wenham cooked curry for them all:

It was Albert's idea that we should all get together to start things off in a friendly, unaffected sort of way. On the second day of rehearsals, Albert arrived looking rather green. I asked him what was wrong and he said that he'd had a late night, or something.

A couple of days later – it might even have been the next day – Albert appeared again, still looking green. This time the reason he gave was that he'd drunk a lot of vermouth. I told him he should see a doctor. He did so and was told at first he had anything but appendicitis – which was, of course, exactly what he did have.

Here, an old Birmingham friendship came happily home to roost. In Finney's first season at the Rep the company's leading lady was Doreen Aris, who had married a local doctor, Bill Lobban. He also took a great interest in the Rep and the actors, and when the couple came to live in London the connection was kept up. Thanks to the ministrations of 'Dr Bill', Finney was now whisked into hospital for an emergency appendectomy, which may even have saved his life. There is a more recent sequel to this medical tale. When 'Dr Bill' finally retired, Finney arranged dinner for him and his wife at San Lorenzo in London. What he hadn't told them was that there were a few surprise guests too: before long, Finney was shuffling old Rep-ites like Kenneth Mackintosh, Geoffrey Bayldon, Alan Rowe and Alan Bridges to the table, much to the obvious pleasure of the Lobbans.

Anderson had found even the handful of days with Finney so agreeable and right that he was desperate no one else should take over the role. A postponement was agreed, but as it became clear that the time Finney needed to recover from the operation might linger on, Bamforth had eventually to be recast. With exquisite irony, the role went to Peter O'Toole, making his own West End début. It is fascinating to note how closely the careers of these two actors had up till this time entwined – and would continue to do so over the next couple of years.

Two parts of Finney's youthful game-plan had been achieved: Rep and the West End. Now, slightly out of the original order, the third, Stratford, beckoned too. In truth, whether it was the new baby, the aftermath of a serious illness, disappointment at losing such a good part or, as he has claimed, the fact that he didn't really respond to the roles he'd been offered, Finney had no great desire to go to Stratford at this juncture. However, Laughton, who was to play Lear and Bottom, wanted him, flattered him and demanded his presence. The protégé obeyed.

That year, 1959, was the much-trumpeted Centenary Season, Glen Byam Shaw's last as director (before Peter Hall, at twenty-eight, took over for the sixties) and perhaps the swansong of the Memorial Theatre's oft-criticized 'Stars Policy', which led to it being called by some just an 'upmarket summer rep'. What stars, though. Laughton, of course; Paul Robeson, recovering slowly from pneumonia, as Othello (with Sam Wanamaker as Iago); Olivier's Coriolanus; Dame Edith Evans as the Countess of Roussillon (in Tyrone Guthrie's production of *All's Well That Ends Well*) and Volumnia. Then there was the Youth – Ian Holm, Vanessa Redgrave, Zoe Caldwell, Mary Ure and Finney, among others – spread across the quartet of plays.

Somewhere in between was Robert Hardy, who'd last played at Stratford under Anthony Quayle's stewardship ten years earlier and was now returning after spending three years in the States. Among the many surprises that greeted Hardy early that year – from very first rehearsal to the final night a Stratford season was virtually an all-year business for the most resident members of the company – was Finney, who was sharing a dressing room with him and another seasoned player, Donald Eccles.

Not surprisingly, Hardy had never heard of the young man and was intrigued to find this newcomer who, refreshingly, 'didn't speak with a standard RADA-type voice'. For Hardy, Finney represented

a new sort of actor. He made one think of the bullfight
critic in Ibanez's *Blood and Sand* who talks excitedly
about the man having 'a quantity of salt'. There was a
great smell of salt in the air with Finney, something
which I'd once felt before with Burton. I remember
when seeing Finney's Cassio [*Othello*, directed by Tony
Richardson, was the inaugural production], thinking,
'Yes, the role's unplayable', but it still had a sort of
strength albeit one covered in puppy fat at the time.

Then it was as Lysander, more than a little lost in Hall's
Midsummer Night's Dream, directed as a wedding revelry
in a lordly Tudor home – so nobody, it was said, 'could
question the authenticity of the production as a journey in
search of origins'.

However, Finney had now, quite suddenly, begun to
question his own worth as an actor. Of this crisis, he said:

> I don't know what was wrong with my work at
> Stratford: it was more wrong then than it has ever been
> before or since. I mean, I was aware of it being wrong.
> It was one of those times when you just feel that you're
> in a kind of tunnel, and there's nothing – nothing –
> you can do to get out of it. The more you try to get out
> of it, the more you're in it. And my work was awful,
> just vile. Every time I went on the stage I felt, 'Get off,
> get off, what are you doing?'

Later that long, hot summer, Finney was invited to go
and talk to the Playgoers' Society one Sunday evening back
at the Rep. Hepton, who chaired the event, recalls quite
clearly Finney telling him how, for a while, he really felt he
was in the wrong job:

He had been badly miscast at Stratford. The things that

had mattered at Birmingham were the work and the camaraderie. If anybody got into difficulties, they knew there was someone with whom they could talk it through. He'd been cushioned for two years and allowed to develop week by week. At Stratford he got quite the opposite feeling. Albert said that when he first went to Stratford he sensed that directors didn't seem to give a damn for what he did. It was somehow a great slap in the face to him.

It was with probably some feeling of envy that he'd stand on the sidelines and watch the towering Guthrie rehearsing *All's Well* – Guthrie, who took the minutest interest in everything and everyone, down to the humblest spear-carrier. If it hadn't been for Coriolanus, Finney told Hepton, he would probably have given up acting altogether.

The early signs weren't too auspicious, explained Hardy:

Peter Hall simply didn't appear to know what to do with the play. I had done a good London production of *Camino Real* with him and thought this was the new Guthrie. Then Hall discovered he wasn't interested in what his actors gave him; that he really didn't like actors at all. We were only ever told in the vaguest terms what he wanted. One day we were working away in the rehearsal room where we had the main blocks of the set and Olivier was taking charge more and more. After ages of shilly-shallying when it was plain that Hall didn't know what to do with the crowd – vital in *Coriolanus* and OK in the end because Albie, as First Citizen, led it – Larry came roaring down.

He said to Hall, 'Peter, there are three positions on this stage which are worth occupying: centre up on your block, up left entrance, down right entrance. Work out which one of these three positions you want me to be in and let me know as soon as you have

decided', before roaring off again. That was one of the
first occasions in the process of hardening Hall up.

As with *A Midsummer Night's Dream*, historical
accuracy here too seemed to obsess Hall as he gave the
production what Ivor Brown described as a 'barbaric, not a
conventionally Roman, background. This stressed the
correct date [490 BC instead of 49 BC] of the proud soldier's
triumph and disasters, and turned the road to the Forum
into no classic avenue but a sinister street where savagery
was natural.' Was it, one wonders, a concession to Finney
that Hall also decided that the Romans should be
distinguished from the Volscians by giving them, respectively, Lancashire and Welsh accents?

As well as playing First Citizen – Billington retains vividly
the image of Finney going up to Olivier and raising his arm
and scratching the pit so Coriolanus got the most
offensively intimate sight and smell of this man – Finney
was also understudying Olivier without, he must really have
thought, a prayer of ever going on in his stead. *Coriolanus*
went into repertory at the beginning of July and from
September Olivier began combining his stage stints, including a breathtakingly audacious death fall, with filming of
The Entertainer, away north in Morecambe. As he wrote:

> I had been doing a whole day of Archie Rice tap-
> dancing for Tony Richardson's cameras, and at seven
> o'clock we were through and I was tired out, when
> Tony asked if I could bear to do one more take.
>   I sighed and said OK and went right into it. I was
> feeling glad we were doing it once more, as it was
> going great guns, when – snap went my old cartilage.

Olivier was due to do two shows of *Coriolanus* the next
day. Quickly alerted to his great good fortune, Finney
moved into Sir's dressing room, the press was summoned,
and the twenty-three-year-old began a six-week spell in the

role. Said Hardy: 'He never gave me the impression of being stretched or nerve-wracked. In fact, twenty-three is a good age to play Coriolanus. Olivier had a great stillness and Finney took that on in the way that an understudy, if he has got his eyes open, will take on much of the original.' Great stillness had also, you may recall, characterized Finney's Tullus in the same play at Birmingham. During understudy rehearsals he had, apparently, insisted on doing it his own way, reckoning that this was probably all he'd ever get out of it.

Far from being in any way fearful of the responsibility, Finney believed this was actually his salvation at the time as an actor. It was 'smashing', he told Clive Goodwin:

All the sorts of difficulties I seemed to be going through just left me, because, first of all, they expect you to come on in flannels with a book: you know, Sir Laurence isn't playing (big groan), his part will be played by Albert Finney. And then I come on, and I have the costume on, and then I start, and they can't see the book, and I actually got through it without a dry. So they think I am very good. I don't think it was a very good Coriolanus [Hardy said he wasn't 'terribly thrilled' either with Finney's performance] and also when you hear Sir Laurence's tones ringing in your ears for the number of times you've done the performance, it's very difficult for you not to be similar, because you're working from his blueprint. What one did learn from that is how a great actor can take the kind of peaks and valleys of a performance, the ups and downs of a character as written, and push them even further apart. He makes the climaxes higher and he makes the depths of it lower than you feel is possible in the text.

Hepton said: 'For Finney, the magic suddenly happened; he went on and claimed the stage.' And what was Olivier's reaction to this 'promising baby' of an understudy? 'I met

Albie in the wings when I was back and congratulated him on the lovely things I'd heard about his performance, to which he replied, "Well, after all, it's much less tiring than the First Citizen." '

To emphasize the Olivier–Finney connection even more, the 'promising baby' had also been invited to work on *The Entertainer* and had come through it completely unscathed. Not surprisingly, considering it comprised just a night's work – 'a living screen test' Finney called it – at Liverpool Street Station: a prologue sequence, not in the play, in which Finney played Archie Rice's son, Mick, a cheeky Army sergeant off to fight, and die, at Suez.

If his acting had been strife-torn – at least up to the moment when he was finally 'freed' by Coriolanus – Finney's painfully brief marriage was no less so.

During *Othello*, he had embarked on an affair with Zoe Caldwell, the exotic Bianca to his Cassio, who became in real life as in art his mistress. That summer too, he actually walked out on his wife and year-old son. For a while, he sheltered with Hardy and Hardy's second-wife-to-be, Sally, at their cottage in Binton, just outside Stratford, and would lie all day in bed, smoking cigarettes, hiding from Jane Wenham. Finally, Hardy said he needed the bedroom and Finney had to leave.

An interview Finney gave a year later to Peter Evans of the *Daily Express* about the reasons for his marriage break-up – 'I felt I was in a cage, so I escaped' – seemed to suggest altogether more deep-seated problems than just actor's block:

It was like having claustrophobia of the soul. Personal relationships drain me and rob me of my concentration and aim and drive and everything. I mean, I'm very selfish. I demand a lot of attention and warmth and love. But I'm no good at giving it back. It was like that during rehearsals. I'd find myself thinking about some stupid domestic problem and get angry and resentful. Gas bills, coal bills, laundry bills. Everybody has them. But for me, they're too much. They defeat me.

In a nutshell, self-obsession and sheer immaturity: the actor's traditional symptoms.

Finney's feelings of inadequacy would still have persisted during the early performances of the Centenary's fourth and final Shakespeare, Byam Shaw's farewell production of *King Lear*, which began in August. The Laughton caravan rolled back into town and then proceeded to roll all over the hapless director. Clasping a first folio and using his wife, Elsa ('even worse than him,' said Hardy), as a sort of meddlesome go-between, he apparently drove Byam Shaw to impotent distraction; according to Simon Callow, Laughton came 'to believe that Elizabethan typography was the clue to the stresses in the verse . . . and was firmly in the grip of the iron iambic, as well'.

This kind of single-minded self-centredness, which all too often in rehearsal seemed to be translated into panic rather than passion, surprisingly had the eventual effect of beguiling the critics, who, one suspects, had come to bury Laughton rather than to praise him. His was a comparatively gentle Lear, not, it's said, at its best in the storm scene but one which 'moved on to a muted majesty of pathos'. The occasion, as far as the press were concerned, was entirely Laughton's. Among the also-rans, therefore, was Finney, who, in a rare acknowledgement for his performance, gave 'a most original Edgar' (Ivor Brown).

It is amusing to speculate how much of his old mentor's Lear would have, even subconsciously, rubbed off on Finney, a great collector of stories and gestures. He has not played the role for real yet; only in passing, years later, during the film of Ronald Harwood's *The Dresser*. Harwood's inspiration was, of course, Wolfit, for whom he once worked in that eponymous capacity, but it's easy, as

Finney played him, to conjure up bits of Laughton as 'Sir' whines, whinges and always gets his own way.

When the final curtain came down on *Lear* at the end of November, the season still wasn't yet quite finished, for Stratford had made a deal with the NBC network in America and some sponsors, Ford, for a 'special television spectacular'. In the theatre, which was effectively turned into a TV studio for a full week, the *Midsummer Night's Dream* company was reassembled, led by Laughton as Bottom, and a condensed version (about seventy-five minutes) committed to camera. Filling up the rest of the fifteen-minute transmission, which was said to have attracted an audience of 40 million the following winter, was a prologue involving Laughton acting as benevolent guide to surrounding Shakespeare Country. Thus America got its first, albeit brief, glimpse of Finney's embryonic talent.

Finney's last sight of Laughton was a couple of years later, in Los Angeles, where Elsa invited him to view her cancer-ridden husband on his deathbed, feeling, she said, that 'as an actor you must be able to see everything, including death and dying'. Finney, on his way to Australia, stayed half an hour by the bedside, but Laughton never knew he was there.

So had Finney merely marked time at that, his one and only Stratford season? Certainly Billington thought the experience was something of a let-down. Having seen at Birmingham a potentially great actor maturing, 'he didn't seem to come across either particularly strongly or clearly; that was disappointing'.

Morley was less critical:

I thought there was no sense of inadequacy or let-down. They were all extremely efficient, eloquent and thoroughly competent turns. Admittedly, there was no feeling, as there was with Vanessa Redgrave, of a sort of coltish embarrassment, which in a way made her all the more interesting. For Finney, the season was seminal. There he was with Laughton and Larry. And those are the models for the way he would stand in the future. A four-square approach. Sheer stardom.

5

Class of the Sixties

Harry Saltzman wanted Peter O'Toole to play Arthur Seaton in *Saturday Night and Sunday Morning*. Woodfall Films, Tony Richardson and John Osborne's company, for whom Saltzman had line-produced both *Look Back in Anger* and *The Entertainer*, bought the rights to Alan Sillitoe's novel from another producer, Joseph Janni, after he'd tried unsuccessfully to set up a movie. Saltzman, though, was overruled by Richardson, who by then had not only worked at Stratford with Finney but also cast him, briefly, in *The Entertainer*. Also Lindsay Anderson heartily recommended Finney to Karel Reisz, who was making his feature début with *Saturday Night*, after a couple of acclaimed documentaries. Like Anderson and Richardson, Reisz too had been an active figure in the Free Cinema movement, which worthily advocated greater social conscience and more 'relevance' in British film themes. As he said:

> I can claim absolutely no rights of discovery. Around that time most of us felt he would be a star. The situation was, if we could raise the money on him, he would run straightaway with it. And that's what we

did. At the time, I found there was an extraordinary God-given natural grace about him. Like working with a puppy; whichever way the puppy jumped, it was fun and interesting. The film was really built around him.

Of all the British films from that fertile period, *Saturday Night and Sunday Morning* – maybe *This Sporting Life* too – is the least dated, in the sense that the near perfect weave of cast, script and direction somehow helped to halt the process of creeping embarrassment, a kind of socio-pseudery, which afflicted so many others of the genre and helped consign almost all of them to obscurity.

A boy and girl wandering mournfully through the drizzle and mist of industrial Britain, looking for a place to live or make love had, as Penelope Houston wrote, superseded the jutting jaw of Kenneth More on the bridge of a destroyer as the most readily identifiable image of British national cinema, but even that 'relevant' image could, and would, quickly pall. Casting could blight too. Burton had been far too mature for Jimmy Porter (had, one wonders, the younger O'Toole been considered after his Bristol triumph?) and though *Room at the Top* temporarily startled everyone, Laurence Harvey's affected 'ee bah goom' Joe Lampton grates with hindsight.

From the noisy opening scenes, sweating at his lathe in Nottingham's Raleigh bicycle factory, there is never any such self-consciousness about Finney's Arthur Seaton. There's nothing upwardly mobile about Arthur: he's trapped, quite happily it seems, by his class and knows there's really nothing he can do about it. 'What I'm in it for is a good time – all the rest is propaganda' and 'Don't let the bastards grind you down' are his twin philosophies. His is, as Ivan Butler so succinctly put it, the 'presentation of a totally self-centred, cheerfully amoral, take-what-you-can-get young man as hero ... a welcome relief from the petulant denunciations of the angry ones'. When he makes Brenda, his workmate's wife, pregnant, he asks her joylessly, 'How do yer' know it's mine?' and offers up his own Aunt Ada as the friendly, neighbourhood abortionist with, 'She's had fourteen kids, and probably got rid of as many.' He drinks, throws up, shoots air pellets at a nosy neighbour, is beaten to a pulp by Brenda's soldier in-laws and finally appears to settle down with the pretty but bland Doreen (Shirley Anne Field).

Arthur's semi-defiant hurling of a stone at the nearby estate (where we know he'll eventually end up with Doreen and a house full of kids) is his last, empty gesture. The morning after has run its course.

Every line of the film is Sillitoe's and, in a way, it works almost better on film than it did in the original, rather over-praised, novel. He and Reisz worked together on the structure of the screenplay for six months and it evolved a considerable amount in that time. It was a long book and Reisz saw the film as more of a 'little folk-tale. I realize that the splash it first made was probably to do with the fact it was about parts of English life that movies then didn't usually deal with, so it felt very bolshie. But, honestly, I never felt like that about it at all.'

There was some pressure from the money men to have Diana Dors as Brenda, but to Reisz's great relief she turned the role down and Rachel Roberts, always his choice, was triumphantly cast. Of all the fine North Country ensemble, only Shirley Anne Field, in retrospect, seems a little inadequate: as Reisz pointed out, 'She was the only person in the film who had absolutely no connection with the North', and it showed. As cameraman, both Reisz's and co-producer Richardson's first choice would probably have been Walter Lassally, who had already collaborated on their distinguished documentaries, *We Are the Lambeth Boys* and *Momma Don't Allow*. But here Saltzman put his foot down. As Freddie Francis, who had already worked on *Room at the Top* and, earlier that same year, *Sons and Lovers* (for which he'd win a black-and-white cinemato-graphy Oscar), admitted: 'I was actually forced on the picture. Harry felt that as it was Karel's first feature, he needed someone more experienced, like me. I remember meeting Karel in a Wardour Street pub and gently reassuring him that I wouldn't make his film look like an MGM musical.'

Filming, on the less-than-awesome budget of £120,000 (which included a £2,000 fee for Finney and for the director, half of which Reisz ploughed back into the music), took place in the autumn of 1959 on location in Nottingham and back in the studio at Twickenham. The riverbanks, the bridge, the factory and the exterior of Arthur's home (in fact, Sillitoe's mum's) were all filmed in Nottingham, mostly the Radford district, the grim area that served Raleigh and is now almost totally razed to the ground. The funfair, where Arthur gets worked over, was actually in Wimbledon. The interiors were all filmed in Twickenham.

Saltzman, a tough Canadian on his third consecutive stint with Woodfall as line-producer, ordered that publicity should be absolutely minimal during shooting. 'Hit 'em with it' just before release was his maxim. Malcolm Feuerstein, the film's publicist, said that Finney, Roberts and Field all made it clear they 'weren't too happy with the way we were having to fight off the press. It was frustrating because Finney, certainly, was great material. You knew, as we discovered subsequently, that you could throw him into an interview and he'd come out very quotable.'

For the film Finney was taught to use a lathe, and in those opening scenes he was actually shaping the spindle that goes through a hub cap. That kind of attention to detail also, said Finney, helped take the weight off the acting. Focusing on the lathe meant he didn't have to worry too much about camera and character. Considering the schedule and the subject matter, shooting went surprisingly smoothly. As Feuerstein recalled:

Karel was quite tense but he managed to cover it

beautifully and he had a calming effect on everyone. I remember him once telling Shirley, who was preparing for a strong scene with Albert, to get some tension by biting her knuckles at the side of the set. Otherwise the only tensions were with the moments that were themselves tense, like the abortion scene and some of the love scenes.

As for the famous pub drinking scene between Finney and Colin Blakely near the beginning of the film, that was real beer – pints of it.

Freddie Francis said that both Reisz and Finney told him that they'd be physically sick every morning before work, but those nerves, he added, never showed on the set: 'Karel was always very positive. He loves rehearsing; in fact, he'd probably love never having actually to shoot, just to keep rehearsing. Nothing ever was much left to chance. He and Albert, who had moved into Karel's house in Hampstead, were very close and never stopped discussing the film so they were well prepared.' Their long discussions would revolve around how exactly Seaton would walk, dress, smoke a cigarette or hold a fishing rod. When filming was finished, Reisz went to bed for a week before moving into the cutting rooms for twelve weeks. They were still, most significantly, short a couple of close-ups of Finney, which then had to be picked up later in last stages of the editing. By then, said Reisz, Finney had put on quite a lot of weight, which can be spotted if you look closely at the print. Rather more secretly, Reisz, Francis and another documentarist friend, John Fletcher, went back to Nottingham in the director's small Ford van to obtain several more atmospheric shots. Francis also recalls Reisz becoming jittery when Johnny Dankworth's score was late arriving; just in case, he'd begun to sort out on gramophone record some suitable pieces of programme music.

The film was due to open in London at the end of October, by which time the belated publicity blitz had got well under way. The policy seemed to work, for the movie enjoyed an explosive opening at the Warner cinema in Leicester Square. Said Reisz: 'It got its money back in the first two weeks of release, which scared the shit out of us.' It was actually quite a week for British X-certificate films. Along with *Saturday Night*, there was *Too Hot to Handle*, with Jayne Mansfield as an exotic Soho stripper called Midnight Franklin, and *Beat Girl*, yet another striptease extravaganza, featuring the pop idol Adam Faith and, back in her more familiar cheesecake guise, the ubiquitous Shirley Anne Field.

It was all simply too much for the critic of the *News of the World*, who beneath a trio of titillating stills from supposed sex shockers like *Room at the Top* and *The Entertainer*, and the headline 'Bed *and* Bored', ripped into Reisz's movie:

Once upon a time the censor wouldn't allow the cinema to show as innocent a scene as a married couple having breakfast in a four-foot-sixer. But now even such great actors as Laurence Olivier and Laurence Harvey are baring their chests and snuggling under the sheets with their leading ladies . . . This week, a new British star, Albert Finney joins the bare-chest brigade in a steamy, sordid piece called *Saturday Night and Sunday Morning*. From a look at our pictures, you can see he is as happy as any Larry. It's the first of three British X for Sex films this week. What are our studios up to? Have they forgotten those homely, happy pictures on which the business was built? . . . My verdict is: Distasteful and disturbing.

Despite this studied outrage, there was little or no trouble with the censors here. In the States, said Reisz, it was very different. Summoned to appear before the Catholic Legion of Decency, he was informed by a Monsignor Sullivan and Mrs Love that they couldn't give the film a certificate because the Seaton character was 'unpunished' at the end. Reisz asked them, 'Unpunished for what?' 'Adultery!' they told him.

The abortion they could accept, and even the fact that a strap had fallen off Brenda's shoulder during a bedroom scene, but they just couldn't stomach Arthur remaining 'unpunished'. Reisz pointed out that this was in fact the story, to which they replied: 'You can change it, can't you? You can create an ending where something bad happens to him.' The director was dumbstruck. Then the Monsignor confided smugly: 'Look, I'm not just talking as a censor, I'm also talking as a film critic. I think it would be much better if there was some retribution at the end.' Reisz politely begged to differ and so no Legion seal was forthcoming, which resulted in several thousand lost bookings across the States and rather dented the film's American distribution prospects.

While serious reviewers here were quite ecstatic about the film, American critics were rather more divided. Pauline Kael felt it was 'over-directed . . . every punch is called and then pulled'; Stanley Kaufmann, on the other hand, described it as 'an extraordinarily able piece of work, free of the exhibitionism that often curses those who come out of the world of theory and cinema club'. Both were united in their praise of Finney. For Kael, he was 'remarkable as the hero whose vitality has turned to belligerence', while Kaufmann saw in Finney 'the seething animal vitality of Brando and the compelling abrasiveness of the young Cagney'. And further:

> His face is not an outstandingly good actor's mask; it's not a distinguished or attractive face and, as yet, it lacks mobility and subtlety. But he forces his way ahead, carrying his fairly deadpan [look] before him . . . he has what might be called resident power; his presence *continues* effortlessly while he is on camera, without mugging or distracting from his fellow actors.

Finney, who picked up British Academy and Variety Club awards as 'most promising newcomer' (Rachel Roberts was Best Actress and the film itself, Best of British that year), and Reisz had got on so well that they were determined to work together again sooner rather than later. Finney's girlfriend, Zoe Caldwell, suggested the story of Ned Kelly, the nineteenth-century Australian outlaw. So, with Columbia's backing, a script was commissioned from David Storey. By then Storey had also adapted his own novel, *This Sporting Life*, for the screen, the idea being that Reisz should direct and Finney star as the Rugby League player, Frank Machin. Reisz declined, suggesting his old friend Lindsay Anderson as director, with him as producer, while Finney, fearing a sort of instant rerun of *Saturday Night and Sunday Morning*, turned down the film as well.

For the Ned Kelly project, Reisz said, they first bought up two of the biographies and then began to invent:

> Ours wasn't in any sense a biopic; it was a drama based around the idea of this brilliantly talented, eighteen-year-old guerrilla who terrorized the whole of New South Wales and then went crazy. He had an obsession about his mother and also a notion that he could become inviolate. He built for himself a kind of armour so that he couldn't be shot, but the problem was that it made him immobile, so his eventual violent end was a sort of heroic suicide. Storey wrote a very good, very long and ambitious script.

Reisz flew off to Australia to start location hunting in the Blue Mountains, and Finney, with a moustache and embryo Irish accent, then joined him out there for a further month's recce. When they returned, they had a meeting with Columbia's London chief, Mike Frankovich, who told them angrily: 'I commissioned a Western and you've brought me *Macbeth*.'

According to Reisz, 'It was certainly a dark, Strindberg-ian sort of tale, and they were clearly frightened of it, but we were so keen to do it that when they actually said no, it came as an absolute shock.'

Yet, less than three months after that, the pair were back in business together, shooting a remake of Emlyn Williams's old Gothic shocker, *Night Must Fall*, about a charmingly psychotic axe-murderer at large in the countryside. MGM, who'd made the first film version back in 1937, caught them on the rebound from Columbia, as it were, for what was to turn out as an undistinguished, muddled return ticket. According to Finney, 'The film fell very heavily between two stools. We ruined the melodrama by trying to make it a psychological thriller, and couldn't pull that off either.'

As Reisz sees it:

We were doing the story of a self-deceiving charmer, a compulsive kind of person who becomes what the women in his life want him to be – a sort of identityless clown. I wanted this quicksilver, chameleon character. The trouble was, by this time Albert had started having all his really huge success [*Billy Liar* and *Luther* on stage, *Tom Jones* in the cinema] and had begun to feel what many male actors often feel about acting. Is this a proper job for a man – to keep smiling for the big world out there? The result was, I think, that he resisted playing Danny's charm and lightness and instead went for the pain and inwardness of the character.

Freddie Francis, reunited with Reisz as cinematographer, was more sanguine: 'I had the feeling that we weren't really making *Night Must Fall*, but what we *were* doing seemed rather interesting at the time: a sort of *What Makes Danny Run*.'

For Reisz, though:

The thing just fell to pieces in our hands, just disintegrated. I knew it wasn't working after about three or four weeks, but couldn't put my finger on it, so we just saw it through. I can remember later having a preview of the film and all the MGM wives rushing up to me like furies and almost tearing me to pieces, saying, 'What have you done to this beautiful boy, Tom Jones?' It really rubbed people up the wrong way.

Meanwhile, back in January 1960, at the end of shooting on *Saturday Night and Sunday Morning*, there was an opportunity for Finney to renew the working partnership with Lindsay Anderson that appendicitis had cut so painfully short more than a year earlier. While Finney was away at Stratford, Anderson had staged a one-night show at the Royal Court called *Jazzetry* – a coordination of jazz with poetry – by Christopher Logue and a pair of talented musicians from Johnny Dankworth's regular band, Bill Le Sage and Tony Kinsey. The quartet decided to collaborate again on a musical version of Harry Cookson's play *The Lily White Boys*, which had in a non-musical form won a prize in an *Observer* competition. Cookson himself wasn't pleased by the prospect and, said Anderson,

took strong exception to Logue's lyrics and the ironic finale we put on to the end of his rather sentimental play. In fact, he tried to stop us doing the play altogether, but since Oscar Lewenstein had bought up the rights there was nothing he could do legally.

It was the period when many of us were rather entranced by Brecht and I was anxious to do a musical with the directness of style and reality of a Brecht production, not the sort of English middle-class musical like, say, *Grab Me a Gondola*. At that stage, I don't think Albert knew much about Brecht and I remember we went over to Paris together to see the Berliner Ensemble there.

The Lily White Boys was about three working-class lads and lasses – Ted, Razzo and Musclebound, and Jeannie, Eth and Liz – who decide they want to be successes and the show good-humouredly follows them through their various picaresque attempts to reach the top: tart becomes star, wide boy becomes Establishment leader, cosh boy becomes policeman, and so on.

The last chorus of the show is sung aggressively straight out at the audience:

> You have seen us come from nothing,
> Seen what industry can do,
> And, in spite of good intentions,
> We're successful – *Just Like You* ...

Finney played Ted, the natural leader of the group, and he had also to sing. 'He was fine,' said Anderson. 'It wasn't *The Desert Song* but it was, shall I say, sung with a will. We were also lucky to have Georgia Brown [as Jeannie] to help steer it through. The show did the usual Royal Court run of about eight weeks and went well.' Ann Lynn was also in the cast, as Liz, and recalls the show as her favourite of all the work she's ever done:

> In a way, it was like a crusade, very socialist in content, decrying materialism and showing how most people fall into the trap of greed, which tends mostly to happen on the backs of less fortunate people. Lindsay created a real ensemble feeling, as opposed to, say, Laughton, who had been traditional and hierarchical, ever the lord and master over us all.

In these rather bald terms, *The Lily White Boys* sounds a pretty parcel of polemic. However, according to critic Alan Pryce-Jones, while not perfect, it was both amusing and refreshing:

What is wholly good about this piece is that it breaks away from the normal pattern of a British musical. The gentility, the fake high spirits, the tonic-and-dominant tunes, the sub-Gilbert lyrics are a thousand miles behind. There is no reason why this should not be the start of a new theatrical form properly equipped to sharpen the edge of social comment.

The exuberant *Lily White Boys* was a kind of rehearsal for what was to be, later that same year, perhaps the best and most successful of the Finney–Anderson collaborations, one which also, according to Finney, represented unfinished earlier business. When he had missed out on *The Long and the Short and the Tall*, Finney had asked Willis Hall if the playwright would write something especially for him. Hall was about to work on *Billy Liar* with Keith Waterhouse, who'd written the original novel. Later, though, when Lewenstein, who was staging *Billy Liar*, approached the actor and director, they, 'in a rather conceited way on both our parts, turned it down,' said Anderson. 'In the end, I think, Oscar was going to cast it with Tommy Steele but he came back to us yet again, and since we didn't have anything else to do at the time, we said, "All right, we'll have a go." And I'm very glad we did.'

Considering that Waterhouse's creation would eventually become part of the language, enshrined not only in a play but also a subsequent television series (1973–4), stage musical (1974–5) and American TV spinoff (1979), Billy's first West End steps were distinctly stuttering.

The story of Billy Fisher, the undertaker's clerk who chronically fantasizes – he becomes, variously, a fop, a legless war hero, a tycoon – to escape his dull North Country environment and an aggressive father, seemed irresistible. But Tynan, among others, managed to resist – along with the first-night audience, if he is to be believed – using the play's opening as an occasion for something of a revisionist attack on the current state of British theatre. His thrust was the increasing divide between the socialism of much new drama and the essential conservatism of most playgoers. The result, he believed, was a sort of artistic deadlock.

He wrote: 'Obviously they [the young playwrights] need a new audience, but in order to attract it they will have to define and dramatize the new values for which they severally stand. We know what they are *against* – the human consequences of class privilege, the profit motive, organized religion, and so forth – but what are they *for*?' As for *Billy Liar*, in a week when Tynan was also reviewing (fascinatingly, from Finney's future point of view) new plays by Shelagh Delaney and John Arden, it was 'a ramshackle piece of purely whimsical entertainment'. Tynan felt that the novel's 'broader implications are skirted or ignored', substituting instead 'pure farce'.

Anderson, even in those days never less than combative, fired off a letter to Tynan telling him how 'totally mistaken' he was. 'The critics, particularly Tynan, were very snooty about the play and said it wasn't quite the thing, and therefore had contrived to give their middle-class readership a poor impression of the play.'

After an out-of-towner in Brighton, *Billy Liar* opened at the Cambridge Theatre in September. Tom Arnold, who ran the Cambridge, told Anderson that he'd help the play as much as possible because it was such a big theatre, but within a couple of weeks he was actively trying to evict his poorly tenant. Two saviours fortuitously came galloping to Billy's rescue. In those days, the BBC used to do live telecasts from West End theatres but, in the case of *Billy Liar*, was reluctant because the play used the word 'bloody'. For one of these occasional theatreland excursions, the BBC was planning to pop into the Globe and transmit an act of Robert Bolt's new play, *A Man for All Seasons*. Until Paul Scofield objected.

Suddenly high and dry, the BBC came back to Lewenstein and Anderson, asking if they could, after all, show some of

Billy Liar. The management readily agreed, and so they moved an audience and cameras into the Cambridge and broadcast the whole of the first act. The next day the show was a sellout. As Anderson has said: 'You see, the moment a popular audience saw even some of the play, they wanted to see the whole thing.'

The second factor for the show's enduring success was that less than a couple of months into the run *Saturday Night and Sunday Morning* opened and from that moment on – and for quite a while after – Finney, the new white hope of the English stage, could do absolutely no wrong. He stayed in *Billy Liar* for nine months, the duration of his contract. Instinct, he has said, told him not to stay any longer. For the character of Billy Fisher, he had tried to make himself physically a little smaller and a little more vulnerable than he normally felt. Doing that eight times a week, when sometimes he had the urge to come onstage and just expand, became not only limiting but also, he felt, bleakly limitless as a long-term prospect. Finney was placed on a percentage as soon as the play began paying its way and, that Christmas, was further rewarded by the management with the munificent gift of a £75 tape recorder.

Even as he and Anderson began rehearsing the play, they started to talk in terms of, 'Oh, we'll do that in the film', but while Lewenstein was away some time later at a film festival in South America, the authors sold the movie rights to another producer, Joe Janni. Janni wanted John Schlesinger to direct the film and Finney to repeat his stage performance; Finney said that he wouldn't do it unless Anderson was asked to direct. The impasse was irresolvable. After a worrying moment when it seemed that Anthony Newley would be the screen Billy, Tom Courtenay, who'd succeeded Finney on the stage, was signed up.

So much of Finney's non-stop career around this time seemed to revolve exclusively around just a small circle of creative people, be it at Woodfall, the English Stage

Company, or both. Perm from Tony Richardson, John Osborne, Lindsay Anderson and Karel Reisz, and there resulted a startling sense of continuity in those years. Now it was the turn of Richardson, who was planning to stage Osborne's *Luther*, a muscular, Brechtian drama about the founder of Protestantism and, said the playwright, 'the nature of religious experience'. The role naturally excited Finney, whose preparatory discussions were predominantly with the director rather than the writer and mostly about the sort of style they were seeking. The centrepiece of *Luther* comprises three Lutheran sermons, but instead of being performed before extras shuffling on to the stage to occupy pews, they are delivered from a pulpit directly to the audience as congregation. Much of the tone, in eleven scenes set across more than twenty years of turbulent history, is vigorous, often scatological.

Finney once described the play's three acts like this:

The first act deals with his perplexity, with his neurotic period when he felt things were wrong and should be changed but didn't know how to go about it. The second act is the angry young man period, when he is demanding changes, causing revolution, forming a new movement. The third act deals with his maturity, when he has mellowed and is taking stock. I should think it parallels John's [Osborne] own development.

Finney tackled the detail of the role with his usual thoroughness. For instance, he had to throw an epileptic fit at one point, so he took advice from a neurologist friend on the actual symptoms of epilepsy.

For Finney, the occasion must have had more than an echo of that peripatetic *Caesar and Cleopatra* five years earlier. First stop on the *Luther* tour was none other than the gilded Sarah Bernhardt auditorium in Paris.

The play was to participate in the international festival of Théâtre des Nations, followed by runs at the Royal Court, the Edinburgh Festival and, finally, the Phoenix Theatre in the West End. It seems to be generally felt that, aside from the actual honour of the French invitation (and it resulted in a Best Actor award for Finney), the play did itself no great critical favours at this 'première' stage: the circumstances were adverse, the theatre unsuitable and the audience foreign.

Despite all this, the English critics raced to Paris, where they pronounced themselves rather pleased with the result. Tynan reckoned it the most eloquent piece of dramatic writing for the British theatre since *Look Back in Anger*, saying: 'No finer Luther could be imagined than the clod, the lump, the infinitely vulnerable Everyman presented by Albert Finney, who looks, in his moments of pallor and lip-gnawing doubt, like a reincarnation of the young Irving, fattened up for some cannibal feast.' It's difficult, if not impossible, to find any dissenting voice, though W A Darlington suggested: 'If he [Finney] does not quite convince us that the man is driven by the force of a deep religious faith, that is not his fault but the author's.' At the Court, Harold Hobson's own 'conversion' seemed complete as he graphically painted Finney's Luther as a man who'd absorbed Protestantism like someone 'who has swallowed a powerful dose of medicine which in the end may do him good, but which at the moment is burning his liver and making his eyes swivel.'

Cut to more than two years on: the plan was to open *Luther* on Broadway with John Moffatt repeating his role as the silver-tongued Cajetan, Peter Bull as Tetzel and, of course, Finney as Martin. But they'd reckoned without American Equity, which violently objected to Finney getting a work permit on the grounds that he was not 'an artist of exceptional ability'. David Merrick, the American impresario who was co-presenting the play, appealed to the US immigration authorities and won. Merrick said that it was all part of a concerted campaign against British casts by

American actors, who resented the 'overwhelming success of British shows on Broadway'. *Plus ça change.*

A month after *Luther*, and Finney, opened at the St James's Theater in New York, *Tom Jones* opened in the States. Following that, any transatlantic doubts as to his 'exceptional ability' no longer persisted.

Before Finney embarked on Osborne and Richardson's second slice of unconventional period storytelling, there were to be the formalities of his divorce from Jane Wenham. Fellow actor Peter Woodthorpe, who'd been the Roderigo in that *Othello* when Finney and Zoe Caldwell gambolled on- and offstage at Stratford, gave evidence supporting Wenham's claim of misconduct. The adulterous couple didn't deny it and Mrs Finney was granted a decree nisi and custody of their now three-year-old son, Simon. Finney was also ordered to pay costs. During this whole period, the only roots he appeared to be putting down were on the stages and locations of his plays and films.

He would seldom spend more than a couple of nights in the same flat as he whizzed round London in his Mini, wearing stovepipe trousers and a battered leather jacket to even the most formal gatherings.

It was as if, having finally left his parents' home, he wanted – for the time being anyway – to keep travelling light and avoid accumulating things like clothes or books. Yet this also contrived in a way to make him dependent on other people, particularly women, who could provide a home and stability – things he clearly needed but was equally afraid of committing himself to. This seems to have resulted in his involvement in relationships that dragged on long after they should have ended because they were simply temporarily comfortable.

During the icy cold May of 1962, Finney dropped in at Lincoln Castle to visit his then girlfriend Samantha Eggar, who was making her film début in a steamy undergraduate drama called *The Wild and the Willing*. With him was a basket of wild strawberries all the way from Greece, where he'd just been holidaying. The castle was doubling as the movie's 'Kilminster University', where Ian McShane, also in his first film, was playing a youthfully irresistible stud dallying with wives and students alike. The producer, Betty Box, remembers that McShane appeared deeply jealous of Finney, berated his strawberries as 'mouldy little things' and even stood on a step at the hotel to appear taller than the surprise visitor. Before Finney took his leave, he played an uncredited role in the film, donning a multicoloured 'Kilminster' scarf as he strolled on the arm of another 'extra', Susan Melton, through the background of an outdoor scene between Eggar and McShane. Soon after this Eggar announced that her relationship with Finney was over.

'We thought,' said Tony Richardson, 'it was time we made a really uncommitted film. No social significance for once. No contemporary problems to lay bare. Just a lot of colourful, sexy fun.' This sense of frivolity was extended to the cast and crew of *Tom Jones*, who, at the untraditional *start*-of-shooting party, were told by the director, 'Now, let's all go and have a lovely ten weeks' holiday in the West Country.' There were certain pressures on Richardson to make a more conventional, studio-based sort of film, but after the freewheeling style of both *A Taste of Honey* and *The Loneliness of the Long Distance Runner* he saw no reason to change tack, even if *Tom Jones* would be Eastmancolorfully epic both in period scale and sweep (though, at £450,000, still not wildly expensive) compared with the previous brace. Despite Richardson's domestic success, the new film still required Hollywood studio finance from United Artists.

The eighteenth-century tale of a young man wolfing and wenching his way from bastard's birth to the desirable estate of man of property and winner of the fair Sophie, via a thankfully brief flirtation with the hangman's rope, was ripe for adaptation into, if not, as it turned out, exactly

Henry Fielding, then certainly the requisite 'colourful, sexy fun'. A whole, gigantic, skilled home movie's worth. However, unlike most home movies, this one was, as history relates, wildly enjoyed by millions way beyond just the 'family' circle.

Trying to watch the film again now, however, proves to be quite a considerable strain. What should be a timeless, insouciant romp looks even more dated, nearly thirty years on, than less ambitious slices of kitchen-sink that by rights should be resolutely stuck in a sixties time-warp.

Awash with contemporary influences, the film has jump-cuts like Jean-Luc Godard's, hand-held shots, dialogue-to-camera, fancy camera gimmicks, silent comedy tricks, and even snippets of Brechtian song. Much of this perpetual *hommage* was achieved later on in the cutting rooms, when Richardson, agonizing over the film's considerable length, decided to insert optical tricks in order to speed it all up. It was also at the editing stage that it was decided to add Micheal Mac Liammoir's fruity narration, because, according to Finney, it was felt an audience simply wouldn't understand what was going on. In fact, said Finney, there was a feeling during the shooting that no one really knew what was going on even then. Osborne's script wasn't that finished. On one occasion, they were shooting a bedroom scene where Finney is searching his trousers for something and there's a row going on, too. He knew that Richardson wasn't going to cut, so he just ended the scene himself, spontaneously.

On lovely locations in Dorset and Somerset, like Cranbourne Manor, they shot the infamous stag hunt using a mixture of low-angle ground and low-level helicopter shots. John Trevelyan, then the secretary of the British Board of Film Censors, was given a script by Richardson and expressed concern at what the director deliberately proposed to shoot as a very cruel and savage hunt. Richardson claimed to hate blood sports and felt that by being as realistic as possible he could point up the mindless brutality involved. Trevelyan told him that he thought this might actually do more harm than good and, after a meeting with the RSPCA, Richardson agreed to modify the scene.

Richardson happily encouraged actor participation, preferring the actors to show him the scene first before he then made adjustments to the staging.

The notorious 'eating scene' – shot one wet day in the stables of a girls' boarding school – between Finney and Joyce Redman, whose sexual foreplay consists of consuming with lascivious pleasure a tavern feast, was, according to the cameraman Walter Lassally, 'largely improvised by the actors, being developed as they went along – an excellent example of the advantages of leaving enough elbow room for the actors to enhance a scene'. This method did, however, have its drawbacks. Finney's hero, the eccentric Wilfred Lawson (playing Black George), would make other performers agonize with concern during the exaggeratedly long pauses in his dialogue. Hugh Griffith (Squire Western) became so wrapped up in his character that during a horse-whipping scene actually struck Finney. The second time it happened, said Lassally, Finney retaliated with a punch and shooting was held up for several hours. Finney found much of the country filming, which seemed to consist of his riding up and down past the camera with a smile on his face, dull and undemanding. Back in London, they used some riverside locations at Southwark, Vauxhall Gardens and also at the now defunct Londonderry House at Hyde Park Corner, refurbished for the occasion with necessary double-glazing.

As well as tricking up the action during editing, there was some more drastic surgery. Lassally said that Richardson 'changed the whole beginning, curtailing scenes that now started somewhat abruptly in the middle, intercutting scenes that might have been better left to run their course, and was just generally panicking that things "didn't hold".' A principal victim in much of this was Diane Cilento (as

Molly), who apparently lost at least half her scenes in the final cut. Gerry O'Hara, the assistant director, recalls thinking at the time that there was a better film in the cutting room than the one that finally emerged.

Censor Trevelyan's discussions with Richardson second time round didn't prove quite so fruitful. Having thoroughly enjoyed the film – 'clean bawdy, not dirty bawdy', they thought – he and his board were anxious to put it in the broader A category. There were, though, two problems: the eating scene, 'where,' wrote Trevelyan, 'oysters were used as an obvious suggestion of fellatio', and also the bedroom scene between Finney and Redman. The first necessitated a cut even for the X category and it was administered 'with some reluctance'. The second query was trickier. As Trevelyan explained:

> There was important action in the scene but I believed that it could be altered in such a way as to keep the action and get rid of our problem. I had a long discussion with Richardson in which I strongly pressed him to do this so he could have an A and so a wider audience, but he resisted it and finally said he would have to consult his board. A few days later he telephoned to say that his board had decided to take an X certificate.

A little later, when the film was submitted to the Catholic Office in New York to obtain the precious seal, the question came up again about a couple of cuts. This time the film-makers, doubtless with the urging of the distributor, United Artists (Columbia had turned down the film), agreed and the editor Tony Gibbs flew to the States to substitute some other previously discarded material for the offending shots.

While Finney waited for *Tom Jones* to be released, he decided to escape from London – not only from the recent treadmill of stage and screen, as well as the abortive *Ned Kelly* foray in Australia, but also from sheer necessity: he was desperately keen to direct but no theatre seemed particularly anxious to offer him a job.

Another bugbear was his feeling that, in the West End at least, the actor was merely a hired hand and had no part to play in the direction process, with the result that there was no sense of full participation. He wrote to a number of repertory theatres; he was turned down by some and received no reply at all from others. The only positive response was from the Glasgow Citizens' Theatre, then under the stewardship of Iain Cuthbertson. He could direct Pinter's *The Birthday Party* and one other play (*School for Scandal* was selected) if he was prepared to play the title role in Pirandello's *Henry IV*. Finney was not too keen on the part but the overall offer was, from a work point of view, too good to refuse, even if, as the newspapers gleefully speculated, his salary of £20 a week represented a pay cut of £480 a week. The stint was to be for two and a half months, before he started filming *Night Must Fall*.

In the back of his mind, though, was an altogether more ambitious project. It seems that Finney wanted to create his own ensemble, producing its own plays and with its own authors – something, thought Finney with admirable *chutzpah*, like the 'tie-up Shakespeare had with the Globe'. The group would be based in London and would, periodically, embark on 'new wave' tours of the provinces. The idea never seems to have progressed.

During his time in Glasgow, Finney lived in a flat north of the Clyde, which was sparsely furnished with health food, a pair of bongo drums and some jazz records. He would commute to the theatre, taking care to avoid the queue which more often than not threaded its way right past the Citz and on to the Palace bingo hall next door.

'Despite being,' wrote Tynan, 'grotesquely miscast' as the 1920s Italian nobleman who, after being kicked in the head by a horse, believes himself to be a German monarch, the constant critic could still find praise amid careful criticism: '[Finney is] too young, too moon-shaped of mien and frankly inept at conveying the razor-edged intellect that underlies Henry's lunacy; but the thrust of his temperament carries him over these hurdles to hard-won triumph.' Writing more generally about Finney's decision to direct in Glasgow, Tynan outlined the deal, noting that 'he plunged into a play that was not of his choosing, and a part well outside his usual range. He behaved, in short, like a serious actor and not a star.'

However, it was very much as the star that he finally prepared for the June opening of *Tom Jones* in the UK with rather more than just a passing interest in the potential box office. To help keep production costs down, Finney had agreed to a modest fee, £10,000, but large numbers of 'points' – a percentage of the profits (Susannah York's representatives, for instance, had opted for a healthier fee and no 'points'). Just before the film opened at the London Pavilion, the British distributor was said to have predicted glumly it would run only a fortnight at best. Reviews were fairly mixed – from 'the bawdiest, funniest, most brilliant slap-and-tickle romp I've seen' to 'in the most costly way – which squanders reputations as well as money – the film is a failure . . . [Finney] has no depth and for Finney to play the part is like hiring Pinter to write a nursery rhyme.' The Cassandras were to be proved wrong, though.

Three months on, Finney was already in New York playing *Luther* when *Tom Jones* opened in the States, mostly to ecstatic reviews and, like Britain, exceptional business. To coin a phrase, it ran and ran. Less than a year later, Finney's 10 per cent of *Tom Jones* had already earned him a further £357,000, making him a dollar millionaire at twenty-seven.

6

National Hero

When, at the end of his commitment to *Luther* in New York, towards the close of January 1964, Finney decided to quit working and just drop completely and lengthily out of sight, it wasn't a spur of the moment decision. The previous autumn he'd been telling friends and even journalists that after eight years' solid grind he felt a desperate need to 'just run away' from it all. New York had brought matters to a head. *Luther* and then *Tom Jones* had turned a relentless spotlight on the twenty-seven-year-old, now being described as 'probably the greatest English-speaking actor in the world under forty'. Being lionized in New York is a heady business and, though he seemed to relish some aspects of the adulation, Finney was still level-headed enough to realize how quickly the fame could fatally snare him. When his parents visited him – coinciding with President Kennedy's assassination – their trip also, more poignantly, served to remind him of the real world outside his gilded profession.

There were also a couple more practical considerations. After *Luther* and *Tom Jones*, what on earth do you do for an encore? And his private life was a mess. The first marriage was long over, he'd had a quite public fling with

Samantha Eggar and, early in 1963, he was cited in actress Judith Stott's divorce and ordered to pay the costs in the case. At the time, he told reporters: 'Judith and I are terrible friends. But I'm not going to marry her. I don't intend to marry anyone.' Finney also rather fancied the idea of a very long holiday. His delayed honeymoon to the South of France had been spent ducking out of the rain and occasional short vacations since then were just that – occasional and too short.

One of his favourite holiday locations was Peter Bull's home on the tiny Greek island of Paxos, in the Ionian Sea south of Corfu. Bull's godson, Sheridan Morley, explained:

> Peter was deeply gay and the twin passions of his life, both completely unreciprocated, were Alec Guinness and Albert, which is interesting in itself because they are so unalike. Albert was very good to Peter and, for instance, insisted on his going to New York with him when *Luther* transferred [Bull was also cast in *Tom Jones*]; I think he rather liked having him around as an eating companion. Peter was deeply in love with Albert and saw in him everything that he would like to have been himself – the flamboyant theatre star. Peter was, of course, only ever a supporting actor and, traumatized by his own gayness, saw in Albert, I think, a sort of native courage which he also deeply admired.

Those Greek trips were also the source of other vivid memories. Ann Lynn, who hadn't seen Finney since *The Lily White Boys*, was once staying on Corfu when out of the mists one morning he suddenly materialized unannounced aboard the ferry boat from Corfu town. Travelling on his own, he then joined up with Lynn and her partner and stayed with them at their hotel for the next three days.

A second Greek encounter was potentially more fraught. Susannah York was holidaying with her then husband

Michael Wells and they too suddenly bumped into Finney. Her mind quickly raced back to a time when they were still shooting *Tom Jones* together:

> It was an in-between sort of time for Albie as he'd just broken with Samantha. Anyway, he suddenly fetched up on my doorstep very late one night while Michael was away. I have to say I found him an attractive and extremely sexy guy, but I told him firmly I was happily married and that was that.
>
> Now when he met us he noticed that Michael was very down at the time [he'd had some bad luck with work] and said to him: 'You know, your wife's terrific. I once landed up on your doorstep but she wouldn't have me – she's much too wrapped up in you.' I'd never told Michael about the incident; there was never really any point or reason. It was a very generous, and typical, thing for Albie to do, and it certainly cheered Michael up a great deal.

Finney left *Luther* after a Thursday night performance. David Merrick asked him to complete the week but, as the two had had a 'slight altercation', Finney chose not to. The end of the contract virtually coincided with the announcement of the Academy Award nominations from Hollywood. As well as *Tom Jones*, it was also the year of *Hud, Lilies of the Field*, Fellini's *8½*, Kazan's *America America*, and that great bloated $37 million epic, *Cleopatra*. After *Lawrence of Arabia*'s seven-Oscar triumph the previous year, there was another good occasion in prospect for the British film industry, with *This Sporting Life* (Richard Harris, Rachel Roberts) and *The L-shaped Room* (Leslie Caron) also in contention for acting awards. But *Tom Jones*, leader by a nose with ten nominations, was really the talking point.

No fewer than three of its actresses (an Academy record) – Diane Cilento, Edith Evans and Joyce Redman – featured in the Supporting category, while Finney was vying for Best

Actor with Harris, Rex Harrison (*Cleopatra*), Paul New-man (*Hud*) and Sidney Poitier (*Lilies of the Field*), and Hugh Griffith was also a contender in the Supporting stakes.

The other nominations were for Best Film, Best Director, Best Adapted Screenplay, Art Direction and Music (John Addison), with Tony Gibbs's editing and Walter Lassally's cinematography the notable omissions.

On the actual April night of the Academy Awards, which were being presented at the Santa Monica Civic Auditorium, Finney was far away to the west in Hawaii, following in the footsteps of his childhood hero, Captain Cook. More than two months into his sabbatical, he'd already travelled through the Eastern states, down into Mexico, up to the West Coast and out to Hawaii.

His own account of that Oscar night is one of Finney's most often told stories, and is regularly and gleefully passed on by fellow actors like Eddie Olmos, with whom he worked much later (on *Wolfen*). That evening Finney was with a Hawaiian couple and was partnered by a local girl on a dinner-and-drinks cruise aboard a huge catamaran out from Pearl Harbor to Diamond Head and back. As they got on the boat, a journalist approached Finney, telling him he had a transistor radio and asking if he would like to listen to the Awards ceremony. Finney firmly turned down his offer. Because of the band noise the journalist couldn't hear his radio, so he climbed into a lifeboat and settled under the tarpaulin with the small set.

When the boat got to Diamond Head about two and a half hours later, he climbed out of the lifeboat, back and ears bent and with a long face. He sidled up to the edge of the dance floor, where Finney was executing some hula steps, and said nothing. Later, as the actor drained his coconut milk and cognac, the journalist asked, 'Was Sidney Poitier very good in *Lilies of the Field*?' Finney, rather puzzled, replied that he was.

As the catamaran approached the dock it had to turn

round to reverse in and everyone aboard was moving towards the points of exit on each deck. Finney was on the top deck looking down when, about 30 yards from the quay, he spied huge arc lights blazing, along with a camera and crew. Then 10 yards, and 5 . . . Suddenly Finney saw a man pushing his way through the crowd, shouting, 'Wrap it up. He didn't win.' Sidney Poitier had. By the time the catamaran tied up, all the paraphernalia had long gone.

There were to be four Oscars for *Tom Jones* – film, director, adapted screenplay and music – making it the first time since *Hamlet* in 1948 that an entirely British-made effort had won Best Picture. Finney's loss was also part of history in the making, as Poitier was the first ever black to win one of the top two performance awards. Sadly, the trio of supporting actresses cancelled themselves out as dear old Margaret Rutherford (in *The VIPs*) bustled through in the final furlong to nab that particular prize.

Some five months into his idyll, Finney had fetched up in Polynesia, on the tiny island of Raiatea, between Tahiti and Bora-Bora. Swim, breakfast, look at the reef, Bloody Mary, occasional native fling, swim, Bloody Mary – it was a backbreaking schedule of self-indulgence as Finney pondered the human dilemma with his toes in the surf. The trouble was, he was so busy doing nothing that any effort, like even reading a book, was becoming a chore. 'I realized,' he said later, 'that I was so wound down that I was about to fall apart.'

Even if the big questions had raised more problems than providing real answers, he did manage to figure a few truths: first, that he wanted more than ever to remain his own man; and, second, that acting, though a living, wasn't the 'be all'. He had, after all, turned down all of £250,000 to co-star with Julie Andrews and Max von Sydow in, ironically, Michener's *Hawaii*. There'd also been talk of his playing the Young Winston (Churchill).

The sound of a jet overhead one day suddenly jolted him. He needed to return home and pick up some of the threads.

Fiji, Australia, Hong Kong, Bangkok, Europe and, finally, London – a full ten months after he'd first set out on his travels.

'Mr Albert Finney,' wrote Bernard Levin in *The Times*, 'signals his return to the stage and his most welcome accession to the National Theatre Company by playing Don Pedro as though he had a red-hot poker stuck in his trousers, staggering about backwards and talking like an itinerant ice-cream pedlar with a cleft palate.' This was Franco Zeffirelli's flamboyant production of *Much Ado About Nothing*, with the not-quite-yet-married Maggie Smith and Robert Stephens as Beatrice and Benedick, Frank Finlay as Dogberry, and two other even younger bloods, Ian McKellen and Derek Jacobi, as Claudio and Don John. Eighteen months earlier Finney had been in New York, still playing *Luther*, when the National Theatre Company of fifty, under Olivier's artistic stewardship, was launched at a refurbished Old Vic with O'Toole – yes, O'Toole, again – as Hamlet.

Working with Olivier were two associate directors, John Dexter and William Gaskill, and against his own initial judgement, countered by the shrewd advice of his wife, Joan Plowright, Olivier also took on Tynan as 'dramaturg', or literary manager, after the critic had written to 'Sir', immodestly offering his services in that capacity. The regime was by all accounts extremely democratic and the presence of Tynan at least ensured Finney had one friend at court.

Soon after his return from what became known as 'The Trip', Finney contacted Olivier, asking if he could join the company and adding humbly that he was perfectly happy to 'play as cast'. Zeffirelli had originally asked Olivier if he himself would play Don Pedro, and it was then suggested that Finney should take it on as part of working his passage with the company. The director was delighted to have Finney, though surprised, after all the acclaim and the awards for *Tom Jones*, that the actor should be prepared to accept something rather less than a starring part.

The comparatively small role of Don Pedro towards the end of the National's second season was an ideal vehicle – only two speeches of more than two lines – in Finney's bid to return to what he called 'match fitness'. He explained to Clive Goodwin: 'I found that the breathing equipment wasn't functioning properly; I couldn't quite time when to take my breaths any more. I felt that it took me about three months of being back in the theatre to feel match fit. The environment was such that one could explore. Such varied style. Not of plays, but of directors.'

For Finney, there were to be no fewer than six plays and six different directors over the next year or so. Zeffirelli staged *Much Ado* as broad Sicilian-style comedy. Strapped into a corset to make him look rigid and adopting a strong Spanish accent, Finney played it as broad as ordered. Billington's recurring image of him in the play is his 'sitting alone at the end of the play, puffing a cigar, while everyone else has paired off, as they do in Shakespeare comedy, and he's left in his little pool of solitude and loneliness. Finney had made something very good and concrete out of that small part.'

His next role could not have been any greater in contrast or more demanding in its scale and ambition; match-fitness was essential. Inspired, loosely, by the role of the United Nations in the Congo during the early sixties, John Arden devised *Armstrong's Last Goodnight*, set not in twentieth-century Africa but instead in the sixteenth-century Scottish borders, where King James in Edinburgh is attempting to establish his authority over the local barons, notably the Armstrongs of Gilnockie. As if this wasn't exotic enough, Arden had devised his own patented dialect of medieval lowland Scots, which was then further overlaid by a dialect-within-a-dialect, as it were, to contrast the wild language of the Armstrongs with the more cultured tones of the King's Scottish representative. The play, which had started life at

the Glasgow Citizens' in 1964 – with Iain Cuthbertson as
Gilnockie – found a perfect arena the following summer in
the unlikely setting of genteel, south coast Chichester, at its
Festival Theatre.

The playhouse, with its large Elizabethan-style apron
stage, made ideal use of a medieval convention of
'mansions' – that is, three simultaneous settings, Castle,
Palace and Wood, which then consciously reflected three
kinds of lifestyle and the journey between them.

For Frances Gray, an expert on Arden's work, of all
modern plays this one seemed born for

> the spacious intimacy of Chichester. The characters did
> not, as they seemed to in most plays, simply walk on
> and say their lines or do their business and walk off;
> they created a whole pattern of energy on the stage so
> that not a moment was wasted. The dialogue had an
> amplitude that filled the massive space and which was
> clearly a joy to speak – the verse in particular seemed
> to charge the actors with power. It was a phenomenon
> I had not seen outside the Jacobean drama.

Wild-haired, straggly-bearded, feather-hatted and mightily
cod-pieced, Finney was a great bull of a border chieftain for
whom fate finally decrees the hangman's rope. During the
production, he told an actor friend of Billington's: 'You've
got to go out there and look as if you're enjoying every
moment you're on stage.' And Billington has said: 'I think
that's one of the clues to Finney as a stage presence. It's that
looking as if he owns the stage by right, not as if he's crept
on to it by default.'

Following Chichester, *Armstrong's Last Goodnight* was
selected to open the National's 1965–6 season, with Finney,
Robert Stephens (as the devious royal herald, Lindsay),
Geraldine McEwan and Paul Curran all repeating their
leading roles, and in the absence of the original directors
(Dexter/Gaskill) it was revised for the Old Vic by Finney

himself. Recalling Gray's earlier words, it might be tempting to suppose that Finney was fighting a losing battle with the proscenium.

Clearly pinching himself in disbelief, W A Darlington, who'd not enjoyed the play at Chichester, wrote in the *Daily Telegraph*: 'I had arrived at the Old Vic with no hope that I should dislike it less so. To my amazement I found myself enjoying it, and I went on enjoying it all evening. There was no arguing with my feelings; I had had an almost complete change of heart. A play which had seemed distant and dead now seemed close and warmly alive.'

As Darlington continued to ponder this inexplicable notion, he received a letter from Finney, who, he said, waved aside any suggestion that it was cleverness on his part in restaging the play that had altered its impact. It was, Finney wrote in his note, the Old Vic itself which had caused the improvement to 'which my reaction had been so immediate and so powerful. He did not enlarge on this theme, but it was quite clear what he meant. Once again, and this time in a play which I had thought ideally suited for the open stage, the greater intimacy, the closer concentration of a proscenium, had brought an increase of vitality.' J W Lambert, in the *Sunday Times*, was less convinced, for, while noting that the action had been speeded up, he wrote:

> [Finney's] own performance is as strong, as knotted, as shaggily vulnerable as before; and this is still, though it seems ungrateful to a fine actor giving a fine performance to say so, not enough. This bull to the toreador of Sir David Lindsay doesn't quite hold the ring, for all his bellowing; and something indefinably mannered in Robert Stephens's Lindsay removes this devious character into a different kind of play.

It is impossible to leave that 1965 Chichester season without reference to another altogether different, if only marginally less trail-blazing, production, Peter Shaffer's one-acter *Black Comedy*, paired at the Festival (and later in London) with Strindberg's *Miss Julie*. Shaffer's principal source was a celebrated scene in Chinese classical theatre in which two swordsmen fight a duel in a completely darkened room. The scene is actually performed with the stage fully lit.

Tynan, anxious to keep attracting new plays to the National – in those days Chichester served regularly as a kind of dress rehearsal – began talking with Shaffer, who the year before had been responsible for the memorable *Royal Hunt of the Sun*. Shaffer told him of his Peking Opera idea and on that slender basis, just an idea and a title, *Black Comedy* was announced in March 1965. Over the next four months Shaffer, Tynan and John Dexter, who was to direct the piece, went into regular huddles, underscoring the basic premise that, as Tynan put it, 'all the laughs must be directly connected with the light–darkness convention'. As the play entered rehearsal in Chichester, there was still, apparently, no actual script, just an idea and a few scenes which, explained National Theatre historian, John Elsom, 'were rapidly brought together into neat farce, conventional in structure though with an original idea, with Peter Shaffer rewriting the script to the very days before the opening'. As the play begins, the stage is in total blackness and the cast are saying things like, 'Oh, what a lovely chair.' Then, suddenly, the lights blaze on, and with a chorus of, 'Oh my God, what happened? The lights went out', the lights come up full on a South Kensington apartment where an engagement party is in full swing.

So, for the rest, it's a question of split-second farce as, as if in darkness, the cast begin to stumble over chairs, into one another, and so on. For perhaps the first time in his professional career, Finney was cast entirely against type as the camp, indeed positively mincing, antique dealer Harold Gorringe, complete with hand on hip and effeminate North Country accent. It would doubtless be regarded as excessive these days, but in the context of the sixties and as counterpoint to Maggie Smith's increasingly drunken insults, it was extremely funny.

The 1965–6 season also marked Anthony Hopkins's first major London engagement. Though only a year younger than Finney, he was almost a generation behind in experience and confidence, having attended RADA a little belatedly and then paid his Rep dues in the early sixties. Later, he enjoyed an extraordinarily coincidental 'break' when, like Finney in 1959, he had to go on for Olivier in the starring role (the Captain in *Dance of Death*). Now, though, Hopkins was understudying Colin Blakely as Ben in *Love for Love* and expected to play the riotous Restoration role once Blakely left to go on tour. In fact, though, it was decided at very short notice (only ten days) to ask Finney if he'd step in for his old chum, which he happily did. Hopkins remembers being called in to meet Finney because they were going to rehearse some songs together: 'Hello,' he said, 'I'm Albert Finney. Can yer' sing. No? Welsh aren't yer'?' All done with great charm, said Hopkins.

Tom Jones was still of fairly recent memory when Finney went on as Ben and the audience was packed with university girl students. Hopkins recalls:

There was a pretty heavy cast in *Love for Love* – Olivier, Geraldine McEwan and so on – and you must remember that he hardly knew the part, so he was having to mug along. As he walked on, the audience went berserk and Finney just stood there, milking the applause. I'd never seen such bravura. Olivier went quite red and even turned a somersault on stage to see if he could steal a scene. They were having a drink afterwards and Olivier said to the assembled, through tight lips, 'Albert's doing so well!' Finney replied quickly, 'Cos' I'm a bloody big star.' He was so friendly and accessible: just the sort of four-square, full-frontal actor I really admire.

Hopkins also admitted to more than a trace of envy regarding Finney because he himself was such a late developer: 'He . . . has a healthy arrogance and confidence. Michael Gambon once asked me during rehearsals if I'd ever seen anyone that confident. The answer's never. And that confidence is also tremendously charismatic.' Later that season, the company was on tour in Birmingham and Hopkins approached Finney: 'I was rather tongue-tied and for want of anything else to say, I said: "I hear you're leaving the National?" He said: "Where did yer' hear that?" I said: "I just heard it. Are you coming back?" And he replied, giving that grin, "One day. As a director." '

There was still the last, and perhaps the best, to come: his award-winning spring double in Feydeau's *A Flea in Her Ear* as Victor Emmanuel Chandebise, the impotent Parisian bourgeois, and Poche, the lookalike idiot hotel porter.

Billington recalled:

> As Chandebise, he was with his stiff-jointed walk, ramrod-straight back and arms pinned to his side, erect in all but the most vital sense; as Poche his shoulders drooped and his knees sagged as if from a lifetime of carrying insupportably heavy loads. But his masterstroke – a real sign of acting intelligence – was never to exaggerate the difference between the two men so that the confusion of one for the other became totally plausible.

The production was doubly blessed by John Mortimer's elegant translation ('I am ready to commit a folly. Will you join me?') and the presence of the Comédie Française's Jacques Charon, a fine farceur himself, as director.

Finney was very impressed with Charon:

> It was marvellous to have a director doing that play who you knew could do it better than any of the cast.

When you're playing a double role, an actor's instinct is first of all to show how clever he is, to say, I'll make him as different as possible, so one's A and one's Z, to show what versatility you've got. Charon said no, what's interesting is to make them as close, because they're different. And, of course, he was absolutely right.

The production was full of other deliciously memorable performances, like Edward Hardwicke's cleft-palated nephew, Geraldine McEwan's henna-haired wife, head darting 'like a lobbed tennis ball', and Frank Wylie as Carlos Homenides de Histuanga, the absurdly jealous husband with a Spanish lisp, all cross-cutting in furious unison at the Hôtel Coq d'Or.

At the heart of the piece, however, wrote Trewin, was Finney:

> now with a dignified glare, now with a faithful-dog smirk. He hurries upstairs with logs, swings round on the bed, changes cap and jacket, chases himself in at one door and out at the other, and contrives always to get himself into the right scene at the most disastrous time. Moreover, he never fails to look like one of the halves of that apple cleft in two.

From Feydeau's fictitious suburb of 'Montretout' to, later the same year, France proper; or at least as proper as an unashamedly glossy Hollywood movie on location would permit. Apart from a rather good cameo as a drunken Russian soldier in the grim climax to Carl Foreman's well-meaning wartime saga *The Victors* back in 1963, Finney had not worked on what he called a '*movie* movie' before Stanley Donen's *Two for the Road*. Till now, he had been with friends, in familiar places, everything reassuringly British.

Now he was being asked to play a sort of Cary Grant in

De Luxe colour and Panavision opposite, for the first time, a real international 'star', who looked and acted disconcertingly like Audrey Hepburn, whose elegant, non-stop wardrobe – by Paco Rabanne, Mary Quant, Tiffin and sundry others – seemed to count for as much as the words. Happily, the words were pretty elegant too in Frederic Raphael's time-leaping story of a twelve-year-old marriage that appears to be faltering. As Mark and Joanna Wallace, Finney and Hepburn run the gamut of emotions from breathless students to bored marrieds – though not necessarily in that order.

Hepburn, whose previous film had been with O'Toole, looked even more relaxed in tandem with Finney, who was seven years her junior. In retrospect, their amusingly combative, sexually quite frank on-screen relationship gains an extra frisson with the knowledge that the two really were 'close', as they say, during filming. Hepburn's first marriage to Mel Ferrer was almost over, Finney was between engagements and so the timing and the setting were perfect for the showbiz equivalent of a holiday romance.

It became clear that Hepburn was extremely nervous and 'strung up' before filming started, so Finney was able to call into play his often-used powers to help ease his co-star into her new, earthier image.

They were shooting in the Paris suburbs when William Daniels, that fine American character actor, arrived on the set two months into the three-month schedule. He immediately noticed that the two stars were 'having a hell of a good time together'. Daniels and Eleanor Bron, sporting a reasonably convincing accent, were playing a tiresome American couple who, with their ghastly spoilt daughter, encounter the Wallaces during a spot of sightseeing.

On his own admission, Daniels was more than a little nervous when, on his first day of shooting, he found himself out on the road filming his own last scene in the picture:

The scene is where the couple split up after a fight and they leave our car. It was meant to be kind of emotional. I remember that we had this funny old station wagon and Finney was sitting in the back with Audrey, kidding and teasing her; they were both giggling away. He'd call her funny names like Tawdry Audrey or Audrey Sunburn. Since they seemed so relaxed, I decided to move 10 or 20 yards away and practise my lines while he stayed in the car with her and smoked his Monte Cristo cigar.

Suddenly, I heard a voice shout, 'Billy!' I looked round and it was Finney and he was beckoning me over to the car. I leaned in and he said, 'Not to worry. She gets all the close-ups.' We all laughed and it broke the ice. After that, I was relaxed too — and he also introduced me to Monte Cristos.

Despite Raphael's Oscar-nominated script — full of predictably sharp one-liners — and Hepburn at her most irresistible, the movie's never really amounted to much more than glossy fluff. It also, in a curious way, suffers from the fact that Finney simply isn't Cary Grantish enough to make it convincing fluff. There's charisma without charm; a certain loutishness, even, which distracts rather than helps. And despite the concerted attempt to update Hepburn's sweet image, it's almost as if the stars are performing in two different kinds of film. Hepburn did, however, manage to figure in that year's Academy Awards, but not for Donen's movie. Her nomination was for the more familiar, bewildered-kitten image in the nail-biting thriller *Wait Until Dark*.

7

Albert's Memorial

Lindsay Anderson, Stephen Frears, Mike Leigh, Bill Naughton, Julian Mitchell, Ted Whitehead and Peter Nichols – just to mention a magnificent seven – have all at varying stages of their respective careers had much reason to be grateful to Finney – or, more specifically, to his and Michael Medwin's production company, Memorial Enterprises, which helped foster their work. Finney once explained:

> Up to 1964 I could have a company called Albert Finney Inc and put myself under contract to that company, which would buy my car and so on. Then they changed the tax laws. I also had this company called Memorial – because of the Albert Memorial – and it was really just a joke between me and my accountant. We never really intended to do anything with it; it was just a personal company that employed me. Anyway, when the law changed, we decided to activate it. We never meant to threaten Twentieth Century Fox!

Finney first met Michael Medwin when he was making

Saturday Night and Sunday Morning. At the time, Medwin, who had already enjoyed a string of minor film roles from 1946 on, was one of the stars of the hit TV sitcom *The Army Game*. The pair were introduced through a mutual friend, Norman Rossington, who was in both Finney's film and Medwin's TV series. Though the two men could hardly have been more different – Medwin, thirteen years older, ex-public school – they became firm friends, united in a desire to make a small contribution to the creation of quality film and theatre productions.

As Finney said: 'We're both actors, temperamentally strolling players. I certainly didn't want to go into the office at seven o'clock in the morning and endlessly read scripts and do deals. The idea was that we might come across something from time to time. We didn't ever intend to get a great machine working.'

Memorial opened for business in 1965 and, after gently turning away the man who came through the door with a series of headstone designs, it invested first in Bill Naughton's *Spring and Port Wine*, bringing the play to the West End via the Mermaid Theatre in 1966. The same year, on his thirtieth birthday, Finney announced that he'd not only star in but also direct a new film written by his fellow Salfordian, Shelagh Delaney. Though they'd grown up in the same city and achieved fame around the same sort of time in collaboration with mutual friends, the two didn't actually know each other before *Charlie Bubbles*.

Delaney, a one-time salesgirl and cinema usherette who'd left school at sixteen, was just nineteen when her first play, *A Taste of Honey*, became one of the key works of the kitchen-sink era. Finney now heard that she'd written an eight or nine page outline for a possible film and decided to get in touch. They met, and continued to meet, and as a result a script began to evolve. According to Finney:

It's very difficult to make a film about someone being a little doubtful of their success. 'He's got lots of money.

What's there for him to be worried about?' is an obvious reaction. Both Shelagh and I were successful quite young, and for her I think that was an intense experience. *Taste of Honey* was, after all, her first play. Suddenly, she was *a playwright*. Anyway, I felt very close to what she was trying to explore.

As early as 1961 there had been hints that Finney was interested in much more than just the traditional actor's role and especially in the status of cinema *vis-à-vis* stage in this country. In a rather intriguing question-and-answer session conducted by *Sight & Sound* between him and actress Mary Ure, he expanded on his thoughts.

Asked about the difference in attitude to cinema between an older generation of stage actors and his, he said:

> An old actor who came to see *Billy Liar* asked me if I'd enjoyed doing *Saturday Night*. I said, 'Yes, very much', and he said, 'Well, they're all right for the money.' I can't feel about the cinema that it's just a sort of hobby which pays a little extra on the side, while the theatre is the place where I do my real prestige work. I want to do my prestige work in the cinema as well, and I think this feeling is growing. But the cinema has always been a kind of club . . . a special place where the people are very nice, all the films are very nice and nobody does any real work.

And he might have been defining the role of film director when he answered: 'Preparation's essential. Making a film involves such a long period of creation and in theory at least the first day's shooting is intended to be part of the finished film. So, it's important, even on the first day, that you should all know what you're aiming at.'

His further frustration over what he felt was the prevailing concept of actor merely as 'hired hand' had led to his short but, by all accounts, quite successful directing stint at Glasgow. As his preparation on *Charlie Bubbles* progressed, he became certain that he no longer wanted to participate in the project as actor only. He declared: 'I want to be totally involved in everything I do. Just to act by itself is not enough.'

Charlie Bubbles is an endearing compendium, virtually a style guide, of all you might expect from a comfortably-off first-time director who is self-flagellating on the one hand and fulsomely acknowledges all his cinematic influences on the other. It's the film equivalent of stream-of-consciousness autobiography in full cinematic flow.

Charlie/Finney is a rich and acclaimed London-based writer whose elevation to wealth and success from a modest background appears to have left him not so much self-satisfied as completely apathetic. He can summon the drunken energy for a restaurant food fight with a less successful writer, Smokey, but is simply too tired to care when his adoring American fan-secretary, Eliza, tries fumblingly to seduce him in a Manchester hotel after the requisite return home to the North in his gold Rolls Royce. He takes his nine-year-old son Jack (from a failed marriage) to the big match, loses him at the end of the game when he's distracted and, after a frantic but fruitless search – which seems to provoke a rare bout of real flesh-and-blood emotion – eventually finds Jack back at home with his mother.

Beautifully framed, even if the relentless close-ups do become tiresome, and intermittently droll, *Charlie Bubbles*, set over a forty-eight-hour period, seems as a whole to be afflicted by a terminal joylessness. Not even the more picaresque moments – Charlie's rather dreamlike encounters up the motorway and his climactic 'escape' over the Pennines in a convenient hot-air balloon – do much to alleviate the studied gloom. It is, however, a neat visual summation of some of Finney's old stamping grounds – from the Salford streets to the Derbyshire peaks at Edale via Old Trafford soccer stadium.

Apart from about four days in his own clothes, Finney was always involved in front and behind the camera. Wearing costume and make-up, he'd find himself working out set-ups and talking with actors with Kleenex clamped in his collar. In a *Sunday Times* interview with Hunter Davies, he graphically described the nuts-and-bolts of directing *Charlie Bubbles*:

We had this location which was a slum clearance area in Salford, about 2 miles of it. I got up there about an hour early, at 7.30 in the morning, still in the dark, to see how we could do the sequence. It was an area I used to know as a boy. I was walking round it when this copper stopped me, wondering what I was doing. 'Oh, it's you Albert.' He knows I'm filming in the area. It gets to 8.00 and I'm still looking round. At 8.10 I can hear the trucks coming round the corner, about half a mile away. It's getting lighter. I know they're going to be here in a minute. They roll up with all the technicians and the gear. All I want to say is go away, go away. I just don't know what I want to do.

They all pile out. 'Hello, Guv, lovely day, isn't it? Where's the tea?' Then the rest of the lads start arriving. At 8.20 the first assistant asks, 'What's the first site, then?' I look around, about sixty people, all waiting for me to make up my mind. They're talking about last night's TV and where they're going for a drink. I think, I've got to get moving. For the fourth time, the first assistant says, 'What's the first set-up?' I just can't think. In order to get everybody's energy moving, I just say anything, though I've no idea. Just to get that first shot in.

I know it'll probably end up not being used, but I know I have to. I'm the director. They would still be standing there otherwise, or all have gone home ... I've been completely responsible for something for the first time in my life. I haven't got a get-out clause this time. Actors always have. You can blame the director or the script.

Finney's casting was a mixture of the familiar, the unorthodox and perhaps the downright sentimental. Billie Whitelaw, playing the ex-wife Lottie, was a colleague at the National. So too was Colin Blakely, as Smokey, in a sort of extended sequel to their *Saturday Night* shenanigans. Then there was another old Salfordian, Joe Gladwin, as a waiter at the Piccadilly Hotel in Manchester. Much less obvious was the choice of twenty-year-old Liza Minnelli as the gauche Eliza in her movie début (if you don't count a final-scene shot with her mother in the 1949 musical *In the Good Old Summertime*) – and very good she is too, briefly breathing some transatlantic life into the native torpor. As for his own performance, Finney felt that if he'd been directing another actor he'd have made him a 'little looser' than the way he played Charlie. The performance, he has adjudged, was 'a little heavy'.

As Finney went location-hopping in Manchester and Salford on the first six weeks of the shoot, it was a bit like the return of a local hero, and for his part he thought nothing of stopping at the bus stop and picking up a Roller full of natives, who clucked with pleasure as he drove them to work in the morning. They filmed the Edale cottage scenes early on, as well as the balloon ending.

According to Terence Clegg, the first assistant director: 'No one really knew what that was all about; not even Albert, I think. I'm pretty sure the ending wasn't in the original script in quite that form.' Clegg confirmed that there was generally a very relaxed feeling on the set throughout shooting. Sometimes, a little too relaxed. Apart from playing, rather well, a small featured role in the film, the late Alan Lake was also employed to be Finney's stand-in when the guv'nor was behind the camera preparing a shot.

Lake, who had a major drinking problem, would become

legless on the set two or three times a week, having started
quaffing around lunchtime and becoming incapable by
afternoon tea. According to Clegg: 'After that you couldn't
use him. Frankly, he was a pain in the arse and most people
would have fired him, yet Albert always remained loyal to
his friends.' Lake's boozing reached its unfortunate peak at
the film's wrap-party, held in the old St John's Wood
Studios. He was drunk even before the party started and
then proceeded to smash and crash his way in, knocking
over everyone and everything in his way. After he was,
literally, thrown out, he began to make a noisy fuss on the
steps outside and Clegg was sent for to deal with the
nuisance.

> I remember getting hold of his lapels and, as I did so,
> Alan lost his footing and he fell back down the steps,
> cracking his head at the bottom. I thought I'd killed
> him. Anyway, Albert then left the party to go and sit
> with him and the next day rang me to say that I might,
> or might not, as the case may be, be relieved to know
> that Alan would be all right. It certainly had a
> dampening effect on the party.

Any problems with Minnelli were simply to do with her
age and screen-acting inexperience. Accompanied during
the shoot by another American girl who acted as secretary-
cum-companion, she was certainly nervous and typically
edgy in a Garland-like way, but with Finney's careful
shepherding – which some wickedly say extended to a bout
of 'deep research' in Weaste Cemetery – she came through
with flying colours. Clegg remembered just one tricky
encounter:

> There was a scene where she had to come down the
> stairs, then say some dialogue and it all had to be
> perfectly timed. Twelve seconds for the walk, seven
> seconds for the line, and so on. She fluffed it a few

times and, in my impatience and inexperience, I made an audible noise of disapproval, with the result that she absolutely flew at me. Albert just smirked.

After filming in the North and for several nights at the Newport Pagnell service station on the M1, the unit returned to London. A large house in St John's Wood was taken over and furnished to double as Charlie's luxurious home, and Clegg recalled some problems shooting the scenes showing the closed-circuit surveillance operating from the study: 'There's a bank of television screens and each one had to be shot individually and then be timed into the whole picture so that they fitted correctly. It was extremely complicated.'

No less so was the sequence in which Charlie and Smokey emerge into the street following their food fight. The restaurant was, in fact, re-created in an empty building next to Universal Pictures (the film's financier) in Piccadilly.

The idea was that the two men would walk down the street, covered in spaghetti, attracting considerable attention from passers-by. The police wouldn't allow a camera on the street itself, so one had to be set up on the first floor of Jaeger and, with a long lens, then follow the men's unsteady progress. First glance at the rushes confirmed the worst: only about one in twenty pedestrians reacted. The British, being British, simply ignored all the fuss. They tried the process again and again but with much the same result. As a final throw, they moved on to Regent Street and, with a camera set up in the back of a van, they tracked the pair as far as they dared. The upshot was that very little of the material was usable and they were twice caught by the police.

Finney, based in Wardour Street, was working with his editor Fergus McDonnell one day when he spotted Lindsay Anderson walking past the cutting-room windows. He leant out to ask Anderson what he was up to and was told that

he and writer David Sherwin were hawking round a
finished script called *if. . .*, a black comedy about three
boys at a public school. As there was no production
company yet attached to the project, Finney suggested they
should give Medwin the script. So began the long and often
dispiriting saga of trying to get the film fully financed.
Despite Memorial's involvement, certainly no other major
British company appeared remotely interested.

A year later, when Finney was in New York preparing to
star in *A Day in the Death of Joe Egg*, he and Medwin
played what may have been the final trump card for *if. . .*,
especially as another American company had just backed
out. They arranged a meeting with Charles Bluhdorn, head
of Gulf & Western, Paramount's parent company, a move
which was fraught with danger because Paramount's
London chief, 'Bud' Ornstein, had already turned the film
down. Bluhdorn's first question was, 'How much is the
director getting?' The modest sum mentioned seemed to
please him. 'That's good. At least he's not trying to make
money out of it,' he told his visitors, and although Bluhdorn
had thought that Finney himself might make the film, he
eventually agreed to the package as presented.

Ornstein was now instructed to OK the project, though
only after an elaborate charade in which Anderson had to
appear hugely grateful so that it could seem that the
executive was magnanimously changing his mind about the
film. The cynical game was played and filming finally got
under way, with Medwin as producer.

Mention of *Joe Egg* reintroduces another long-time player
in the Memorial stakes. Peter Nichols, then still making his
living as a teacher, had just won a BBC West Region
playwriting contest when he met Finney for the first time
during the Stratford Centenary Season through a mutual
friend, Michael Blakemore. He remembers sharing Finney's
cakes at the As You Like It Tea Shoppe. A few years on,
using the money he'd earned scripting the Dave Clark Five

film *Catch Us If You Can*, Nichols set out to write his first stage play, a savage and often surreal comedy based on his and his wife's own domestic experiences dealing with a young spastic daughter. Nichols's agent at the time remained pessimistic about finding a sympathetic producer and various feelers confirmed a less than lukewarm reaction.

Blakemore, who by this time was acting and directing at the Glasgow Citizens', asked Nichols if as a last resort he could try and stage the play, rather mysteriously called *A Day in the Death of Joe Egg* (part extracted, it transpires, from a children's school rhyme). Nichols agreed and, with some finance from an adventurous local businessman, worked on a further draft of the play. The next problem was to get a licence from the Lord Chamberlain's Office (this was the year before the abolition of stage censorship) and with a few bizarre concessions, including one which meant that the handicapped child (actually played by a healthy fourteen-year-old) should not be present on stage to hear a married couple proposing sex, *Joe Egg* finally opened in Glasgow in May 1967.

The play enjoyed good local reviews and the question now was whether a London transfer was on the cards. Nichols had already resigned himself to a Citz-only three-weeker when, belatedly, a rave *Observer* review appeared, causing a flock of West End producers to scurry to Glasgow. The National wanted the play and, Nichols was told, a company called Memorial, of which he'd never heard. If the National took it, it would mean a new production and a gentler easing into the repertoire. Tying up with Memorial would, however, ensure that Blakemore and his cast – Joe Melia, Zena Walker, Joan Hickson, Phyllida Law and John Carson – could come to London and, said Nichols, 'profit from their loyalty to the play'. By the time *Joe Egg* won Best Play of the Year, it had already closed after just four months at the Comedy Theatre. There was more than an element of expedience in all this. *Charlie*

Bubbles was due to open in the States early the following year and Finney thought he could help publicize the movie by also playing Bri in *Joe Egg* on Broadway.

On most people's admission, including Nichols's, the play had been Joe Melia's finest hour. As Bri, the frantic father, the balding Melia was a loose-limbed comic — stand-up, slapstick and pathetic, in the best sense. According to Nichols: 'I think Albert was smashing but I suspect he'd admit himself that he was miscast. Joe was fraught, seedy and thoughtful — that was the character — while Albert was really too handsome, healthy and confident. Still he must get the credit for taking the play to New York.' Blakemore agreed that Finney wasn't the 'quicksilver comedian' Melia had been, 'though he made sensible suggestions which led to some definite improvements'.

It was, said Nichols, extraordinary arriving in New York 'with this great "store" [star]. Like going with Harrods.' Bookings started long before the play opened, because everyone wanted to see the man who'd been Tom Jones. 'Mind you,' said Nichols, 'it made it a bit difficult for the play. People would get up in the interval and say, "Is this a play? What is this?" *Joe Egg* didn't really conform to most of the things they'd normally expect of a play.' The show attracted a strange, almost bewildered press reaction as well: mostly good reviews, particularly for Zena Walker (who won a Best Supporting Actress Tony award), though a little cooler for Finney. Business, however, was splendid. You knew it was a hit, said Nichols, when they told you they were putting in extra phones because they couldn't cope with the bookings, or were thrusting what seemed like thousands of dollars into your hands for 'expenses'.

Joan Hickson recalled that Finney became quite affected by his role. Nichols, who left New York about a week after the opening, said he was told about the strange night nearly all the cast broke down:

Albert was having an affair with someone who'd been

to New York then left again; Joan didn't like travelling in lifts and insisted on being on the second floor, only to be found often wandering aimlessly down service stairs; John Carson was parted from his wife; and Zena was rather pining for her most recent husband. The only one who seemed happy with things was Elizabeth Hubbard [who'd taken over from Phyllida Law], and she was a New Yorker anyway. One night, everything, including the play, got too much for them and they all just started crying on stage.

Finney played the role for just eleven weeks before handing over to Donal Donnelly; *Charlie Bubbles* had opened and probably the 'store' was getting bored.

Nichols felt it wouldn't have been 'unreasonable' for Finney to do a six-month stretch: 'You might say, he gave us the very, very least he could to make the thing pay.' Despite those reservations, it did pay off handsomely for Nichols; so much so that he was able to buy a new £12,000 home in Blackheath, which he jokingly nicknamed 'Albert Hall'.

Over the next ten years, until after *Privates on Parade* in 1977, when Nichols and Finney had what the writer described darkly as 'a bit of a falling out' (though he wouldn't elaborate), Nichols's new plays were roughly divided between Memorial in the marketplace and the National's subsidy.

Phil, in his fourth play, *Chez Nous* — after *The National Health* went to the National and Memorial brought *Forget-Me-Not-Lane* in from Greenwich — was the first and, to date, only time Nichols has written a part for a specific actor, after Finney had asked him if he'd create a role for him in a new play. The character, said Nichols, was based on a friend, an architect, who'd been with him in the airforce and who was, physically at least, a bit like Finney. They also shared the same rather formal way of making jokes: 'Whenever I read *Chez Nous*, I can only hear Albert speaking Phil; though the character is not like him as such, it has his speech patterns.'

Chez Nous centres on two couples, Dick, a paediatrician, and Liz (Denholm Elliott, Pat Heywood) and Phil, an architect, and Diana (Finney, Geraldine McEwan) – old friends, spending a summer holiday together at Dick's smart new farmhouse home in the Dordogne, which has been bought with the proceeds of his bestseller, *The Nubile Baby*. The title has a dreadful resonance since it transpires that Dick's youngest child is actually a grandchild, fathered by none other than Phil, who'd once seduced the hosts' fourteen-year-old daughter.

When Finney first read the play, he felt that Phil's part wasn't as good as Dick's, and Nichols agreed, even though this hadn't been his original intention. Finney, though, decided that he didn't mind: 'It'll be all right,' he said. 'I'll have a go, and it'll be nice to do a commercial play after all that stuff at the Royal Court.'

Directed by Robert Chetwyn (reunited with Finney for the first time since they were actors together at Birmingham), *Chez Nous* is, like so much of Nichols's work, a superbly crafted comedy of middle-class, mid-life desperation. Although Denholm Elliott may have got the meatier role – and no one comes to the end of his tether better – Finney conjured something exceptional out of the lazy, hedonistic Phil, especially at the dreadful moment of revelation. As Billington said:

> I remember Finney padding around in his shorts, with stocky, muscular legs, looking as if he was cock of the walk. Then, suddenly, he exhibits a quality of naked, unadulterated shame. He presses his palms flat against his skull, as if to beat down the awful truth, the colour drains from his big, cratered face, tears prick his eyes. It was like watching a man age twenty years in three seconds. When Finney lets his defences drop, he can actually be extraordinarily moving on the stage.

At the time, John Barber of the *Daily Telegraph* put it another way: 'It has the effect of a silent scream. I do not think that even Olivier has shown more vividly what calamity can mean. We are in the presence of an actor who can enlarge the understanding of human distress, and we can only be grateful.'

The play received better reviews than its six-month run would seem to suggest.

Nichols has said: 'With Albert, it should have been longer. I suppose you could say that it was at the point when his extreme fame was already a bit on the decline. Nowadays I don't think you can say he's a major box-office name in the theatre any longer; it very much depends on the play itself being good.'

They collaborated closely one more time, in 1975, for a television version of the autobiographical *Forget-Me-Not-Lane*, in which Finney played the adult Nichols, contrasting with flashbacks of his younger self (played by Robin Davies) growing up during the war at his parents' home in Corinthian Villas, Bristol. Nichols found it 'misdirected and very disappointing'. This was Finney's first work for TV since appearing in four episodes of *Emergency Ward 10* before he went to Stratford in 1959 and he admitted to being 'terribly nervous', particularly with the speed of the whole enterprise: two and a half weeks of rehearsal, followed by a rapid four-day shoot.

He explained to Sheridan Morley why he so enjoyed Nichols's work:

He wrongfoots his audience; he uses its sensibilities and then sharpens it by surprise, so that people come away from a play of his feeling more alert than before they saw it. There's an edge to his work which I've always liked; he writes the kind of lines people say to themselves when they're alone at night after the rest of the family has gone to sleep. He worries people. He'll

suddenly say something which a middle-aged, middle-
class audience may not like much, but which they
ought to hear. He uses his own blood on the page, and
he writes for all the poor bastards who can't. Once,
years ago, making love to a girl on a beach in Hawaii, I
thought, 'I'm doing this not just for myself but for all
the Finneys who never got here.'

Nichols could have written that line.

Finney's promotional push for *Charlie Bubbles* in the States
had an extra edge, for the $1.2 million film, despite its
essential Englishness and not to mention the considerable
standing of its star-director, had already been turned down
by Rank for circuit release in Britain. Charles Champlin of
the *Los Angeles Times* was one of a number of influential
American critics to acclaim it. Recalling it now, he said:

Yes, I gave it a rave review, because I thought it was
terrific and found that ending especially interesting: the
writer and Albert didn't quite know what to do with
their lives, so the balloon was an evasive answer for
want of anything more solid to say. When I put this to
him at a later date, he just laughed and wouldn't give
me a yes or no. I still think I was right. Shelagh
Delaney and he had both experienced that isolating
thing that happens with success where you're cut off
from your roots because you're now rich.

Pauline Kael, who had just begun her long and
distinguished reign at the *New Yorker*, was one of the
dissenting voices:

The movie is glum, Charlie's life seen through his eyes,
and since he sees people joylessly, with apathy and
distaste, much of it consists of close-ups of semi-
repulsive faces that look cold and dead. The entire

painfully monotonous movie is based on this single, small, unoriginal idea – the kind of idea that could be one element, or good for a short sequence.

The film was not a box-office success in the States.

A year on, Finney was to be found introducing his movie and answering questions at small provincial English cinemas like the Cinecenta in Sheffield. 'The theme of the movie,' he told one audience, 'is the struggle for identity that starts when you begin believing a lot of stuff people tell you when you're getting your name in the papers.'

He claimed not to have been concerned at Odeon rejection: 'In those large emporiums, it wouldn't evoke the kind of interest it was meant to evoke. If you see a film in a quarter-full cinema, it affects your response to the film. Smaller cinemas can help offbeat pictures to find their own audience, and there aren't sufficient houses of this size.' In other words, *Charlie Bubbles* was what would now firmly be termed an 'art house' film; the fact that it was English language rather than foreign subtitled made it even more uncategorizable – unplaceable in broad circuit terms and also a tricky hybrid for the specialist market. With these drawbacks, the film wasn't a success in the UK either. Did Finney really care that much? According to Terence Clegg: 'The feeling one got making the film was that it was all a bit off the cuff. The idea was that it should be fun doing it – if it worked, fine; if it didn't, well . . .'

Not long after, Finney was already beginning to talk of another collaboration with Delaney, this time on a script in which the hero gets eaten at the end. Too offbeat? 'I'm waiting till cannibalism is in again,' he said, later.

Twenty-five years on, *Charlie Bubbles* still remains his one and only film as a director. It was also another very useful rung in the rise of a Cambridge law graduate, Stephen Frears. After university, he went to the Royal Court as an assistant director before working, first, for Karel Reisz on *Morgan, a Suitable Case for Treatment* and then with

Finney. According to Clegg: 'He seemed to be a great buddy of Albert's. I didn't quite know what his actual function was. A sort of creative assistant, I suppose. He'd talk about the script but was not really involved in the technical aspects.'

A year later, Memorial financed a thirty-minute dramatic short called *The Burning*, set during an uprising in South Africa but directed by the novice Frears in Morocco. Around that time too the company, in collaboration with the British Film Institute, also helped back another pair of shorts, Tony Scott's drama *Loving Memory* and Paul Joyce's comedy *The Engagement*, written by Tom Stoppard.

Gumshoe arose out of Frears's and writer Neville Smith's enthusiasm for Bogart and Raymond Chandler. An amusing pastiche of 1940s movies, it was the story of Eddie Ginley, a Liverpool bingo-caller who variously dreams of playing Vegas, recording 'Blue Suede Shoes' and writing *The Maltese Falcon*. He starts the process by attempting to become a Bogie-style sleuth, after which matters begin to take a rather more serious turn as he finds himself way in over his trenchcoat. Finney, who had been weaned on Bogart movies and had also practised his impersonation during *Two for the Road*, said he'd like to play Ginley. With that sort of clout, despite an untried feature director, the film was 'on the floor' under Columbia's patronage only ten months after the script began to be written.

Although the references are clear and the film is craftily tailored for the Scouse setting, beautifully photographed by Chris Menges and wittily scored by the twenty-two-year-old Andrew Lloyd Webber, it never becomes too bogged down in *hommage* at the expense of narrative. It's a nice, small film – and it performed equally modestly at the box office. Finney said later: 'One of the problems was that not everyone who saw it felt the same way about those old thrillers as we did. Some just thought it was a not very good thriller and simply didn't realize it was a fond tip of the hat.'

Over the years, Memorial has stuck closely to its brief of 'infrequent production'. For EMI it produced the film version of *Spring and Port Wine* (resisting the notion of changing its title to *Dance to Your Daddy*); Anderson's *if...* follow-up, *O Lucky Man*, brought Warner Brothers back into UK film-making after a long absence; Mike Leigh's début, *Bleak Moments*, cost only £18,000 but it began his powerful if too infrequent flirtation with film; Medwin went to the States to produce Ivan Passer's satirical comedy *Law and Disorder*; filming E A Whitehead's *Alpha Beta*, with Finney and Rachel Roberts, was a logical way to keep on record the same pair's short, sharp and shocking stage two-hander; and David Gladwell's *Memoirs of a Survivor*, with Julie Christie, was an ambitious, though dourly doomed, attempt to try and capture Doris Lessing's fantasy novel of urban decay. It invested in Julian Mitchell's hit play *Another Country*, though it decided to pass on both *Love Story* and *Oh! Calcutta*.

Various other projects, which included Gerald Durrell's *My Family and Other Animals*, Wyndham Lewis's *Snooty Baronet*, scripted by David Mercer, and an Adrian Mitchell screenplay, *Off the Rails*, eventually came to naught.

Memorial, reckoned Finney, has averaged between 0.1 and 0.42 films a year – and that was in its most productive years. The cupboard's been pretty bare of late. But even with this kind of infrequency, the company would still warrant honourable mention on one of the man's headstones.

8

National Hero Too

Finney was still a ten-year-old at primary school in Salford when Anouk Aimée made her film début in 1946, though admittedly she was just fourteen then. By the time he made *Saturday Night and Sunday Morning*, she'd already completed more than a dozen movies. Born in Paris, the daughter of an acting couple, Anouk (*née* Françoise Sorya) studied drama and dancing in France before making her first film, *La Maison sous la Mer*. She first really attracted attention a couple of years on in André Cayatte's *Les Amants de Vérone*, playing a Juliet-like role especially created for her by the poet-screenwriter Jacques Prévert. After that, there was a series of indifferent roles in a series of even more indifferent films in the fifties before she finally became a major international star in the sixties.

Dark and sensuous, almost feline, Anouk (as she was known) made *La Dolce Vita* and *8½* for Fellini, *Lola* and *The Model Shop* for Jacques Demy and, most popular of all, in 1966, Claude Lelouch's incurably romantic *Un Homme et Une Femme*, which earned her an Oscar nomination, while the film itself won awards for Best Foreign Language film and Original Screenplay (though not, surprisingly, even a nomination for Francis Lai's hummable score). By this time, Anouk was on her third marriage, to actor Pierre Barouh, and had a teenage daughter, Manuella, from a short-lived marriage back in the early fifties with second husband, the director Nico Papatakis.

Anouk was filming the title role in *Justine*, a mangled, Hollywood version of Durrell's *Alexandria Quartet*, when she and Finney began quietly seeing each other.

Justine's shooting schedule was interminable, compounded by the fact that after a month's shooting in Tunis, director Joseph Strick was fired and his work scrapped. Twentieth Century Fox relocated the production to Hollywood and signed up the veteran George Cukor to start the movie again from scratch. Anouk's co-star, Dirk Bogarde, described in his autobiography *Snakes and Ladders* how in Tunis, she

> was wan and sad for most of the time, since she had suddenly realized, too late, that her decision to accept *Justine* had most probably been, for one reason or another, a serious error of judgement on her part, and was now feeling abandoned and lonely. She had brought her two cats from Paris to keep her company and fed them on fillet steak, which angered the waiters in the hotel who had to make do with chick peas.

Between leaving Tunis and setting out for the Fox soundstages in Hollywood, Finney took Anouk home to Gore Crescent to meet the family and then at Heathrow amid inquisitive reporters, saw her off to the States.

The following spring they were to be found holidaying together on Corfu and the message seemed to be that Anouk was in the process of suing Barouh for divorce and that she and Finney would be marrying soon and even honeymooning on the same Greek island. A year later, in May 1970, they were still not wed and instead Anouk, described tactfully as 'a very good friend', was visiting Finney on the Shepperton set of his latest movie, *Scrooge*.

It was his first sustained work since *Joe Egg* on stage in New York two years earlier and his first film since a curiosity called *The Picasso Summer* more than six months before that. The idea for the Picasso film had originated with American animator Wes Herschensohn, who in the early sixties met the painter in France and showed him some samples of his animations of Picasso's paintings.

He explained how he wanted to make a film based round these and more, and the old painter apparently gave an enthusiastic endorsement to the project. After he'd begun developing the story and the animation, Herschensohn learnt that the science-fiction writer Ray Bradbury had written a short story about an American's chance encounter with Picasso on a French beach, so the two decided to pool their ideas. The story was now to be of a young American couple (Finney, who said he wanted to meet Picasso, and Yvette Mimieux) who go to the South of France one summer in search of Picasso.

They meet his children, his women, his bulls and bullfighters, and eventually spot – it is hoped – Picasso himself on a beach, drawing in the sand with a lollipop stick. And the film, which was first conceived as a one-hour television 'special' for Eastern Airlines, then grew, with funding of $1.6 million from Warner Brothers–7 Arts, to theatrical feature proportions.

What actually followed was as mysterious as some of Picasso's canvases. Serge Bourguignon, a Frenchman who had enjoyed much success with the arty Oscar-winner *Sundays and Cybele* and rather less with a subsequent Western, *The Reward* (also starring Mimieux), started directing *The Picasso Summer* on locations in France and San Francisco.

Some months later, he was directing the film all over again because the studio considered the first version virtually incomprehensible. The following summer it was reported in the Hollywood trade magazines that Robert Sallin, an experienced maker of commercials, had been drafted in by the producers to replace Bourguignon and make his own version of the story. When the finished film bypassed cinemas altogether and ended up on American television in 1972, the Frenchman's credit was still intact. More intact, to be sure, than Herschensohn's trail-blazing animation.

The former Disney man wrote an open letter to the network:

Thank you, CBS, for the massacre of my movie, *The Picasso Summer*. You sure as hell wouldn't have bought the movie if what you first saw was your own version of it. You cut virtually one-third of the film, including the bullfight and the entire animated EROTICA sequence, and chopped up the WAR and PEACE animation at the precise moment of transition from WAR to PEACE. Brilliant. How did you do that? I understand you plan a second showing. Do us both a favour and forget it.

Variety reviewed the film, scheduled in a throwaway late-night slot, with barely concealed ennui:

It is more of a travelog in quest of a confrontation with the post-impression painter than a serious profile. Not until the fading seconds of the film is the back of his neck seen, strolling along the beach. He was the main topic of the dialog and the center of life in Spain but not even a painting of his was seen.

Animation [albeit abbreviated] of his surrealist art and haunting theme by Michael Legrand were a bigger help than the two adventuring leads, Albert Finney and Yvette Mimieux, who played like tourists from the midwest without any dramatic force ... What slowly developed was a meandering through the South of France with a way stop in Spain by Finney to try his hand at bullfighting. That ended with the bovine snorting his revenge ... So as not to make it a complete débâcle, Miss Mimieux did manage to catch up a blind artist, ate at his table and was rewarded with his canvas. It was payful and playful for the roving art buffs but as an acting chore it was a breeze. Never was acting so alluring without any real thespic effort.

And after all that, Finney never even got to meet Picasso.

When Anouk visited Finney at Shepperton, there was another happy reunion: with the director Ronald Neame. Twenty years earlier, when she was still only eighteen, he'd directed her in *The Golden Salamander*, a gun-running thriller starring Trevor Howard. Neame had rather stumbled into *Scrooge* after walking off *Hello Goodbye*, an absurd romance personally produced by the Fox boss, Darryl Zanuck and starring his latest girlfriend. With 'You'll never work for Fox again' still ringing in his ears (just a couple of years on, Neame was responsible for one of the studio's biggest-ever hits, *The Poseidon Adventure*), the director was pondering on what to do next. Less than twenty-four hours later he was called up by another producer and asked to fly to New York to meet the songwriter Leslie Bricusse, who, he was told, was working on the screenplay of a new musical, *Scrooge*, based on Dickens's *A Christmas Carol*.

Richard Harris, who had enjoyed much success in another musical, *Camelot*, was due to play the old miser, but with just ten days to go before shooting, he suddenly became unavailable after taking over the directorial reins of a footballing drama in which he was also starring in Israel. Second choice for *Scrooge* was Finney, but when first approached he told the producers he wasn't in the mood for making films.

Next on the wanted list was Rex Harrison, who was in a play at the time, which meant that filming would have to be put back three to four weeks. While Harrison pondered, they cast Michael Medwin as Scrooge's nephew. He had left his script in the office at Memorial when Finney, at a loose end one day, picked it up and began to read. When he'd finished it, he quickly put a call through to the producers and said that if the part was still open, he'd now love to do it.

As Neame said: 'Though we appeared to have Harrison, we knew that Albert was better casting. Rex would just play Rex, while Albert has, like Guinness, that quality of being able to play completely different characters. We decided to use the excuse that we simply couldn't afford to put the film back the time Rex required. So we got Albert instead.'

It would be nice to report that it had all been worth while, but apart from some clever trick effects and a handful of cheerful cameos (by the likes of Guinness, Kenneth More and Dame Edith Evans), *Scrooge* amounted to little more than a poor man's *Oliver* with the additional handicap of an almost entirely forgettable musical score.

Finney's modest baritone voice wasn't unduly stretched though everyone agreed that his last song, as first written, wouldn't do at all. So, over the phone from the States, Bricusse piped out a new tune on his wooden whistle, which was then arranged by Ian Fraser into 'I'll Begin Again', warbled by Finney as he realizes he's not in Hell after all.

More hell with the make-up, a two-hour job each day to turn Finney from a bright-eyed thirty-four-year-old into a miserable old codger. 'Show us yer' hands, Ronnie,' Finney said one day to Neame. 'Why?' asked the director. 'Because we want to know what an old man's hands really look like,' he said mischievously, turning to the make-up man.

A couple of months later Finney and Anouk were married at Kensington Register Office, with a minimum of fuss and ceremony. Medwin was best man and the bride had her eighteen-year-old daughter in tow. There was, the *Daily Mirror* reported dolefully, 'no wedding ring, no wedding reception and there'll be no honeymoon'. A 'happy occasion,' it concluded, 'but something of a non-event.'

Like *Scrooge*, *Murder on the Orient Express* was, from Finney's point of view, all about 'dissembling, disguise and broad strokes'. But there, apart from half a ton of make-up and more than two hours each morning in the studio dressing room, the resemblance ended. Not only does Finney's Hercule Poirot remain the most enjoyable big-screen version of the little Belgian detective but the film itself is far and away the most successful ever adaptation of an Agatha Christie tale – a thoroughly sustained exercise in style.

EMI's Nat Cohen, who claimed he first had the idea for the film of one of Christie's most popular whodunnits, signed up the producers Richard Goodwin and John Brabourne. There were two positive side effects to this. They had previously produced *The Tales of Beatrix Potter*, which Christie liked, and also Brabourne's father-in-law, Lord Mountbatten, was both influential and extremely persuasive. Pressure was needed, because Christie had roundly disliked earlier film versions of her books, none more so than the most recent Poirot, *The Alphabet Murders*, made in 1965 with an American, Tony Randall, as the lead.

Sidney Lumet, a self-effacing American with a peerless reputation for bringing in his films on time and budget, and a track record that already included a 'chamber' classic, *Twelve Angry Men*, was sensibly hired to direct.

According to Goodwin:

We had an extremely good script by Paul Dehn and needed a resourceful director to deal with what could easily have become rather flaccid material.

We thought of the film as being quite small in scale and felt we could do it inexpensively but still with a good cast. His agent went on at him about why should he want to do 'that dumb train movie'. Which turned out to be the one way of getting him to do it.

There was no 'ideal Poirot', said Lumet. 'I thought we should just get the best actor possible and go from there.' Lumet suggested Finney and also wanted to get Sean Connery, with whom he had worked happily in the past on three movies, involved as well. For Goodwin: 'Albert–Sean, Sean–Albert. It was a question of persuading these two leviathans that if the other was in it, it must be a good film. They were pivotal to each other. Sean was, perhaps, the key; he made Albert feel happy.' It also helped that Finney was more than keen to work with Lumet.

And so the idea of the 'star package' – a 'glamour train' – was born. Bearing in mind the famous line-up that was eventually assembled – including Ingrid Bergman, who had actually wanted to play Wendy Hiller's wizened Princess until persuaded she'd be ideal as the mousy Swedish missionary – the film was ludicrously inexpensive at around $4.5 million. Everyone was persuaded to accept a flat fee; Finney, Connery and Lumet were also awarded a generous percentage in potential net profits.

Profits were still a long way off as Finney began one of the most arduous periods of his working life – Poirot at Elstree by day, *Chez Nous* in the West End at night. How, though, to turn a muscular, 5 foot 11 inch, auburn-haired thirty-eight-year-old into a short, tubby, middle-aged Belgian detective with the famous moustaches?

A couple of months before shooting began, Finney started talking to and experimenting with make-up artist Charles Parker, to try and evolve the right 'look'. Lumet added his suggestions and, by the time filming began, another fine make-up man, Stuart Freeborn, was putting into practice the fruits of those discussions as Finney began his daily transformation into Poirot at five o'clock every morning.

Facially, there were a false nose, padded cheeks, gleaming black hair and a ferociously waxed moustache. Tape round the neck brought the flesh up tight at the collar, while body padding rendered him pear-shaped. No heels on his black patent shoes made him look much shorter. All this was set off finally with impeccable clothes, his head tilted, birdlike, to the left and an accent which owed something to a spot of domestic coaching by Anouk. 'Fussy, pedantic and dapper,' said Finney.

Lumet was as good as his reputation. Filming took just forty-two days, which included a day on the Bosphorus, some snow scenes in Yugoslavia and, for the sequence showing the arrival of all the passengers, a goodsyard outside Paris. The rest was done on re-created train sets at Elstree. Lumet fondly recalled a 'trouble-free' film:

> The other actors knew Albert was carrying the load; they all had their individual arias, so to speak, but Poirot ran through the whole thing and his great aria is the final one. Between that and his theatre schedule, he must have been exhausted.
>
> Although there was quite a lot of chit-chat and kidding going on, everyone let him have his concentration and, for his part, he generally sat to one side, slightly closed off, thinking of his next scene coming up. From my point of view, he had the extraordinary ability to give you absolutely everything you wanted, and immediately.

Goodwin gives Lumet particular credit for Finney's performance: 'He is the sort of actor who needs to be gingered along by his director. If he isn't, he doesn't do it. Also, it was something that could have become extremely camp but, happily, didn't.' Finney remained uncomplaining despite the heat on a cramped set which meant that within half an hour his 'look' started to become extremely uncomfortable.

Relief would come at lunchtime, when he could extract his padding and pop it into the fridge to cool down and, later, cool him up. He also clearly thrived in such distinguished company. As he has said:

> There were a lot of people I'd never met before – like Bacall, Bergman and Widmark – and, being a movie buff, I liked talking to them about their films. We all started saying how we should perhaps do one of these films every year, like a glamorous repertory company. When they did actually ask me a couple of years later if I'd play Poirot again, I wasn't so sure. They said they were going to the Nile this time; it had been quite hot enough for me at Elstree.

Although the budget wasn't exactly excessive, it was large by British standards and so the producers were anxious to get American involvement, not only to share the load but also to secure future distribution in the crucial US marketplace.

Goodwin and Brabourne, who had produced Zeffirelli's *Romeo and Juliet* for Paramount in the late sixties, met Charles Bluhdorn and were greeted enthusiastically with, 'Ah, I remember the Orient Express. I was a waiter on Vienna station and we would see the train coming through and think how glamorous it all was.' Paramount was in for half of the production costs and also gave EMI a percentage share in the American gross profits. Yet Goodwin still got the feeling that no one actually believed the movie would do much business over there.

The American opening was on a Sunday at the Baronet Theater on New York's Third Avenue. A queue had already formed before the doors opened and the producers were on hand to watch ticket sales. Goodwin quickly rang Bluhdorn and told him there was a queue round the block, adding, 'Didn't you realize it is going to be a big hit?' Within an hour, all the top distribution and marketing brass of Paramount had been summoned to the Baronet, with orders from on high to 'sell the picture'.

Part of that sell, from Nat Cohen's point of view, was to employ a PR consultant, Jerry Pam, with a brief to raise the British profile of the film and make sure that the heavily disguised Finney got proper recognition, since nobody seemed to know that the man who was once the revered Tom Jones was the same actor now lurking within Poirot's heavy padding. Pam told the producers that if he was allowed to design an interesting campaign, it should at least help Finney get nominated for an Oscar.

Among other things, he put together a mock newsheet called the *Orient Express Gazette*, which had a picture of the real Finney alongside a shot of him as the detective, and that was sent to all the Academy members. Ten years after *Tom Jones*, Finney duly got his second Oscar nomination.

This time round, the opposition was even tougher: Dustin Hoffman in *Lenny*, Jack Nicholson in *Chinatown*, Al Pacino in *The Godfather Part II* and one other outsider, Art Carney, in *Harry and Tonto*. To everyone's surprise, the veteran Carney won. In fact, the film's only winner out of six nominations (Costume Design, Music, Adapted Screenplay and Cinematography too) was Ingrid Bergman, who added a Best Supporting statuette to her brace of Best Actress awards, playing the part she hadn't even wanted in the first place.

Happily, the lack of Oscars didn't slow down business and the film proved to be a hit not only in the States, where it earned more than $20 million, but also all around the world. Even Agatha Christie seemed pleased, though she is reported to have expressed a preference for a Poirot armed with an even finer moustache.

As with *Tom Jones*, Finney may have lost out on an Oscar but, thanks to the 'points', became a percentage millionaire all over again.

David Warner, Nicol Williamson, Julian Glover, Corin Redgrave, Charles Kay, Robert Lang, Samantha Eggar, Lynn Redgrave, Rita Tushingham and Finney – was there ever a more representative or better cross-section of fledgeling British talent gathered on stage together at any one time? The occasion had been early in 1962 for one of the Royal Court's famous Sunday night 'productions without decor': *Twelfth Night*, directed by George Devine, who had founded the English Stage Company at the Court seven years earlier. For Finney, who played Feste, it was a brief Shakespearean respite from the rigours of *Luther*, then well into its West End run.

Finney's return to the stage in *Alpha Beta* in 1972 marked not only his first work in an English theatre since his mid-sixties bout at the National but also a renewed acquaintance with the Royal Court for the first time in a decade. Since Feste, in fact. Even by his own relaxed standards, and allowing for *Joe Egg* in New York, it had been a long sabbatical: golf, lunch, girlfriends, a few films, nice holidays, accumulating wealth, new wife, in between pondering who he was and what he should be doing with his life apart from golf, lunch, girlfriends ... Finney certainly didn't feel his time away from stage-acting had been in any sense wasted:

> I would call these 'fallow' periods; not really inactive periods. I don't think anything's a waste of time – even wasting time! And maybe five years of indecision and worrying have been necessary in order for me to become reassured by this play that acting is one of the things that I love doing. That I need to do. But maybe I needed that five years in order to be convinced so strongly.

Alpha Beta was certainly the ideal vehicle to regain match-fitness. A lacerating account of modern marriage, set across three acts and nine years, it demanded the utmost concentration.

Finney warmed to it not just because he admired the writing but also because it dealt with a working-class marriage — something of a change from the usual British theatrical preoccupation with middle-class *angst* — it was modern and it was a two-hander which reunited him with his *Saturday Night and Sunday Morning* 'mistress', Rachel Roberts, this time in unholy union. Indeed, it's rather too tempting to suggest that if Arthur Seaton had ever wed Brenda, *Alpha Beta* might well have been the map of their marriage.

Irving Wardle vividly described the two sparring partners, Mr and Mrs Elliot:

> She rams home the anti-marital argument by changing from a gawky peasant with protruding top teeth to an implacably bourgeois householder who regards her husband, like her washing machine, as material property. Finney undergoes an equally interesting change: at first a bottled-up youth plagued with fears of middle age, he steadily thickens and coarsens, going through a phase as a clubland buck, putting up a defensive barrage of pop songs, and finally slumped into booze-sodden middle-aged defeat.

Before *Alpha Beta*, Finney claimed not to have been that keen on naturalistic plays and, despite occasional evidence to the contrary, he is not a naturalist. Though he was for so long — too long, he often complained — identified with *Saturday Night and Sunday Morning*, this was deceptive, and very soon after that he became altogether larger than life.

Giving, then, the rare lie, his Elliot seemed entirely naturalistic, from loutish, boastful youth at the start to the final act where, separated from his wife and slumped ale-bound in a chair, he indulges in a moving *mea culpa*. Though leavened with sardonic wit, *Alpha Beta* remains, nevertheless, a fairly relentless display of raw, naked pain as the couple tear each other apart in a display of verbal and even physical assaults.

After its run at the Royal Court, *Alpha Beta* transferred for a short season to the Apollo. At the same time, with his appetite for the theatre clearly refreshed, Finney was also appointed an associate artistic director at the Court, which then helped sustain one of the most intriguing phases of his stage work in the seventies. He had last directed for the theatre up in Glasgow ten years earlier. For his first Court assignment, he chose Brian Friel's controversial play *The Freedom of the City*, a thinly disguised re-creation of and elaboration upon the fairly recent events in Londonderry which became known notoriously as Bloody Sunday. By way of flashbacks from a subsequent tribunal, the play follows the fortunes of three unarmed protestors seeking sanctuary after the break-up of a banned march through the city. The trio, two youths and a middle-aged housewife, while away their time in the Mayor's parlour before giving themselves up, only to be shot dead by the Army, who claim they were armed and so are exonerated by the tribunal.

Put that baldly, the play appears to be an anti-British diatribe of great insensitivity. It was, of course, criticized that way on the one hand, but also as too weak and not political enough on the other. Finney admitted that when he first read Friel's play he was jolted into wondering whether he should be directing plays or building houses for the underprivileged in Derry.

Indeed, one of the prevalent criticisms of the play was that it almost wilfully stood aside from matters like sectarian violence in order to project an arguably more simplistic view that the issue was just a case of rich versus poor. The point of the play, according to Finney, was that 'lives are gone. It does not attack the man who pulled the trigger but shows that the situation is possible. *That's* what has to be altered.'

To help convey the right atmosphere, Finney had taken some of the cast to an aeroplane crash inquiry at a West End hotel and also rehearsed in the Irish Club near Sloane

Square. He gave full rein to Friel's use of irony as the situation becomes exploited on all sides, from Army intransigence and Bogsider rumour-mongering to the priest's ideology and even a resident balladeer's instant myth-making. And he earned plenty of marks for not only extracting maximum humour but also expertly weaving the time-shifts and multiple settings, even if many of the critics still remained convinced the play was nothing more than entertaining propaganda.

As Finney rehearsed the Friel by day, by night he was to be found at the Court under a grey wig and thick stubble performing Beckett. This was the playwright's eerie one-act monologue *Krapp's Last Tape*, paired in a double bill with Beckett's even odder *Not I*, in which Billie Whitelaw's mouth, painted white, babbled pain-filled gibberish out of the darkness surrounding it. Appearing elsewhere in the West End at the same time was a frothy musical called *I and Albert*, so the Court double inevitably became nicknamed 'Not I and Albert'.

Finney likes to tell the story of how Beckett, who was not technically directing *Krapp's Last Tape*, turned up at the first rehearsal to offer the actor some advice about his physical performance. According to Finney, 'He was just illustrating certain aspects of the part, but I found it very over-facing to have this *exactitude* when I hadn't had time to work out what I was doing at all and I couldn't link it to any inner reality in myself.' So, it seems, he told Beckett, in so many words, to be gone. For his part, Beckett made it clear that he felt Finney was miscast.

After working together abortively on *Ned Kelly* a decade earlier, Finney and David Storey eventually collaborated rather more fruitfully at the Court on *Cromwell*, a rare excursion into historical expressionism from a playwright best known for strong contemporary and naturalistic themes in plays like *In Celebration* and *The Changing Room*. Despite the title, Cromwell himself remains merely a spectre hovering over a desolate setting which suggests seventeenth-century Ireland but in fact could probably be any land ravaged by a futile religious war. Finney played O'Halloran, one of a pair of opportunistic Irishmen caught up in a brutal drama in which high style is eventually surpassed by even loftier melodrama.

When the Royal Court decided to mount a season of three Joe Orton plays, to be shown in the order they were originally written in the sixties, Finney agreed to direct *Loot*, tucked in between *Entertaining Mr Sloane* and *What the Butler Saw*, supervised by Roger Croucher and Lindsay Anderson, respectively.

An intriguing view of how Finney approached the work and his actors emerged from the story of one of that cast, James Aubrey, a young jobbing actor who had enjoyed an early encounter with fame when, as a fourteen-year-old, he was picked to play Ralph in Peter Brook's haunting film of *Lord of the Flies* in 1963.

Aubrey was now in his mid-twenties and had just made his first television programme, an episode of *Z-Cars*. The story goes that as Finney was at home one night doing the washing-up, Anouk called him through to inspect an 'interesting' young actor appearing in the popular cop-show cast that evening. Finney took a look, seemed to register some interest and then went back to the washing-up. A year later he was preparing *Loot* and remembered Aubrey's face but not his name, so he rang the BBC to ask if they could line up for him any new young actors who'd been in *Z-Cars* around the time. Naturally Aubrey's name came up, and the Court's casting director rang him at home to ask if he would mind popping into the theatre and poking his head round Finney's door to see if that triggered the memory. Which he, along with a number of other hopefuls, proceeded to do. 'That's the one,' said Finney, as he spotted Aubrey, who wondered what the hell was going on. Bemusement turned to delight as he was handed the role of Dennis, one of the two gay bank-robbers who hide their 'loot' in a coffin.

His co-stars were David Troughton (as Hal, his fellow conspirator), Jill Bennett (as the homicidal nurse, Fay) and Philip Stone (as the appallingly corrupt Inspector Truscott). The first of four weeks of rehearsals took place in a tiny room in the Irish Centre. For four days, they just sat round a table reading the play and discussing it.

On the fifth day, their legs began flexing instinctively under the table. The actors wanted to get up and start moving around, but Finney wouldn't let them. On the sixth day, he took the table away and said, 'There's no audience. Just feel how you would like to do it. I'm not going to say whether the audience is here or there. One hour I'll be sitting in this corner; another, I'll be sitting in that one. Don't play it towards me, though. Just do what *you* want.'

In the second week, they all moved to a slightly larger room in Paddington and slowly Finney began building up the characters. From, said Aubrey, 'the inside out. I don't know if he liked the word "method", but that's the way he worked. We spent about a week doing that still without any idea of where the audience was, still doing what *we* wanted. We were creating the relationships and providing a very solid base to the production.'

For week three, they repaired to an even larger room and Finney said, 'By the way, the audience is out *that* way.' Very slowly over the course of that week, they turned out performances, and yet, as Aubrey has said, 'We didn't perform as such. What we were doing seemed very, very real. We didn't seem to be acting as such.' Finney's instruction was that Orton had to be done 'straight'; that the situation, however horrible or funny, must be put over with complete seriousness, the actors behaving as if everything was quite normal.

In the fourth week, they went into the theatre itself. The *Mr Sloane* sets were taken down every night and the cast began to work onstage. At the start of the week Finney was seated in the front row, and as each day went by he moved further and further back until, by about day five, he was in the gods, saying, 'Can't hear you. Speak up. Project.' What had started from nothing and progressed through tiny performances, gradually became a fully-fledged stage production that filled the Royal Court.

According to Aubrey:

[Finney] wanted us to discover the characters for ourselves. Being an actor himself, and a very fine one, he, like most of us, had worked with good and not so good directors in his time, but he had his own very definite way of working which seemed to me more American than British. It was round about the second week he would ask us what we were doing and then maybe guide us slightly in the direction he wanted. Basically, anything we did was our own creation but with his own absolute confidence in our performances and talent backing us up. If he got a little cross, it was an actor getting cross with another actor. Yes, he had the odd snap at me. I thought I knew Orton better than he did, and he'd occasionally say, in a slightly sarcastic way, 'Oh, yeah, you knew him, did you?' He never became authoritarian about it, never, 'This is the way I want it and who's directing this anyway?'

The direction didn't end there, though. There were ten days of previews and every night Finney recorded audience reaction on audio tape and the next morning would come in and give the cast notes, saying things like, 'Rather than pause in the middle of that sentence and get two little laughs, run the whole sentence together and get a really big laugh at the end of it.'

By opening night, said Aubrey, 'it was one of the most secure and confident productions I had ever been in'. Finney was involved in every aspect of the production, from personally organizing Fortnum and Mason hampers for his players every lunchtime during the rehearsal period, and entertaining them on Sundays too, to making sure there was the right kind of lino for the floor and that the cast had the appropriate sort of shoes and the nurse's costume fitted correctly.

The set itself was extremely solid, more like a film set; if someone slammed the door, the pictures didn't wobble. Finney was so completely wrapped up in the work that even though the show didn't finish till half ten or quarter to eleven, he'd still often be seen hanging round the theatre at that time.

There was one occasion when the show was about to begin previews and Finney was onstage with all the cast. Jill Bennett said, 'Albert, what are you in this production?' He replied, 'Well, I'm the director.' She said, 'Yes, love. Now what do directors do? They sit in the stalls, off the stage. This is where *we* live.' Finney, said Aubrey, 'had become so involved in our performances he thought he was invisible. He thought he could move around with us onstage during the show, with his eyes riveted on us as if he were some kind of concealed camera.'

The critics were divided about the production. Irving Wardle wrote:

> Wherever the text specifies physical violence or gruesome spectacle, the production anaesthetizes it ... Whatever the stage directions, I believe this is the right procedure. There were two Ortons: one a superb stylist who converted states of moral anarchy into patterns of rigorously disciplined high comedy; and the other a practitioner of juvenile shock tactics. Finney's approach may make for a cosier evening than one associates with this author, but at least it gets the hooligan out of the way and lets you attend to the artist.

Eric Shorter was quite enthusiastic too, writing that Finney's revival understood 'the driving need for solemnity amid Orton's whimsical circumlocutions'. For Milton

Shulman, though, the production was 'sticky and hesitant'. And Jack Tinker was even sharper in the *Daily Mail*: 'Albert Finney's production is as rigidly embalmed as the manhandled corpse. He has caught little or nothing of Orton's wicked paradoxes.'

But there's still a bitter-sweet postscript to Aubrey's tale. Towards the end of *Loot*'s run, he was approached by London Weekend Television to do a major TV series called *A Bouquet of Barbed Wire*. His current contract had stipulated six weeks at the Court and then, if the play transferred, another six months. Aubrey met the LWT people, who said they'd be prepared to work round him. Fine, until the theatre's management, then still negotiating a possible West End transfer, stepped in, telling him that he would have to be permanently available in case of illness and understudy rehearsal. Even on Wednesdays and Thursdays, just the two days LWT needed him.

One evening in the theatre bar, Finney asked Aubrey what he had lined up in the future and was told of the *Bouquet* impasse.

Albert got quite cross and said he would sort it all out himself. What it seems he said to the Court contract people was, 'Give Jimmy a break. He's a good little jobbing actor who hasn't made very much money or done a lot of television.' It so happened that the play didn't transfer – the reviews were not as good as for the other two productions, which did. Maybe Albert was conscious of this when he spoke to the management. Anyway, it was the gesture of a fellow actor, for the last thing he wanted was to see me signing on the dole and possibly not working for six months. If I'd had to turn down *Bouquet*, which proved my big break, that's what would have happened. So I owe Albert a great deal.

While Finney plied his various trades at the Royal Court, an altogether more ambitious theatrical venture was slowfully and painfully beginning to take shape at last on the South Bank, more than twenty years after the foundation stone of the National Theatre had been laid by the river. Building plans were eventually agreed in 1969 and the first 'sod' dug in June 1970.

As costs began rising – from £7.5 million to £17 million – the construction itself continued to stutter along in line with a severely receding economy during the early seventies. The 1973 opening date was put back to 1974, and then that was abandoned too.

Away from the public gaze, there was another kind of reconstruction going on too: the search for a successor to Olivier, who was becoming older and iller, creating, as he would have put it, 'a dangerously unhealthy situation in the National Theatre leadership'.

Olivier pondered various possible candidates, among them Richard Burton, Richard Attenborough, Michael Blakemore, John Dexter, even his own wife, Joan Plowright. And Finney too. As Olivier wrote: 'I tried to interest Albert in the idea, but his own acting prowess was so marketable that he could naturally see little point in vastly increasing his responsibilities and decimating his income.'

Had Finney accepted, Sheridan Morley believes, the experiment would have been very interesting:

It would have carried on that actor-manager tradition and so there wouldn't then have been the great gap between Olivier and Kenneth Branagh. One of the reasons why Branagh has been able to clean up so flamboyantly is the vacuum created by Albert. The problem can be, however, that other top actors don't necessarily want to work for an actor-manager. For instance, Branagh finds it difficult to collect good supporting players around him. If Finney had gone to the National in that capacity, I doubt if he'd have got people like Ian McKellen or Brian Cox.

The upside is that I believe it could have been the making of Albert. It's such a high-profile job, you can't be seen to pack it in. If that pressure had been on him, he would have done his best and, I think, have stayed with it.

Whether he would have wanted the day-to-day administrative grind of such a job Michael Billington rather doubted: 'I think he'd have liked the play choice, the casting and directing. It seems to me that Glasgow and the Court notwithstanding, he's never fully explored that side of his talent. He's also a man of some considerable discernment and he likes spotting talent.'

History relates that while Olivier was thinking along his lines, Peter Hall was being secretly approached on behalf of the theatre's board to see if he would be prepared to succeed to the directorship. After a brief interregnum, Hall eventually took over in November 1973, but still with no firm date for a South Bank opening of the three new theatres, the Olivier, Lyttleton and Cottesloe.

On the morning of Tuesday, 2 July 1974, Finney met Hall at the director's flat on the thirty-eighth floor of the Barbican. From his balcony, you could see straight down into a deep hole below that was being prepared for the foundations of a new Barbican theatre. It had been ten years since Finney last played classical roles at the National and getting on for twenty since he had actually tackled some of the big-name Shakespearean parts like Henry V and Macbeth.

Now, according to Hall, Finney, at the age of thirty-eight, told him he felt ready to take on the challenge, to try and, in Hall's words, 'examine a rougher, more instinctive form of classical acting'. They settled on *Hamlet*, to be followed by Marlowe's *Tamburlaine the Great*, both hopefully to be staged on the as yet unfinished Olivier's thrust stage.

With building delays still going on, it soon became obvious that *Hamlet* would have to open at the Old Vic before becoming the South Bank trail-blazer, though not at the Olivier but instead at the more conventional Lyttleton.

The following May, with *Hamlet* scheduled for December, Hall agreed to direct both productions – the Shakespeare with some reluctance, he said. Blakemore had been pencilled in first for *Hamlet* but Hall called him to ask if he'd mind standing down. A couple of months later, with rehearsals still some way off, Hall began to consider the idea of presenting *Hamlet* with an uncut text – more than four hours' worth.

When rehearsals began in late September at the new theatre – at least the rehearsal rooms were usable even if the stages weren't – Finney was sporting a beard and a fine level of fitness after months of working out at the Grosvenor House Hotel gym, ready to tackle, at thirty-nine, what Hall described as 'a thirty-year-old failure'. Then, as the production proceeded into its dress rehearsal phase, there was a double blow. First, Angela Lansbury's mother died in Hollywood and then, less than a week later, Finney's father also died, at Lytham St Annes, back up in Lancashire.

Lansbury had been finishing a Broadway run in *Gypsy* when Hall approached her to play Gertrude. It was her first ever Shakespeare role, daunting enough in itself but also full of reminders of her mother, Moyna McGill, a fine character actress who had taught her daughter well. They used to study Shakespeare together and Lansbury's youthful audition piece would be conducted with mother playing Nurse to her Juliet. Her death came as a great shock. As she recalled:

> I'm not sure it didn't colour the whole experience a bit. It wasn't the happiest time for me. We were doing what I would call an extremely Anglo-Saxon sort of *Hamlet*. We were really rooted to the ground. It was very, very spare. At times, Albert resembled a kind of black-clothed paratrooper, while I felt like a rather

roughly hewn chesspiece as the queen – chained to the ground. There was no sexuality in the piece at all, which was curious. I was extremely disappointed about that because I felt that one of the reasons that I could be cast in this role effectively was the fact that I had a somewhat shady reputation for playing rather incestuous mothers.

Yet I didn't have a chance to display any of those qualities in the production. I suppose I was a little young anyway to be playing Albert's mother. That didn't matter too much – I've played everybody's mother. But I simply couldn't help feeling at the time that I was miscast. I had to play her as a rather annoying, puddingy sort of woman and I wasn't ever comfortable with that.

Finney had been playing a scene with the King, his father in the play, when he got the news about his own father. It took another twenty-four hours and another complete performance for the sad news fully to sink in. Hall has recorded how Finney once told him that he felt he'd never properly conveyed to his father what he felt about him, how fond he was of him and how he respected him. Finney once wrote him a long letter, attempting to put these feelings into words, and when there was no answer rang him and asked if he had received the letter. 'Oh yes,' said his father, 'there's a reply in the post for you.' It read:

Dear Albert
   Thank you very much for your letter.
   Love Dad

While the National performed another play in its repertory, Finney returned home for the funeral. Before Finney Sr was finally laid to rest in Lytham, there was a bizarre episode as the funeral cortège wove its way through

Salford. Apparently it got lost and had to turn round. To do so, it just happened to reverse into the drive of the old Castle Irwell racecourse. This, explained Finney, must have been the driver of the hearse giving his father a last look round.

For many of those with particularly fond memories of Hall's previous *Hamlet* – a passionate, often anguished, barricades-style production with David Warner at Stratford in 1965 – this one was an indigestible marathon – processional, pageant-like and passionless – as stark as John Bury's single set, a great wall with one portal at its centre. Finney was not so much a thirty-year-old failure as a bluff comrade monotonously rasping his lines, appropriate to, in Harold Hobson's words, 'an age that puts only a low value on grace, style and subtlety'.

Memory, however, can play strange tricks and this *Hamlet* tends to be remembered perhaps less generously than it should, judging by the notices it received. They seem as much afflicted by a sense of occasion as the production itself. They ran from, 'I do not believe we shall ever see a finer representation of the play as it is written' to 'a ponderous cultural event which will attract the star-following public [indeed, the production was sold out three weeks before opening], gratify spectators of the "Shake-spearean intentions" school . . . I can recall few productions less coloured by a directorial viewpoint.'

For his part, Finney's reception ranged from 'dreadful' to 'the best Hamlet since Redgrave's'. Somewhere in between, but still clearly weighed down by the historical perspective, Bernard Levin was moved to offer up his view of events, coloured by thirty years of *Hamlet*-going. Beginning portentously, 'Albert Finney's Hamlet has not been received with the kind of unanimous acclaim that he has hitherto received for almost every part he has played – and not only received but richly deserved, for this great actor brings to mind what Dr Johnson said of Goldsmith: truly Finney touches nothing that he does not adorn . . .', he went on to say that he would be reserving judgement on this particular prince until he had seen him again, for what he had observed was 'a sketch for a portrait, not a finished performance'.

Opinions about Lansbury were pretty much in line with how she felt herself to have been moulded. This, as well as the recent bereavement, made her feel even more depressed and she would sit for long stretches in her Old Vic dressing room sewing a quilt and scoffing sweets.

As she recalled:

One night Albert came in to chat about something or other, took a look at me and said, 'You do rather like sweeties, don't you, darling?' I realized that what he really meant was that I was putting on weight. Which indeed I was. That stopped me in my tracks. I went on a diet and lost twenty pounds, which meant that all my costumes were now hanging off me because they'd all been constructed when I was rather heavy.

As 1975 drew to a close, Finney could also have been forgiven for feeling less than exultant, despite the obvious exhilaration induced by his *Hamlet* and the imminent move to the South Bank. On the personal level, not only had his father died but it also seemed that his five-year marriage to Anouk was now suddenly over after a comparatively long period of model domesticity. At first, and as unlikely as it might seem in retrospect, the glamorous French actress appeared only too happy to shut down her career and become the second Mrs Finney, cooking and keeping house in Brompton Square. The pair appeared inseparable; she was supportive of his work, which fitted in neatly between exotic holidays, and he was suitably attentive. They made an attractive, often photographed couple-about-town. They were even invited to sit for a fashionable painter – Finney politely declined on both their behalves, saying they'd 'hate to have to sit still for such a long time'. Anouk had also become a grandmother with the birth of Manuella's daughter, fathered by the Duchess of Bedford's son, Gilles Milinaire. But, according to Finney, being just Mrs Finney or, for that matter, a glamorous granny eventually wasn't quite enough for a woman who had started working for a living in her teens.

Then a cuckoo began to flutter round the nest. Ryan O'Neal was filming Kubrick's period epic *Barry Lyndon* in London when he met Finney and Anouk at a party. He and Anouk, nine years his senior, appeared to be instantly attracted to each other and O'Neal, who was between marriages, started phoning her regularly at home. When domesticity finally palled, Anouk flew to Los Angeles to try and revive her film career. There was talk of her starring in Hemingway's *Islands in the Stream* and while talk, for it proved only that, continued, Anouk moved out of the Beverly Hills Hotel and into O'Neal's Malibu beach-house. It appears she actually sought Finney's approval first, and he gave it to her.

Finney has said of this:

I simply knew that Anouk and Ryan were going to have a relationship – *should* have one. It was time for Anouk to move on, and she did so with my blessing. I do believe that when you're together out of habit, *I* have the right to say, 'It's been grand, *but* . . .' and so does my partner, if she feels pulled towards another man – or a woman, for that matter. With all the freedom nowadays comes the responsibility of accepting this possibility in each other. I mean, one of the reasons we may *be* here is to find out a bit about ourselves – and relationships are a *big* way to do so.

The marriage had atrophied for both of them, so after Anouk had returned to Brompton Square following her long, hot West Coast summer with O'Neal, Finney moved out and into a room at the Dorchester. Months earlier, as the newspapers began chewing over their transatlantic separation, Finney confided to Hall that he was seriously thinking of going back to the simple life – one room and living out of a suitcase. 'Better,' he remarked brightly, 'if the one room is at the Dorchester or the Savoy, with perpetual service!'

As the National Theatre company moved into the Lasdun-designed complex, there was no disputing that Finney was the leader. Maybe not as actor-manager but certainly as *the* actor, leading by example and spiritedly raising morale as a mass of logistical problems still beset the auditoriums. When Olivier ducked out of spearheading the last-night celebrations at the Old Vic, Finney cheerfully took his place, and he continued to remain at the forefront as the company began a tempestuous new chapter in its chequered history.

There was hardly time to draw breath as the Lyttleton opening, with *Hamlet*, came and went, followed immediately by the start of rehearsals for *Tamburlaine*, another four-hour marathon and, line for line, an even longer role for Finney. He and Hall had settled on the play because it was so rarely performed – the last time in London had been twenty-five years earlier – and because it so vividly represented the dawning of Elizabethan theatre. Finney also rather liked the idea that, unusually, here was an immorality play in which a terrible man died quietly, unpunished.

The opening date, in the Olivier, was first scheduled for July, then for the end of August and then finally, come hell or high water – and neither was completely out of the question with all the National's problems – for the first week in October. The company had originally met for ten weeks of rehearsals. These stretched on for no less than six months as, all around the actors, the complex was plagued by temperamental equipment, striking workers and continuous media flak. It was not unlike something out of a Lindsay Anderson movie.

These prolonged preparations also did nothing to help

the nerves of 'a company, lost in limbo-land, without hope, it seemed, of even performing,' noted John Heilpern, who was assistant to the director.

Brian Cox, who was playing Theridamas, relates a particularly good rehearsal story about how Finney was exhorting the company with, 'Listen, fellas, we're like magicians, we've gotta pull the rabbit out of the hat', to which Oliver Cotton, as Techelles, responded acerbically, 'You've got to get the rabbit *into* the hat in the first place!' Cox's own concerns centred more around what precisely Hall intended as he would spout on endlessly about 'emblematic acting' and '*chutzpah*'.

The public got its first view of the production, rabbits or no, a full two months before the official opening when Hall took his players outdoors for a full run-through on the terrace because the Olivier was still unfit for theatrical habitation. The company wore their own summer clothes but some essential props, like crowns and swords, were provided, as was mood music, from a group comprising percussion, saxophones, trombones, oboe and flute. The rather good public-relations angle on this alfresco freebie was the sheer orthodoxy of the exercise: the play was, of course, originally written to be performed out of doors.

Just three days before the opening, Hall discovered that Finney was afflicted not with, as he had first thought, just a heavy cold but with serious bronchitis. A preview had to be cancelled and then fingers strenuously crossed that his therapy, which consisted of being hung upside down and having his chest tapped to drain the fluid, would work.

Looking far from well, Finney attended the Sunday night rehearsal and on Monday, 4 October, was given a medical go-ahead for the evening's opening. Hall recorded: 'Albert sounded badly bronchial for the first three-quarters of an hour, but gradually the tubes began to clear and his confidence grew as he realized he would be able to get through. At the end there was the sort of ovation that is usually reserved for opera and ballet.'

With Liza Minelli in *Charlie Bubbles*. (*Universal/National Film Archive*)

Singing and dancing as Scrooge. (*Cinema Center/National Film Archive*)

With Anouk Aimée after marrying in London. (*Associated Newspapers*)

In *Krapp's Last Tape* at the Royal Court. (*Douglas Jeffery*)

As Hercule Poirot in *Murder on the Orient Express*. (*National Film Archive*)

(*Below left*) As Tamburlaine the Great. (*Associated Newspapers*)

(*Below right*) As the National Theatre's Hamlet. (*Associated Newspapers*)

With Diana Quick in 1979. (*Associated Newspapers*)

Directed by Alan Parker in *Shoot the Moon*. (*National Film Archive*)

As Daddy Warbucks with his Annie, Aileen Quinn. (*Columbia/National Film Archive*)

As 'Sir', with his Dresser, Tom Courtenay. (*Columbia/National Film Archive*)

As Geoffrey Firmin in *Under the Volcano*. (*Twentieth Century-Fox/ National Film Archive*)

As Pope John Paul II. (*CBS TV*)

As Maurice Allington (*centre*), in *The Green Man*, with Sarah Berger and Linda Marlow. (*BBC*)

With Gabriel Byrne in *Miller's Crossing*. (*Twentieth Century-Fox*)

With Kathryn Erbe in *Rich in Love*. (*UIP*)

As Sergeant Hegarty in *The Playboys*. (*Samuel Goldwyn*)

Billington thought it was heroic that Finney had performed at all:

I never went back to see it again so I don't know how it developed. But on that first night, one was giving him marks just for getting onstage. It was powerful, big and had all the confidence you might expect for a man portraying a sort of Saddam Hussein conqueror figure.

Physically, he was breathtaking too. Figure-hugging tunic draped with armour, metal high on the arm and at the wrist, then bare-legged down to calf-high boots; full-beard set off by a Genghis Khan-style moustache; jagged crown and mighty curved sword. Supremely fit for what the *News of the World* captioned, in typically pithy style, 'an X-certificate study of brutality and bloody conquest'.

After almost eighteen solid months of classical turbulence on and off the stage at the National, and with an eight-month break before his next scheduled bout at the Olivier, a still fired-up Finney resisted what must have been a deep-seated urge to go walkabout and instead pressed on with his revived theatrical ambitions.

He had last worked with director Michael Elliott in the National's *Miss Julie* in 1965 and once even before that, in the BBC TV play '. . . *View Friendship and Marriage*', when both men were still in their twenties. Elliott was now the founding artistic director of Manchester's new Royal Exchange Theatre company, whose remarkable construction in the round had been officially opened by Olivier in September 1976.

It seemed logical that a local boy made good should be invited to become an integral part of the theatre's plans in its first full season. And what could be more appropriate than to follow in Olivier's footsteps by playing Astrov in Chekhov's *Uncle Vanya*. As far as Finney was concerned, the change was almost as good as a rest.

Yes, he told local journalists, it was partly because it was so different he was doing it and, after the long classical roles, here was a play

> where acting doesn't seem to consist of you doing all the talking all the time. You are working on one of the founding fathers of naturalism in the theatre. The difficulty is the amount of inner life and intensity you have to communicate – they are extremely elusive.
>
> It is different from plays written to be performed on a platform in the open air; so much more concerned and felt. That is partly why I am drawn to it. But perhaps I am also trying neurotically to prove my versatility.

The last time Finney had played in Chekhov was at school, when he had had one of the female roles. Now his Astrov, the self-disgusted doctor, and then Lopakhin in the National's *Cherry Orchard* – more of which later – suggested that here, belatedly but welcome none the less, was a closet Chekhovian who had, for whatever reasons, been sidetracked into marathon classical roles. Which only proved, the *Daily Mail*'s Jack Tinker suggested sharply, that he had 'a phenomenal memory and he should use it to remember never again to speak Elizabethan verse'. Tinker, while considering the *Vanya* production itself 'dully routine', was ecstatic about Finney: '. . . a revelation of delicate shadings. The very stuff great character acting is made of, and I shall dream on it whenever I see Chekhov trampled underfoot by the deadly earnestness of the English.' Peter Hall also visited the theatre in the last week of the six-week run and found both Leo McKern's Vanya and Finney 'definitive . . . Albert's Astrov was a country doctor wading through shit and mud in order to save the peasants from cholera.'

The second leg of Finney's Manchester double was a kind

of revelation too and seemed to confirm that Finney was indeed, as he had been fond of saying, trying to 'push out the boundaries' of his career. Perhaps the last person you'd think of casting as preening actor Gary Essendine in Coward's clipped, epigrammatic *Present Laughter* would be Finney. Yet here he was, remembered fondly by Billington, playing 'muscular camp, if you can imagine such a thing. What was so particularly funny was seeing this square-shouldered, heavily built figure as the dressing-gowned matinée idol uttering the Coward lines. The performance was full of mischievous touches, like the ritual glance every time he passed a mirror to ensure that his wavy locks were still unraped.'

Finney made an earlier return to the National than expected when he agreed to appear in Bill Bryden's Cottesloe production of *The Passion*, replacing a colleague, Pitt Wilkinson, who'd suddenly died of a heart attack. Finney had accepted the comparatively minor roles of Annas and The Blind Man in Tony Harrison's adaptation of the York Mystery Plays because his build and his Northern accent were both perfect for the piece, and was still trying to learn his lines when Hall's rehearsals for *The Country Wife* officially started.

From the start, as later with *Macbeth*, Hall was wracked with uncertainty over the Wycherley play. It was his first Restoration comedy, and throughout its preparation, the fear kept dogging him that 'nothing was happening'. Finney confided his worries about the production but, like an unstoppable engine, it just ploughed inexorably on. As Mr Horner, vociferously feigning impotence so he can bed a succession of ladies without alerting their husbands, Finney seemed unsure quite how to approach a role that can seem misanthropic, misogynistic and downright absurd unless blitzed through.

There was a hint of his supposed confusion in an otherwise droll letter he phoned in to the *Evening Standard* following the opening night:

You may have saved my life. In Monday's *Evening Standard*, you stated that I was opening at the National Theatre in *The Cherry Orchard*. Well, that's what I thought too, but apparently that was not the case. My fellow actors and the director told me that it was *The Country Wife* I opened in last night. I did think it odd to be doing a Chekhov play dressed in seventeenth-century English costume and I'm glad that your error helped to clear my confusion. Actually *The Cherry Orchard* opens in February and *Macbeth* in May, or is it Mac the wife?

Hall recorded a meeting with Finney later at which he felt that both he himself, and his leading actor had, with all the continuing pressures at the National, perhaps been trying 'too hard'. Hall told Finney that it had 'affected his voice, his freedom, his whorishness as an actor'. They resolved to make the next piece of work 'freer, less puritanical'.

The Cherry Orchard was as confident and focused as *The Country Wife* clearly hadn't been. Billington thinks it was also one of Finney's best-ever performances in his National years:

The quality I most remember was that instead of playing Lopakhin in the obvious way, which is as a kind of country peasant who has become part of the middle classes, the motivating factor here was that he was obviously in love with Ranyevskaya (Dorothy Tutin). He'd obviously nurtured this quiet passion for years and buying her estate was therefore a way of registering his emotional regard for her rather than an act of class revenge.

It also happily reminded Billington of Finney's character-actor days at Birmingham as he watched Lopakhin, 'squat, barrel-chested, an ambulatory toby jug with a fob-watch'.

Strangely, Finney hasn't played any Chekhov since.

As Hall fiddled disconsolately with his preparations for *Macbeth* – he claimed he was only doing it as a favour to Finney – his empire began to smoulder even more in a succession of garish newspaper headlines about everything from his salary to the alleged drain on taxpayers' money. There couldn't have been a worse climate for concentrated work.

Yet, according to fellow actor Nicky Henson, Finney remained the

> great company man. He held us all together when the National was going through these dodgy times. For example, I remember that I was playing the lead in another play that was rehearsing at the time and I was having tremendous problems with the director, who was also the author. He was being especially difficult with my leading lady and I didn't know how to handle it. I naturally went and knocked on Albert's door, not taking any account at all of the fact that he was playing a stonking great lead in another play at the time. Yet, while he changed his costume or whatever, he talked to me reassuringly and was prepared to give advice if asked.

True to its traditional reputation, this *Macbeth* also looked a bit jinxed from the word go. Aside from Hall's own doubts, there was the added pressure of trailing in the wake of Trevor Nunn's Royal Shakespeare Company studio production, with Ian McKellen and Judi Dench, which had just completed its hugely successful Young Vic run nearby, so proving a happy exception to the familiar hex.

As Henson said:

> I think we all really knew that we were in for a hard time from the press. Ours was a much more old-fashioned, operatic kind of production than they'd done first at Stratford. We were working from the first

folio and Albert would refer to it all the time to get nearer to the original text. He and Hall were delving as deep as they could to find out what Shakespeare really meant.

On the day the National was opening its *Macbeth* to the press, Hall gave the assembled company a pep talk but also warned, ominously, that they were going to get bad reviews. For Henson:

We thought that was rather extraordinary. That night, I was getting ready in the dressing room – they're built round a horrible well in the middle of the building and all look out across to each other – and I suddenly heard this most colossal drumming noise. I looked out the window and saw Albie out on this glass roof, banging a drum. There he was, in his underpants, completely sober, about to play Macbeth, whipping up company spirit. It gave us all a lift and we then all hung out the windows, cheering away.

As feared, most of the reviews were, inevitably, predicated by memories of Nunn's recent chamber triumph. J C Trewin, who had, of course, seen Finney's Birmingham Thane a full twenty years earlier – writing at the time: 'To see anybody else doing what Albert Finney has done, at a first attempt, will astonish' – was much more direct this time around. 'For all his clarity, he is not primarily a classical tragedian or a haunted speaker. We know his talents; they do not take him immediately towards Macbeth, even if he occasionally surprises us. I remember him when he was half his present age and there were one or two moments that the elder Finney has lost.'

Finney had also finally lost patience with Hall, who, a month after *Macbeth* opened, recorded a meeting with their mutual agent in which the director was told that Finney felt he had been 'overworked, abused, mishandled'. Finney later explained that he felt Hall's 'interest in getting the text right can smother the spirit. I thought Peter and I would complement each other, with his academic view and my freelance spirit, but it didn't work out that way.'

It is often the case that people without too much formal education become overly impressed with academe. Finney, like Anthony Hopkins, for example, was no exception and there's no doubt that, despite a scratchy start with Hall at Stratford in 1959, when he and the Cambridge-educated Hall started working together, he was very much prepared to listen to the master. But eventually – and it was sooner rather than later, bearing in mind Finney's public pronouncements about staying at the National for a decade – Hall's specific approach – in particular his notions of speaking verse – finally palled for Finney.

As Sheridan Morley put it:

He is no introverted scholar poet. That's why, for instance, *Hamlet* went so wrong. What you see with Finney is what you get. There's no great iceberg. Onstage, he does what he's paid to do; he delivers. And I find that very refreshing and admirable when so many have been into the Cambridge, intellectual, tortured-soul thing. He doesn't pretend to be a professor of drama.

Coincidentally, Hopkins was another Macbeth who, for his own particular reasons, had quit the National – in his case, even more prematurely. Unlike Hopkins though, Finney has never returned since to this cradle of subsidized theatre.

In November 1978 Finney had one more National commitment: to Charles Wood's droll, even prescient, satire *Has 'Washington' Legs?*, about the making of a movie on the American War of Independence. Finney played the director, John Bean: Huston, by any other name (his real-life assignments with Huston were yet to come).

That same month, Finney and Anouk were finally divorced. In their original petition, Finney alleged desertion by his wife and she claimed he had committed adultery. Later they agreed the marriage should be dissolved on the grounds of two years' separation by consent. The Brompton Square house would have to be sold, with Anouk receiving a third of the net profits.

A few years on, Anouk explained to Sheridan Morley that when she married Finney she didn't ever plan to act again:

> I'd been at it a long time, there was no script around that I particularly wanted to make and I genuinely thought that maybe I should take up painting or writing instead. I even bought an easel, on which the canvas turned slowly from white to yellow as it lay untouched in a corner of the house. While the marriage was good, I saw no point in being an actress; when it began to fail, I went back to work.

The most tangible legacies of the marriage were the ability to make a fine Yorkshire pudding and a passion for Rugby Union.

On the day the decree nisi was granted Finney told journalists outside the court that he was still on 'friendly terms' with Anouk. As for future marriage plans? 'All matters have to be considered,' he muttered mysteriously.

9

Wine, Women and Song

They were shooting a scene outside the Fairmont Hotel in San Francisco: Finney and his wife, played by Diane Keaton, arriving in their car to attend an evening awards ceremony, as a rain machine lashed torrents of water across a tight set. Then something went wrong. The director, Alan Parker, can't remember quite what, but it was enough for him to come running over to Finney and, in front of everyone including extras, 'let loose' with his mouth, before storming back to the camera position. Then he heard: 'How dare you? How dare you speak to me . . .'

Parker turned round:

Suddenly there we were, the both of us, face to face, standing under the rain machine getting drenched. Here were the same lungs that had stood on stage declaiming Hamlet and Luther yelling at me in the middle of San Francisco. It was not an experience I would recommend. After all that, and more than a bit dampened, I said to him: 'It's good you're letting me know what you feel.' He said: 'What is it? What is it?' So I told him: 'It's just that I know you can be *great*. That's all I want.'

This extraordinary encounter came some six weeks into filming the intense drama *Shoot the Moon* and was the climax of growing tension between Finney and Parker. After various 'takes', Finney would corner the director with 'You always say, "Great Diane. Very good, Albert." ' To which Parker would as regularly reply, 'Well, Albert, *she* is always *great*.' Inwardly, Parker was getting increasingly concerned: 'You watch someone walking and you want them to run. You know they *can* run, but won't. There's something holding them back; they're not trying too hard, as if it's rather vulgar. To Albert, I never seemed happy, and he'd become irritated by that and would ask me why – and maybe I couldn't properly articulate it.'

At the core of the problem, as well as at the centre of the film, was the clash of two great acting titans. According to Parker:

What we had was the man thought to be the greatest actor of his generation, theatrically trained. Rehearse, get it right, repeat. Then there was Diane, who, at the time anyway, was absolutely the top American movie actress. Her style is naturalistic; the film set is her world. She's very unusual compared with most other contemporary American actors, in that unlike most Americans, who are only loose and improvised, she also keeps an extraordinary discipline within the framework of a scene. She then adds to that a fresh sense of improvisation – bend a line here, take a line there. We did the fight in the kitchen very early on and I could see that Albert was very impressed with her. I remember him sitting in the corner, in a sort of boxing-ring stance, and I said, 'You OK, Albie?' and he said quietly, 'She's very good, isn't she?'

Every single moment that Diane was on the screen, he knew deep down that he couldn't afford to be anything but as good as he could be. He was suddenly realizing that after all the years of not being an actor, he would have to go up a gear. He'd never been acted off the screen before in his life and now this was actually happening. Yet I was also beginning to think that if he could get away with walking through a scene, he would. That's nothing to do with laziness; it's to do with the fact that he had to rekindle the passion he once had for the job. For the moment, after walking through his last couple of films, he seemed to have lost it. For too long he'd been enjoying lunch more than acting. I knew that in order to push him where *he* knew he had to go, and for the sake of the film too, I had to risk my friendship and confront him head on.

Up to about eighteen months before *Shoot the Moon* in 1981, Finney hadn't done any really substantial film work for five years – since *Murder on the Orient Express*. He had opted for hunks of stage work at the Court, a couple of Peter Nichols's plays and then the National stint, so when he finally did decide to tackle movies again, he made the conscious decision to take on a whole block of work.

The *Alpha Beta* factor this time round seems to have been the actress Diana Quick, whom he'd first met when they were rehearsing *Tamburlaine* together. Quick, ten years his junior and a fiercely bright Oxford graduate, was ambitious about her own career and is also likely to have prodded Finney at a time when it seemed that he might simply lapse into a less-than-dizzy round of meetings, lunch and theatrical anecdotes. As well as *Tamburlaine*, they also worked together at the Royal Exchange in *Present Laughter* and, in his case very briefly, on Ridley Scott's first film, *The Duellists*.

This was an elegant, though extremely inexpensive, adaptation of the Joseph Conrad story about two Napoleonic officers (Keith Carradine and Harvey Keitel) engaged in an absurdly prolonged personal vendetta. Scott needed 'a major element' for the tiny but significant role of the sinister

French secret police chief, Fouché, and with added persuasion by his producer, David Puttnam, managed to snare Finney for four days' work (in St James's), resulting in three minutes' screen time. All in exchange for two crates of Dom Perignon and no screen credit. The film's distributor, Paramount, doubtless delighted by the modesty of the first, wouldn't agree to the second because of Finney's nominal clout. So the producers had to go back to the actor and, with some embarrassment, ask him if he minded being credited after all. He did not.

Finney and Quick, who were living together in her pretty Georgian house in Camberwell by the time the divorce from Anouk came through, became inseparable, and when he completed his final commitment at the National, they set off together for South America. After the carnival in Rio, they joined a slow boat for the Galapagos Islands. Too slow, it seemed, judging by the furore and headlines that followed. According to Michael Medwin, the couple had been due in Hollywood for meetings and when there was no sign of them on the appointed date, he told journalists that he was beginning 'to get very worried'. He had visions of them lost up the Amazon and even contacted the Foreign Office about instigating a search. LOST? NO I'M NOT, SAYS STAR, roared the tabloids a short while later, as the dauntless couple exchanged South for North America.

If Finney's film career at that stage could be considered sporadic, then Michael Wadleigh's was technically non-existent. Back in 1969, Wadleigh, just twenty-four, had directed arguably the definitive rockumentary, *Woodstock* (brilliantly edited by Martin Scorsese, among others). It scooped Warner Brothers more than $14 million in the US alone, made Wadleigh a millionaire and also earned him and his producer partner, Bob Maurice, an Oscar. Between *Woodstock* and *Wolfen* in 1979, he had not made a single movie. Ever consistent, another decade on Wadleigh hasn't made a feature film since *Wolfen*. These days he prefers teaching film at Harvard and Boston, making the occasional documentary in the Third World and occasionally writing well-paid screenplays which never seem to go beyond the development stage.

Back in 1979 Wadleigh was fascinated by the material he'd read in the galleys of Whitley Strieber's new book, *Wolfen*, a distinctly surrealistic shocker about wolves – or could they be werewolves? – violently stalking the streets of modern-day New York. Their nemesis was a rumpled city cop, Dewey Wilson. Dustin Hoffman made it very clear he'd like to play Dewey, but Wadleigh, engaged by Orion Pictures to make the movie, said he wanted Finney for the role. Though the studio thought it strange that anyone would prefer Finney over Hoffman, they went along with his idea. Still lurking in the back of some concerned executive's mind was Finney's last screen image: a 'fat, oily fellow' called Poirot. Was this, they queried, how he looked for real?

For Wadleigh, *Wolfen*, cruelly mocked by one critic as 'the first pro-ecology, anti-gentrification, lupine-revenge horror movie', was never intended to be a horror film as such. He saw it as an allegory, 'a classy metaphor', not unlike Moby Dick. As he recalled:

> I was pleased that Albert also felt this way. Here were wolves treated in two different ways. There were these rather mystical Indians, who saw the wolf as almost a surrogate human being, as an equal; as a smart, very tribal, family-orientated animal. The Indians never killed wolves. The white man, however, somehow believed wolves were the devil and tried to wipe them out. However, at the end of our film, Albert, representing a more thoughtful white man, softens up and lets the wolf get away.
>
> It was basically a film about one of society's hunters who has begun to doubt the justice of protecting that same society. When I eventually met Albert after we'd

first sent him the script, he looked perfect too: quite long hair, brooding, shaggy.

Apart from the unusual subject matter, *Wolfen* was also a remarkable-looking film, with much of the shooting done from a wolf's-eye point of view, thanks to the gliding, sliding but always stabilized, hand-held Steadicam.

Its inventor, Garrett Brown, who two years earlier had won an Oscar for the device, actually operated the Steadicam himself for most of the filming. An exceedingly tall man, 6 feet 7 inches, he organized an especially low rig for his camera as, with knee-pads and helmet on, he simulated the movements of stalking wolves. There were many extremely difficult locations, notably the Dresden-like South Bronx – 'a vision of Western civilization dropping into post-holocaust decay', as Wadleigh described it – so Brown was often literally risking life and limb as he darted through rubble or tried to avoid crashing down on to the detritus of endless redevelopment.

Another intriguing visual element was the use of what special effects supervisor Robert Blalack called 'thermagrams' to represent the wolfens' ability to perceive their potential victim's body heat and even their level of hostility. For this, he experimented with a wide range of black-and-white stocks and colour filters to separate out flesh tones from the rest of the scene.

Then, of course, there were the wolves themselves. According to Wadleigh:

> Yes, real wolves. To give you an idea of their size, I'm 6 feet tall and occasionally these things would stand on two legs and put their paws on your shoulders, and with the size of their head too, they'd be looking *down* at you.
>
> Albert had one wonderfully consistent trait; he'd do *anything*. He'd even go up on high steel despite having a fear of heights. The same applied to his close work

with the wolves. It helped that he had complete faith in our wolf wrangler, George Toth, a great bear of a man who came from Hungary and whose father was a wolf-trainer before him. I remember one particularly tense scene near the end of the film when we were working in a penthouse and this wolf had to be inches away from him and seething. Try and imagine what would happen if it had suddenly lunged forward with its jaws; your face would be gone just like that.

We had about a dozen wolves altogether, and for our epic scene in Wall Street we had, as we'd had all the way through, police marksmen standing by in fenced-off enclosures with orders to kill if the wolves got out. I doubt if Hoffman would ever have done the stuff that Albert did.

Finney had occasionally mugged an American accent during other roles but this was the first time he'd really gone for the rounded native, as it were. If the resulting inflections do seem to veer wildly between Bronx and Broughton (Pacino advised him on the Bronx bit), the rest remains a decent enough impersonation of your average cigar-chomping, junkfood-eating, maverick New York cop. Wadleigh would prefer 'wobble' or 'wander' to 'veer wildly', yet he was slightly surprised that Finney didn't manage to get a better handle on the accent. Still, he felt that was less important than the overall characterization: 'We talked a lot about the role and both felt that, in Dewey's case, actions spoke a great deal louder than words. So it was a question of stripping away dialogue and playing up the irreverence and irascibility of the character where possible.'

Almost as scary as the time Wadleigh made Finney totter on top of the Manhattan Bridge was when he took Finney and Diana Quick to a concert by gravel-voiced Tom Waits, who also had a small cameo role in the movie. As Wadleigh recalled:

The place was full of drugged-out freaks but, no matter, Albert was getting into the music and all. I remember he was sitting next to this long-haired, drooling kid and they were all drinking and having a good time. Then, suddenly, in the middle of the goddamn concert, the kid rears back, throws his head forward and vomits all over Albert. I was trying to laugh it off with something about this being part of the experience of attending a Waits gig. It was outrageous, but Albert stayed cool and just wiped it all off. But I'll never forget the way he looked at that guy!

Though considerably re-edited beyond Wadleigh's brief, *Wolfen* remains an unusual and effective thriller, full of good supporting performances too, notably by the dancer Gregory Hines, in his movie début as a young assistant coroner. Hines had first read for his role a long while before he was eventually cast and, though fairly nerve-wracked about his first movie, was quickly put at ease by Finney. 'You and I are playing very good friends in the film, so I think we should spend some time together,' Finney told him when they met. As Hines recalled:

I was hoping he'd say that because I knew I could learn a lot just by being around him. Mind you, I almost became an alcoholic hanging out with Albert. He was really drinking in those days and I was doing my best to keep up with him. He also turned me on to Cuban cigars. And the crew loved him – until he won $10,000 in our Superbowl pool.

Towards the end of filming, it became extremely cold in the city, so cold that Hines was finding it increasingly difficult to concentrate. As Hines sat in a van between takes, Finney told him: 'You know what we have to do, Greg? Think of something that will help us here. Why don't

we think of Hawaii? Let's imagine ourselves in Hawaii
when we go out there to do the next take.' Hines was
beginning to relax and thaw out nicely as he took Finney's
advice. Then, just as he stepped out of the van, Finney said
to him, 'Hey, no. Hawaii's just too much of a contrast.
Let's think of Alaska!'

Another day, another location. This time, it was London
and an altogether more conventional thriller called *Loophole*,
which at the time boasted that it was the most costly
independent British-financed film ever made.

Of its $6 million budget, $750,000 went to Finney and
the same to his co-star Martin Sheen, for nine weeks' work.
The story revolved around a criminal mastermind (Finney)
who snares an architect (Sheen) into helping him and his
gang rob a bank. According to director John Quested:

Our film was less about a robbery and more about
what it takes for one man to corrupt another. Albert's
role was loosely based on a couple of the Great Train
Robbers, particularly Bruce Reynolds. In fact, I had
thought first of Michael Caine because he actually
looked like Reynolds. But it's funny how things stay
with you, and I always remember that scene in
Saturday Night and Sunday Morning when Albert's
looking at his beer and you just know he's going to
throw up. He has that quality of keeping still, which is
the best thing a film actor can have. I just knew he was
right for this.

Quested, who now runs Goldcrest Films, had come up
through the ranks, working as an assistant to film-makers
like Huston and Losey before making his own directing
début with Brian Friel's *Philadelphia, Here I Come*. From
Huston, he had learned the virtues of letting the camera
work itself, avoiding unnecessarily flamboyant camera

moves, and ever since *The Servant* he'd also been fascinated by the idea of conflicting characters, where one is so much more strong-willed than the other. All this, and Finney's admiration for the Friel adaptation, made for, if not one of the most memorable films, at least a solid entertainment and, during its production, an enjoyable set.

Quested again:

Albert's an unselfish actor and helps create a good atmosphere on the set. He's always prepared to take that extra risk as an actor, not necessarily keeping to the trunk of the tree but sometimes bouncing on the branches instead.

That can make him a dangerous actor, which is good too. Talking of corruption, he certainly corrupted Sheen into betting on the horses.

Sheen had missed out on meeting Finney twenty years earlier when both had plays at that 1961 Théâtre des Nations festival in Paris, but there was a more unorthodox encounter a couple of years later in New York. Finney was appearing in *Luther* and decided one afternoon to visit a movie house on 61st Street where *Tom Jones* was playing. 'Resting' at the time, Sheen and his fellow cinema usher, Al Pacino, spotted Finney and fought for the privilege of seating him. When they eventually paired up on *Loophole*, they'd both already enjoyed a lot of living and, in Sheen's case, nearly dying, when he had a heart attack while filming *Apocalypse Now* in the Philippines. Though he was a jogging fanatic, Sheen was also mightily fond of his Guinness, and Finney would kid him about how Irish he was. For his part, Sheen, who was actually half-Irish and half-Spanish, often joked with Finney about how he had royal blood and was really a marquis. Sheen's sister, Carmen, was visiting the set and so Finney embarked on an elaborate charade, pretending to treat her brother like royalty. He came into Sheen's caravan, bowing and scraping and asking if it was time to do the hoovering. Carmen was suitably nonplussed until she was finally let into the joke.

Perhaps all this fun and frolicking took its toll because, though *Rififi*-like in concept and agreeably cast, *Loophole* simply didn't manage to catch fire and Finney seemed barely stretched. But at least he achieved the vertical, which is more than can be said for his next role, in Michael Crichton's *Looker*. In this deeply confusing sci-fi porridge, Finney was so laid back that he was almost prone, playing a rich plastic surgeon whose gorgeous clients seem to be dying off at an alarming rate.

It must rank as one of the laziest performances on film, edging an already comatose movie close to flatline. Pauline Kael described it best when she wrote: 'To the rescue of civilization as we know it comes Albert Finney, like a lame tortoise; boredom seems to have seeped into Finney's muscles and cells – he's sinking under the weight of it, and the only part of him still alert is his wiry hair.'

Finney finished *Looker* on a Thursday, flew to San Francisco, met Diane Keaton the following Tuesday, rehearsed on the Wednesday and, by Thursday, was throwing plates at her. *Shoot the Moon* was a brooding movie about the disintegration of a fifteen-year marriage, further complicated by four noisy young daughters in the domestic battlefield. Written by Bo Goldman, it was originally called *Switching*; then someone came up with the term used in the card game Hearts when a player tries to win all but knows they will probably lose everything.

Keaton was cast first, as Faith Dunlap. Parker had met her when she was still engaged on the marathon *Reds* and still emotionally involved with its producer-director-star, Warren Beatty. By the time she started *Shoot the Moon*, she had broken up with Beatty. Parker thinks he probably tried first for Jack Nicholson to play George Dunlap, a successful writer who's having an affair. Parker said:

I know I've asked Nicholson to do every one of my last five films, so I must have done here too. I also talked to Al Pacino and for a moment it really looked as though it might be Diane and Al, but he wanted something else from the part which he couldn't articulate. I thought about Albert as well, but it was around the time he'd sort of given up on movies.

Albert had been a hero of mine and to most of my generation of film-makers, but when we started to get the chance to make films, he wasn't there and it was very frustrating. You'd see him having lunch, telling wonderful stories, but offer him anything, and he'd always say no. I originally thought that he was plain lazy, but then he did things like *Hamlet* and *Tamburlaine* on stage, so it wasn't that. Suddenly it all changed and I got lucky. I knew he'd done that weird thing *Wolfen*, but I probably thought that was just him being bloody-minded, choosing some weird subject, considering that he turned down anything that was good in previous years. I remember talking about it to David and to Puttnam's one-time partner, Sandy Lieberson, who then worked for Twentieth Century Fox. 'What about Albert?' they said. I said I thought probably not. Then Sandy said, 'No, really. Albie wants to work.' I told him I thought it would just be a waste of time, but Sandy insisted. 'Just send the script to him. See what happens.' So I did.

As Parker feared, Finney said no. He told Parker: 'I'm at a point in my life where I don't want to re-examine the darker corners of my life and put them on to film. Which is what I know you want me to do.' They all kept on at him: Parker, Puttnam and Lieberson. Then he changed his mind, said yes and, after completing *Looker*, joined the unit in San Raphael, about an hour's drive north of San Francisco. The production offices were in an old converted schoolhouse and there, soon after he'd arrived, Parker arranged for a read-through with him and Keaton. Finney did an American accent and Parker stopped him:

I was never fond of Albert's American accent – you never know whether he's taking the piss or not. I said to him that I didn't think the character had to be an American. It seemed that it just lost a degree of truth, from the point of view of whether his accent would be believable, particularly when it wasn't really necessary. After all, it wouldn't be unusual for an English writer to reside in northern California. He said, 'Fine', and read it again as an Englishman.

Before filming started, Parker indulged his usual practice of writing to cast and crew to let them know what he thought the film was about, 'because I once heard that Ingmar Bergman did it'. He saw it as the story of an American marriage,

two people, fifteen years married, with four children, seemingly with everything and yet torn apart by the summation of a thousand vague and tiny reasons that come with the passing years. Two people who can't live together and who also can't let go of one another. A story of fading love, senseless rage and the inevitable bewildering betrayal in the eyes of the children.

He also pointed out that although the schedule wasn't 'horrendous', it would be made difficult by 'all the familiar problems of working with kids'. At times he further warned, 'This will mean we all need to be a little more patient.'

The opening sequence of *Shoot the Moon*, which Kael has, perhaps a little extravagantly, described as 'perhaps the most revealing American movie of its era', is as uncompromisingly bleak as anything that follows and sets the tone perfectly. Finney, face drawn and preoccupied, walks

straight into camera and, with sounds off of wife and
children, treads slowly downstairs, moves into his study,
sits down and weeps bitterly. It's an immediately arresting
start. Parker said that it may have needed only one, perhaps
two, takes, after which he went up to Finney, put his arm
round him and asked if he was all right. Finney just said,
'Oh, yes.' Self-control, Parker thought, adding, 'You know,
Albert, that's amazing, because it looks like you're really in
pain.' Finney replied matter-of-factly: 'That's acting. If you
don't feel it, fake it. That's what I do for a living.' For the
director, this made an intriguing contrast with Keaton: 'If
Diane cries, she has to cry, has to be in pain as an actress. She'd
put on a Sony Walkman and play some music that reminded
her of, I suppose, Warren, then she'd cry for real. No faking.'

Unusually, much of the film was shot chronologically, so
the first few weeks of filming mirrored the break-up of the
marriage. As Parker has recalled:

> Diane and Albert did the professional and respectful
> thing that actors do; they kept their distance from one
> another. When we did the kitchen scene in which she
> first talks about the fact she knows he's having an
> affair – that's when the plate-smashing happens –
> they'd go to opposite corners in between shots. I think
> they were quite fond of each other, though I'm not sure
> they could really figure each other out as people. But
> there again, nobody else could, so they weren't unusual
> in that respect.

It was now that Parker began gradually to notice what he
perceived as a widening gulf between their performances
and started to fret about how he might have to risk his
friendship with Finney to prevent the gulf becoming
unbridgeable. He was also getting increasingly irritated with
aspects of Finney's olde worlde theatricality:

> Albert's very charming to have around, but I have to

admit I'm not at all interested in theatrical anecdotes. To me, it's the most boring thing in the world to hear an actor tell his Gielgud or Wolfit stories for the umpteenth time. However, the make-up or set-dresser people seem to like it. I would say, 'We're ready, Albert!' and he'd reply, 'Just a minute ...' as he'd be coming to the punchline of yet another Wolfit story. For the first five times, it may be quite funny, but when it happens endlessly and you're on a film set in the middle of nowhere and everyone's ready and working their balls off ... I wanted him to be there when I called him.

And so they clashed. Parker reflected:

Albert's a street boy like me. He knew; he absolutely knew. It was a fiery moment. He was once the most brilliant actor in the whole world and then became someone who enjoyed lunch more than acting. I pushed him further than anyone had ever pushed him. The decision he had to make within himself, regarding this film, was whether he just had to please this wanker from Islington, who might not know what he was talking about anyway, or else confront the truth about his own worth as an actor. I really believe that was the dilemma.

For the remainder of the shoot, Parker found Finney 'extraordinarily reflective'. Yet he believes that 'the filming moved on to a higher level, as he began to dig deeper and went to a place where he wouldn't have been before my argument with him'.

The process wasn't all one way. 'He was tough on me too. I expected that. He's not only a great actor but also a fine director, and there's no way you can pull the wool over his eyes. On the other hand, film has moved on a great deal and I don't think he could fake it any more either.'

On his own admission, Finney became extremely miserable during the filming. Fourteen weeks was a long time to be playing around in the area of human relationships and to keep 'digging deep for memories'. He had, after all, been initially reluctant to begin what was tantamount to an exploration of the darker corners of his own life and now here he was, in Marin County, doing just that. It was interfering with his sleep and even impinged, heaven forbid, on his weekend golf.

And as if this wasn't enough, there was child-beating too. After the Dunlaps split up, George moves out. He still has restricted access to the children, but despite feeble attempts at civility, any sort of communication is disintegrating fast. The oldest daughter, thirteen-year-old Sherry (actually eighteen-year-old Dana Hill), says she hates her father, but he's still determined to press on her the birthday present she always wanted – a portable typewriter. Even if it means breaking into his own house, throwing his wife out and violently barring her re-entry. Then he terrifies the three younger kids, and beats Sherry with a coat-hanger after she's threatened him with scissors and a torrent of abuse. Finally he leaves the devastated household, still clutching the rejected typewriter. The harrowing sequence was shot over three or four nights, with Hill suitably padded, wearing a diver's wet-suit under baggy trousers. And she needed it, as Finney/George vented his impotent rage with a shocking violence.

When the film was shown some time later on the cable channel in Los Angeles, Finney was interviewed in the studio by *Los Angeles Times* critic Charles Champlin. Champlin showed a Sherry-bashing clip and, when it came back to camera in the studio, the interviewer found himself briefly at a loss for words. Before Champlin could say anything, Finney chipped in with, 'So unlike the home life of our own dear Queen!'.

As the domestic strife ebbed and flowed, Finney and Keaton found that if, between set-ups and takes, they were able to latch on to the right emotion, they'd retreat to separate rooms to preserve it for the next scene. The children continued to remain cheerful, until Hill got caught up in the atmosphere and would retire on her own. By the end, Finney recalled, 'even the seven-year-old was in her own corner. I began to think we must be corrupting them by making them as neurotic as we were.'

Dealing with the children must have been quite tricky for both actors. Keaton, who had wanted the role because it gave her a rare chance to play a mother, told Parker, 'I don't know about children. I only know about cats.' Finney, who hadn't really been a conventional father to Simon, did his best to achieve a rapport with the quartet here. Karen Allen, who was playing his mistress, remembered the way he tried to keep the atmosphere on the set 'light and fun for the kids. The image I have of him most is one day being a gorilla and playing all over the room with them.'

Towards the end of the film, there is a splendid confrontation in a restaurant between Keaton and Finney. George is already seated when Faith comes in and settles down at a separate table. He moves across the room to join her and they begin to row noisily, much to the consternation of the staff and other guests. 'This is a restaurant, not a gymnasium,' they're told. 'I'm just having a nice quiet fight with my wife,' George tells the exasperated *maître d'*.

For Parker:

It was after my row with him, and was an electric scene in that he was word-perfect. We were shooting on a bluff in the city and, before we started, Albert went off for a long walk along the beach. If you look at the scene, it's as sharp in its timing as a piece of theatre. I cut towards the end of it, but most of it played like a theatrical two-shot. Albert was very concerned about the timing on how he was cutting up a piece of salmon. Maybe to catch me out on continuity, or something. I said to him, 'Don't worry about it. Go for it. What happens happens.' So then he cut a little piece of salmon and he held it out – he was immaculate with the matching – when, suddenly, and this hadn't been rehearsed, Diane leaned forward and smacked the fish off his fork. He just went with the moment. And at that moment, he escalated from where he was to where she was. He simply wasn't going to let her get away with the scene and, I think, he actually stole it from her brilliantly.

The film ends with George descending into more mindless violence. He smashes up Faith's new tennis court before being smashed up himself by her new lover (Peter Weller). Lying on the ground, he raises a hand towards her in supplication. Parker apparently canvassed the unit about whether they thought she'd be likely to take hold of Finney's hand or spurn it. They shot three different endings before settling, somewhat predictably, for a contactless freeze-frame. Finney's own theory was that matters had gone too far between them and their struggle was likely to continue. Reconciliation was somehow inconceivable. There were reports that women hissed at previews, resenting Finney's loutishness so much they couldn't enjoy the film. They also seemed appalled at the possibility that Keaton might simply take him back.

Bearing in mind what had taken place between Parker and Finney during shooting, the reviews, particularly of Finney, make fascinating reading. Kael wrote:

Finney, who has been sleepwalking in his recent movie appearances, is awake and trying out his reflexes. There's a profound difference in Finney; this is not a performance one might have expected from him. He uses all the impacted sloth and rage that show in the sag and weight of his big, handsome face. His scenes seem to be happening right in front of us – you watched him with an apprehensiveness that you might feel at a live telecast. Keaton *is* Faith, but Finney seems both George *and* Finney. He's an actor possessed by a great role, pulled into it screaming and kicking by his own guts.

David Denby, in *New York* magazine, was also obsessed with visual clues:

As he's grown older, Finney has lost the cheerfully raffish grin, the physical grace and ease that made him so appealing in *Saturday Night* and *Tom Jones* . . .

He's become a heavy-bodied, heavy-spirited man, surly, a bit of a lout, his face frozen in baleful frown, almost as if he were suffering permanently from cramps in the jaw and neck . . . In the recent *Looker* and *Wolfen*, Finney was clearly a zombie star trying to pass as cool . . . the locked-in sullenness works for George.

Finney's face was also described variously as 'a sensitive potato' and 'as finger-marked as a second-hand Rubik cube'. Nigel Andrews, in the *Financial Times*, drew the bigger picture: 'Keaton and Finney sink themselves so deeply, so completely, in their roles that no film has ever so well caught the pendulum pulse of domestic stoicism and domestic misery.'

For a film expressing such naked emotions, just the kind that Hollywood usually hugs to its bosom on an awards night, *Shoot the Moon* was conspicuous by its absence. And to add insult to injury, Alan Parker had also lost a friend.

Finney's last scene on *Shoot the Moon* was shot in the stilly watches of a Tuesday night. He was cleared to leave on the Wednesday evening, and arrived present and correct for tap-dancing lessons in New York at ten o'clock on Friday morning. The fifth and, for the time being, final leg of his turn-of-the-eighties film quintet was *Annie*. Based on the long-running Charnin–Strouse stage musical, which itself was derived from a famous syndicated comic strip by Harold Gray, the film rights alone had cost Columbia a record $9.5 million.

The movie, which eventually cost anything between $35 million and $51.5 million (depending which estimate you believe), began bottom heavy and could only sink. It cannot have helped the cause when the producer, Ray Stark, normally a reliable purveyor of old-fashioned screen entertainment, became simply old-fashioned – 'out of touch' might be a better expression – when he decided to entrust this latest froth to his great friend John Huston. Huston, who was seventy-six, had never before directed a musical, but Stark said: 'I thought it would be classy with John – because John *was* Daddy Warbucks.' Quite what he meant by this is difficult to fathom. If he meant big spender, then judging by *Annie*'s inflated budget he was quite correct. His probable intention was to equate Huston with a larger-than-life character who seemed part of the nation's fabric.

Warbucks is, of course, the gruff, profiteering, bald billionaire who becomes irredeemably softened by the American Depression's most famous foundling, Little Orphan Annie; a sort of Scrooge without hair. Sean Connery, who was originally considered for the role, would have had a head start, but Finney had played and sung *Scrooge*, so that was even more helpful.

He was also prepared to undergo one of the unkindest cuts of all – to remove his proud, auburn locks. The idea of a cap was briefly toyed with, but a cap takes an hour to seal sufficiently so the camera can't spot it and as soon as the head moves it can begin to wrinkle at the back of the neck. Sweaty, too. Off came the hair, but that wasn't the end of the story. Finney would have to be shaved twice a day to prevent the hint of a shadow interfering with his gleaming pate.

Finney claimed that becoming properly bald helped him with the role: 'Having a shaved head makes you feel quite different. Normally, I slump a lot, but with my head shaved I found I was thrusting my jaw forward and extending my neck a lot. It even affected the way I walked.' Then, after careful research of Gray's original strip, they conveniently discovered that Daddy Warbucks was not quite so native American as first imagined: he'd apparently been a young immigrant from the north-west of England. So Finney was now eminently qualified on all three counts.

Apart from yet another hefty pay day, the lure for Finney had to be Huston, a long-time hero and author of many of the tough-guy movies the actor had so enjoyed at his local cinemas back in the forties. For a forty-five-year-old Finney, Huston rapidly became a surrogate father figure. He even gently spoofed Huston's speech in the film. He particularly admired the old man's endless curiosity and he was also awed by his reputation as a *bon viveur*. One of Finney's most regularly repeated anecdotes concerns the night he planned dinner for twelve at the huge New Jersey estate (doubling for Warbucks's lush Fifth Avenue home) where *Annie* was shooting. The guest list included Huston, Ray Stark and veteran editor Margaret Booth.

Before the meal, Finney asked the *maître d'* to decant four extremely expensive bottles of Château Lafite-Rothschild 1959 and to leave them on the table in carafes, as if they were house wines. Later, Huston was talking to Booth when the wine waiter filled his glass. After he'd taken a sip, he pondered for a moment and then, with a glint of recognition, asked rhetorically: 'Isn't this a Lafite-Rothschild '59?' After the meal, Finney asked if anyone wanted a liqueur and Huston replied: 'I don't think so. But perhaps we can have another decanter of that nice red . . .'

Wine has for a long time been a bit more than just a hobby for Finney as well. When he was at the National he kept a fridgeful, of blessed memory by his then colleagues. Nicky Henson remembered popping into Finney's room one night for a chat and was invited to help himself to a glass of 'white plonk'. Henson thought it delicious and asked if he could check a bottle to write down its name. 'Oh, it's Chassagne-Montrachet. I just keep it for plonk,' said Finney, as Henson spotted rows of the stuff in the fridge. Later, when he tried to buy some, he was informed it was £24 a bottle: 'You tend to forget with Albert,' said Henson, 'that he has done quite well.'

Annie's long shooting schedule also gave Finney an ideal opportunity to indulge his love of horses and horseracing. Though from his earliest youth he had been vicariously involved with the sport and had ridden for pleasure since his teens, it was only after beginning to accumulate his first fortune, following the success of *Tom Jones*, that he started to buy horses and become keen on betting.

Soon after he returned from his world trip in 1965, he took some advice from a friend, the Australian jockey Ron Hutchinson, and bought four yearlings at a reputed cost of £15,000, giving them to his parents as a gift. They were trained at Lewes by Gordon Smyth, a former trainer to the Duke of Norfolk, and ran in his mother's name. Between 1966 and 1972, he had ten horses and won eighteen races. One of that first quartet, Straight Master, wearing the Finney green-and-yellow, won a William Hill Gold Cup at Redcar, got a second in the Cambridgeshire and a third in the Hunt Cup at Royal Ascot.

The game was becoming something of an addiction when, for a couple of years, he even had a 'blower' – a bookie's loudspeaker – installed in his London home. Since then, his equine interests have extended to the US and Ireland. He has had breedings from the champion Seattle Slew and, by the mid-eighties, owned nine horses in the States, reputedly worth $10 million, including the three-year-old colt, Synastry, a declared runner in the 1986 Kentucky Derby until it had to withdraw at the last moment through injury. More recently, he has admitted to owning a brood mare in Wexford and a third-share of three horses at Epsom, though he claimed to bet only rarely.

So, in between strutting his stuff on *Annie* and keeping his eye on son Simon, who was spending the summer with him after graduating from Oxford (these days he works as an assistant cameraman), Finney could most happily be found out on the West Coast at the Del Mar track, immortalized by founder-president Bing Crosby in his song, 'Where the Turf meets the Surf'.

Some 100 miles south of Los Angeles and 25 north of San Diego, Del Mar is a much-favoured playground for the Hollywood crowd. Indeed, it was a Paramount Studios boffin who installed the world's first photo-finish device at Del Mar.

This was the perfect place to get away from work and wade deep in horseflesh and horse-talk. He rented a house from the restaurateur Tony Roma, who was another keen racing man. Regulars in Finney's circle at Del Mar were the owners Edward Taylor and Robert Sangster, trainer Billy McDonald and the American actor Vince Edwards. Edwards had years earlier appeared in a movie with Finney, *The Victors*, but they never shared a scene together and met each other only briefly when Edwards, who had filmed his scenes in Italy, visited the set later. Now they became racetrack chums, enjoying racing parties at each other's houses and dinners at trendy restaurants, like Pisces, just along the coast at La Costa. Edwards always knew where to find Finney. The bald head beckoned like a beacon.

When Carol Burnett, who was playing Miss Hannigan, the dreaded orphanage warden, first met her *Annie* co-star, she thought he would be 'terribly young' for the part. She soon changed her mind. Though in the stage show Hannigan and Warbucks never meet, for the movie a scene was devised in which he goes to the orphanage to get the adoption papers signed. As first rehearsed, the scene seemed too short. 'It needed,' recalled Burnett, 'a song to make it really pay off. I started a campaign for one. Albert joined in. It was push, push, push right up to the moment we won.'

The result was 'Sign', a comic duet in which Warbucks is trying to get Miss Hannigan's signature, while she is trying to instigate a romance. Rehearsed with the ink on the music barely dry, it was filmed two days later, as one of four new songs composed just for the movie.

One of the film's fatal omissions was the theatre production's effective Hooverville episode, combining the subject's escapism with the reality of the Depression. Without that, the movie became pure, undiluted *schmaltz*, which a talented red-haired moppet and an equally skilled dog merely compounded. There was also a problem caused by the strict division of labour, for while Huston directed the actors, it was left to Joe Layton to supervise the musical scenes. The movie had an unwieldy, schizophrenic feel to it. Of Finney, one critic suggested: 'His ability to choose roles to fit his great talent is in question.'

Whatever their eventual box-office score, even Broadway's most successful musicals have seldom failed to make a dent at Oscar-time. *Annie*, however, collapsed on both counts. It scraped a measly two nominations (for Musical Adaptation and Art Direction) and failed to earn back even its original budget in American rentals. The film's slogan was 'The Movie of Tomorrow', referring to its only memorable song. The way things turned out, *Annie*'s day never came at all.

10

In Character

As with so many British film projects that are enthusiastically announced – star, director, writer, often budget and start date too – and then as summarily aborted, *The Girl in Melanie Klein* once seemed a promising venture. Set in a private mental hospital in London in which the rooms are named after donors, it had been adapted from his own 1969 novel by Ronald Harwood and was to star Glenda Jackson, as a sane patient held captive in the 'Klein' room, and be directed by Finney, returning behind the camera for the first time since *Charlie Bubbles*. It eventually ended up among a clutch of no-go film casualties in the early seventies, never to be heard of again. Harwood, though – playwright, biographer and theatre historian, as well as screenwriter, novelist and one-time actor – became one of Finney's closest friends and so it was perhaps inevitable that, despite the disappointment of *Melanie Klein*, they'd link up again sooner or later.

Finney was firmly on his Hollywood treadmill when Harwood's *The Dresser*, became first a West End and then a Broadway stage hit. A thinly disguised account of Harwood's time as dresser to the rampantly egocentric Sir Donald Wolfit on a dizzy round of provincial English theatres in the fifties, the author had shifted the play's setting back to war-torn Britain in 1942. The dresser became the decidedly camp 'Norman', while the Wolfit character was now simply 'Sir'. The success of the play in America made it a natural for film translation, especially with two such juicy central roles (Norman was played by Tom Courtenay in London and New York, with Freddie Jones and Paul Rogers each getting a bite at 'Sir') and an evocative period milieu.

The Dresser swept into production as swiftly as *Melanie Klein* had foundered. It also coincided with a rare high point in the fortunes of co-investor Goldcrest Films, who persuaded the British director Peter Yates to make *The Dresser* for no fee upfront – in Hollywood, after movies like *The Deep* and *Breaking Away*, he could normally command $1 million a picture – but with the promise of substantial profit 'points'. Harwood, who received $60,000 for writing the screenplay ($100,000–$250,000 might have been more the norm), Finney and Courtenay, who'd be playing 'Sir' and Norman respectively, were also persuaded to take points in lieu of a huge fee, so that the film was eventually made for a modest $6 million. From first draft to production at Pinewood took a mere five months, by which time Goldcrest's *Gandhi* had not only scooped eight Oscars but also begun to make serious inroads into the American box office. So when Goldcrest suggested to Columbia that it might also like to distribute *The Dresser*, the US studio jumped at the chance and offered an advance which covered the entire budget of the British film.

As Finney's career had often coincided with O'Toole's, so it has also regularly crossed with Courtenay's without ever actually colliding – until *The Dresser*. Also a Northerner, Courtenay followed Finney at RADA, was also a Woodfall film babe, and followed in the *Billy Liar* footsteps too. If you had to characterize the way that that generation of actors began to take shape early on, you could almost say that O'Toole was becoming Burton, Courtenay, Gielgud and Finney, Olivier.

Finney had first seen the play in its première run at the Royal Exchange, directed by his friend Michael Elliott, and, as he prepared for the film, he was determined not to make 'Sir' too decrepit or far gone, and to give him a 'touch of buried authority'.

Finney told Billington that he was trying to suggest a man who had 'flashes of greatness'. He'd remembered Olivier playing Archie Rice in *The Entertainer* and, when asked how he managed to sing and dance and tell jokes in the character of a third-rater, Olivier had simply said, 'I did it as best I could.' Finney also listened to gramophone records of Wolfit, Wilfred Lawson, Johnston Forbes-Robertson and Gordon Craig, noting particularly how they dwelt on vowel sounds, like the 'ou' in 'ground', how they turned 'my' into 'me', how they enunciated every syllable, and how their voices had a sing-song musicality. 'It's the old thing,' said Finney, 'of getting the details right and then the character, hopefully, follows from that.' He also fondly recalled Gielgud's advice to Charles Laughton when playing Lear: 'Cast a very small actress in the part of Cordelia.'

Pauline Kael had written of Finney and Keaton in *Shoot the Moon* that they gave performances which in the theatre would be considered legendary. She might have said – but, in fact, didn't – the same thing about the pair in *The Dresser*, for the screen was barely enough to contain them as they swapped mannerisms, mugged shamelessly and delivered some great Harwood lines with unashamed theatricality. Forgetting whether he's meant to black up as Othello or preparing to bear the weight of Cordelia as Lear, halting an express in its tracks with a bellowed 'Stop ... That ... Train' or taking curtain-calls with outrageously false modesty, Finney's performance is massively unsubtle and huge fun in equal measure. Courtenay is much more low-key, yet almost too practised – as, after all, he would be after umpteen theatre performances – for the overall good of the film: 'All dried up,' wrote Kael correctly.

When the pathos comes, it seems, after the carefully

limited attempt to 'open out' the action, to belong strictly to the proscenium. In the movies, normally less is more; here, for a change, more is better.

The two actors appear to have had as much fun making the film as they clearly do in the film itself; endless banter on and around the set, jokey rivalry about their respective roles, and so on. A good deal of the shooting took place in Bradford, notably at the town's splendid old Alhambra Theatre, and eagle-eyed cinemagoers would also have spotted an in-joke early on in the film when Courtenay/ Norman is caught polishing a silver plate inscribed: 'From the grateful citizens of Salford, to commemorate a great performance of *Hamlet*, given in aid of local charities, 21 March 1929.' Harwood, who was on the set every day, even got a chance to take over directing at one point when Yates had to fly back to the States for his daughter's graduation. He was permitted to do two shots of Norman making up 'Sir's' hands as Lear. Both, admitted Harwood, ended up on the cutting-room floor.

For Goldcrest chief Jake Eberts, *The Dresser* was 'the most pleasant production with which I have ever been associated . . . Albert Finney, who adored being the star [*sic*] and centre of attention, and Tom Courtenay . . . were in their element: they had so much acting to do.' Eberts's only concern was that the film might have a hard time finding a substantial audience. In fact, all the profit participants did make money, though the overall perfor- mance of the film proved, a little surprisingly, to be as modest as the budget, despite a fistful of Oscar nomina- tions.

In order to qualify for the year's Academy Awards, *The Dresser* had to have opened in New York and Los Angeles before the year's end. The decision to première the film in the States ahead of Britain was fully vindicated when the film received five nominations, including two for Best Actor. The last time that had happened was in 1976, when Peter Finch and William Holden were head-to-head for *Network*, but on that occasion the situation was eased because, by the time of the ceremony, Finch was dead and so could be accorded posthumous honours. There was no such way out for *The Dresser*, and in fact things were made even more fraught when it transpired that four out of the five actors nominated were British. In addition to Finney and Courtenay were Michael Caine for another stage adaptation, *Educating Rita*, and Tom Conti for *Reuben, Reuben*. The only homeboy, as it were, was Robert Duvall, and he duly swept home. So for Finney it was third time unlucky. Variety Club Best Actor (for Courtenay) and Berlin Silver Bear (for Finney) were pale compensation.

The Dresser had, though, proved a highly successful working partnership for Harwood and Finney. As for that other *Melanie Klein* tandem, Finney and Glenda Jackson, they now became 'co-stars' in a rather different kind of enterprise: United British Artists. A more modest version of the Chaplin–Pickford–Fairbanks–D W Griffith Hollywood prototype, UBA was a bold attempt to corral a group of top British talent who would then, it was hoped, provide combined clout in generating theatre, film and television production. The group, formed by producer Peter Shaw and actor Richard Johnson, comprised Finney, Jackson, Diana Rigg, John Hurt, Maggie Smith, director Peter Wood, Harold Pinter and Lew Grade.

However, as UBA conducted its first board meetings in St James's during the summer of 1983, Finney was thousands of miles away: first, in Graz, Austria, for a rather anaemic American telemovie about Pope John Paul II, with Finney playing the pontiff from the age of thirty to fifty-eight; then, in the tiny Mexican village of Yautepac, 30 miles from Cuernavaca, renewing his acquaintance with John Huston.

Finney, who had some initial reservations about playing a character like the Pope, who was still so very much alive, was eventually convinced by a combination of the story and its part of what he regarded as a fascinating recent period of

European history. Michael Crompton, a young English actor, was one of four finalists for the role of Karol Wojtyla from the age of nineteen. He said:

> Albert had agreed to read with all of us and I remember we both arrived early at an office in Soho. As you can imagine, I was incredibly nervous, but Albert told me to relax and, 'just speak it, the camera will do the rest'. Anyway, I got the part, probably because I looked more like Albert than the others.

The film, originally due to be shot in Yugoslavia, had to make a last-minute, expensive switch to Austria because of logistical problems. As they flew out, Crompton noticed Finney scanning the unit list and learning the names of all the film crew so that when he arrived he could quickly fit names to faces: 'I had heard about how well he leads a company and he was determined here too to make everyone feel part of a team.' This also extended to hospitality off the set. Whenever a new cast member arrived from England, they'd all go out to dinner at one of the few local restaurants. At the end of the meal, Finney would invariably get up and disappear for a few minutes, returning to say that the owner had liked his film guests so much that he was donating the meal for free. 'After a while,' said Crompton, 'we finally twigged that it was Albert who was paying for the meals.'

Crompton, nicknamed 'the lad', said that Finney was very protective of him, making sure, for example, that despite his youth and inexperience he received all due perks.

He also cherishes two other abiding memories of the film. 'One was Albert's £600-a-week phone bill to Kentucky to check on his horses, who were about to give birth. The other was his last day, when he arranged a presentation for me in front of all the crew. It was a large jar of my favourite Marmite that he'd especially imported from home.'

Huston and Finney's work together on *Annie* a couple of years earlier and, as importantly, the warmth of their relationship had convinced the old film-maker that Finney would be perfectly cast as the British ex-consul Geoffrey Firmin, one of literature's most stupendous drunks, in his film of Malcolm Lowry's *Under the Volcano*.

Ever since the book was first published in 1947, there had been regular rumours of a movie adaptation. Lowry, a drunk himself, was the first to attempt it, while Burton and James Mason, among many others, had over the years openly declared their passion for the original material. Anthony Hopkins had, most recently, passed on it because of his commitment to *The Bounty* (echoes of Brando in 1960). Directors like Buñuel, Losey, Kubrick and Skolimowski attempted and then abandoned the idea. More than 100 scripts – including one by Dennis Potter which very nearly made it in 1973 – lined film-company shelves.

Under the Volcano, for many an almost impenetrable stream of consciousness veering wildly between the linear and flashback as it explores the last twenty-four hours of Firmin's life on the appropriately named Mexican Day of the Dead, is one of those books known by most, actually read by a good deal fewer, but almost universally hailed as a 'masterpiece'.

Literary masterpieces have a nasty habit of strenuously resisting decent screen adaptation, but the producer-triumvirate on *Under the Volcano* – including Wieland Schulz-Keil, who'd played a bomb-throwing anarchist in *Annie* – got off to a good start when they located a script by Guy Gallo, who'd written it while still a student at Yale Drama School. Gallo had skilfully pared away the obvious complications of flashback and the torrent of words and images to leave a spare, linear narrative following the dipso diplomat through his last day to a sad, violent end under the shadow of Popocatépetl. En route, there were enough references to the past to help fill in a wealth of detail for, during the tumultuous day, Firmin is reunited with his long-estranged wife (Jacqueline Bisset) and journalist half-brother Hugh (Anthony Andrews), late of the Spanish Civil War.

During the preparation a key event was an eight-hour meeting between Huston, Finney and Bisset in which they discussed minutely all aspects of the movie. After that, said co-producer Michael Fitzgerald, 'everything changed completely'. According to Huston, a kind of 'codal communication' existed between him and Finney: 'I mean, I would nod, and he would look at me and smile and that's all there was to it. There was little or no direction required.'

Finney had expressed his concern to Huston about sustaining what was effectively a 100-minute drunk act and was told, 'Look, I don't rehearse much. If I cast someone, it's because they have something I want to be there.' Huston considered that Finney gave one of the finest performances he had ever seen: 'He was never drunk during shooting, only after-hours. His understanding of drunkenness is a very profound one, based on his own experience.'

Finney explained this:

There were times when I was a young actor when I thought in order to be admired I had to drink a bit. And that it was romantic. It was the self-destructive urge that was romantic and I imagined that women would flutter around me to save me. I mean, I might have little excursions into cul-de-sacs where I got a bit far that way. But it was not destined to be my road through life. And so I realized I would have no get-out clause as an older actor. No one would be saying, 'Oh, if only he hadn't become an alcoholic, he would have been the greatest ever.'

In *Film Comment*, Todd McCarthy described watching Finney in action:

A bit plump, powerful physically (as Lowry described the Consul), a wig covering his shaved head (he had arrived in Mexico fresh from playing the Pope), his flushed complexion making him look both baby-faced and pickled. Finney showed the unnerving ability to summon up the twilight of a man's life at ten o'clock in the morning.

The role requires that the Consul proceed through the final day of his life in an increasing state of inebriation and Finney, through will and skill, was pitching his performance, and degree of drunkenness, with extraordinary precision in each take. Dressed in a cream white suit, matching Panama, light-blue shirt, purple Ascot and an Oxford tie pulled through his belt loops, Finney ran through his monologue before the first take.

'Not a performance,' was all that Huston had to suggest. Then the actor would force his transformation, retreating behind a massive tree prior to each take, bowing his head in intense concentration, and emerge with fingers trembling and blue eyes glazed in brilliant alcoholic stupor. Before one take, he violently shook and slammed down a chair to work himself up for it one more time.

Apparently Finney would down a shot of tequila before each take, explaining, 'I like immersing myself in the Consul's world. I like to have the taste of tequila, which I've never tasted before, in my mouth, just as I like smoking Mexican cigarettes and eating Mexican food' – all in pursuit of what he thought the part allowed him to do and what he did best: record 'feeling'.

Finney said that, as with his research on *The Dresser*, he inevitably resorted to memories of Wilfred Lawson in modelling his performance. There is also, in the film, the occasional, almost uncanny, resemblance to Wolfit. Most drunks, particularly when the onlooker is sober, tend to become the world's greatest bores, but Finney's act never becomes dull because he somehow manages to leaven the maudlin with a generous helping of self-mockery.

And so he clocked in once again, and perhaps most deservedly of all occasions, for the Oscars. But 1984 was the year of *Amadeus*, and for a fourth time he was an also-ran, as F Murray Abraham breasted the tape ahead of his fellow Shafferite Tom Hulce, Finney, Jeff Bridges (*Starman*) and Sam Waterston (*The Killing Fields*).

Some consolation was the historical precedent that Paul Newman had also been nominated in two successive years, 1981 and 1982, without winning either time. Newman had to wait until he was sixty-two before acquiring his first competitive Academy Award, so at least Finney still has time on his side.

United British Artists had originally been set up, according to Peter Shaw, as 'predominantly a theatre company. The idea was, we would put on limited-run West End shows, then take them off and shoot them for television broadcast, with America particularly in mind.' With that *raison d'être*, it turned out that the UBA's timing couldn't have been worse, for six months after the company started cranking up some productions, a prime US customer, CBS's theatrical cable channel, pulled out of the business because it couldn't attract enough subscribers. By then, UBA had staged and photographed *The Biko Inquest*, a determinedly low-key account direct from transcripts of the notorious proceedings held in camera in South Africa after the death in police custody of the eponymous black activist. Condensed from thirteen days and 2,000 pages, the two-hour show at the Riverside Studios was directed by Finney and also featured him in the central role of Sydney Kentridge, the lawyer for Biko's family.

Throughout Finney's career, and in his sporadic public pronouncements, there has rarely, if ever, been any solid hint of what makes him tick politically or what, if anything, troubles his conscience; the odd charity show for Amnesty International hardly undermines the dismissive claim, by one commentator that he is simply 'too sybaritic to be an agitator'. He had directed the Friel play, because he said he went along with the play's message that 'it's time we started living for Ireland instead of dying for it', and his stated reason for doing *Biko* – 'I suppose I will from time to time get involved in a film or a play of this sort' – didn't exactly reek of serious political intent either.

In staging *Biko*, matter-of-factness was the key to Finney's approach:

> Nobody is on trial. It is not a court. There is a sort of informality about the proceedings. I don't think it works like a courtroom. There isn't suddenly a climax. How it will work as a play is that we are trying to get the feeling of a polite inquiry among peers openly offering up their experiences and knowledge. Theatrically, how it should work is that the most callous way of treating a human being is discussed as if it is a normal event. The experts go on . . . they forget from time to time that they're discussing a death.

Props were sparse and no accents were attempted. It proved quite a disconcerting occasion for Kentridge himself, who, with his wife, Felicia, another lawyer, was taken by friends to the first night in Hammersmith. Though similar in age to Finney, he's physically quite different: slight, pale, gentle and Jewish. At the original hearing, all the Afrikaner witnesses had replied to Kentridge's questions in Afrikaans, addressing the Coroner, Martinus Prins, in almost inaudibly low voices. To give himself more time and to make sure the inquest heard their evidence, Kentridge would translate the responses for all to hear. The dramatization, by Jon Blair and Norman Fenton – who had previously created a half-hour version for ITV's *This Week* series – eliminated that element, but despite that the Kentridges both pronounced themselves 'shaken' by the evening, and happy with Finney's portrayal.

For UBA's television production, a more elaborate set was constructed at the Riverside and it made for surprisingly compelling viewing. The recording was sold to Channel Four here and then they tried to sell it in America, without much initial success. After rejections from both Home Box Office and Showtime, the principal cable channels, Lew Grade, who had helped finance the production, took the bull by the horns and told Showtime firmly that they should reconsider; it would be good for their image, he told them.

Showtime duly complied and, after a major publicity screening at the United Nations – attended by Grade and Finney, among many others – transmitted the programme eight years to the day after Biko died in Port Elizabeth: a death which, 'according to available evidence, was not caused by any act or omission', the inquest shamefully concluded.

The Biko Inquest was the first and last production that fulfilled UBA's original aims. As Shaw has said: 'We tried to get broadcasters interested in funding TV versions of our subsequent plays, and whilst we managed to get them to take a look, we simply couldn't get their real interest. I think the general feeling in the States was that they didn't want to see something that had the feel of the proscenium.'

Finney's contractual obligation to UBA was that he would do one production within the first year of its existence. In fact, he went straight on to complete another, a new production at the refurbished Old Vic of John Arden's most revived play, *Serjeant Musgrave's Dance*. Between its première at the Royal Court in 1959 – when it suffered almost unanimous critical hostility and just over twenty per cent house capacity – to its most recent, and successful, revival, by the National at the Cottesloe in 1981, the ballad play, set in the 1880s, not only picked up an audience but also occasioned a radical reassessment by reviewers – so much so that it has generally been accorded the status of a modern classic. According to Arden, its original sources were an incident in the Cyprus conflict and an obscure American Civil War B-movie. By the eighties, the play's sense of colonial outrage reflected a much more immediate and poignant model – Northern Ireland. Though ostensibly about pacifism, a rising tide of violence runs anachronistically through the tale of Black Jack Musgrave, who leads a small group of fellow soldiers – actually deserters – to a small Northern town gripped by a pit strike.

Ostensibly there to recruit, Musgrave (Finney) is, in fact, set on some perverse revenge against the community. As with other Arden plays, like *Armstrong's Last Goodnight*, there is song, dance and even a touch of Vaudeville woven in too. It does seem, though, that Finney's commitment to UBA – there were firm plans to record the play as well – did account for a somewhat rushed staging. Sheridan Morley remembered it being 'at best inadequately stage-managed and at worst not even that, so the final marketplace line-up looked as though the cast were assembling for a first read-through rather than as a first night'. He also felt that Finney shouldn't really act and direct at the same time – except on film. These thoughts were underscored by Michael Ratcliffe, who, writing in the *Observer*, said that the production opened 'long before it was ready' but would provide a 'spectacular role for Finney once his directorial responsibilities are shed'. With his mutton-chop whiskers and ruddy face, Finney rightly earned more plaudits for his acting, an explosive piece of bullet-headed bluster, than his direction, which allowed all kinds of curious indulgences, notably a tiresome stand-up comedy routine by Max Wall, and stifled climax, letting it become, too often, something of an anticlimax.

The fact that *Musgrave* didn't follow *Biko* on to film was perhaps the beginning of the end for UBA. Without that extra string to its bow, Shaw felt that the whole enterprise began to lose its real point for the actors involved. As he said:

> It was always a problem finding new plays. Naturally, everyone was very selective, although most of the board were actively associated with one or more pieces of material from time to time.
>
> It's a funny thing, though, about actors: they don't tend to come forward too often. They seem to have been born and bred to sit by the phone, waiting for their agent to call. Inevitably it all began to turn into the old development grind.

After some six shows and glaring evidence that UBA's original aims weren't viable, Shaw, whose background was film and not theatre, offered the board an ultimatum: close the whole thing down or else rejig into a film company, and that is what happened.

Finney finally bowed out of the now rather dormant United British Artists about five years ago.

Finney was fifteen months into his next sabbatical, roaming the States mostly on 'horse business', when he got a call from Michael Medwin in London announcing his impending arrival in New York. He felt that they ought to meet and go immediately to see a much-heralded Off-Broadway play called *Orphans*. They hurried down to the Manhattan Theater Club, where they were treated to a noisy, visceral black comedy from one of America's most innovative stage companies, Steppenwolf, from Chicago. Steppenwolf was established in 1976 – founder members included John Malkovich, Joan Allen and Gary Sinise – and in just eight years it had moved to the forefront of American theatre, transferring plays by, among others, Sam Shepard and Lanford Wilson to New York. Their productions were characterized by an acrobatic, muscular style, often drenched in the music of Pat Metheny and his keyboardist, Lyle Mays.

Orphans, by Lyle Kessler, was no exception. Said to be a pastiche of Shepard and Pinter – one critic suggested an intriguing collision of W S Gilbert and Damon Runyon – it also evoked old Warner gangster movies in the tale of two strange young brothers, one a thief, Treat, the other a recluse, Philip, holed up in a derelict Philadelphia house.

The ménage becomes even odder when Treat returns one day from a mugging expedition with a drunken kidnap victim, Harold, a Chicago businessman, who turns out to be a wealthy mobster on the run. The presence of a powerful and, it transpires, curiously benevolent third force – himself an orphan and lawbreaker, a 'dead-end kid' – begins inexorably to shift the balance of power in the household, as Philip grows more self-assured.

Finney said he was captivated by the play, adding that it reminded him of his early days as an actor when he wanted roles to be 'simple, truthful and direct'. The character of Harold, he said, 'invaded his imagination'. He and Medwin negotiated with Steppenwolf and director Sinise to bring the production to that pearl of London's Off-West End, Hampstead Theatre Club. Sinise, as director, and Anderson, playing the agoraphobic Philip, were part of the transfer and would be joined by another young American actor, Jeff Fahey. And, of course, there was Finney, who, after regular impersonations of Bogart, would now get a chance to do an all-stops-out Cagney.

The trio began rehearsing in New York before moving back to London and Finney had in Sinise a Chicago native to help him perfect the accent. For Billington, one of the most fascinating aspects of the Hampstead Theatre production was the clash between two different acting traditions. It was, he believed, Finney's best performance in years: 'compact in Celtic roguishness, paternal love and the kind of bull-like self-possession that bespeaks profound loneliness'. And the performance actually gained power from the contrast between this and the 'furniture-pounding' style of Fahey and Anderson.

While generally ecstatic about Finney, other British critics were less convinced about the play itself, with its 'dislocating jerks' between comedy and tragedy, and an ending which bordered dangerously on the mawkish.

Yet, in the midst of the 'furniture pounding', it was Finney's stillness that elevated *Orphans* to something extraordinary. Jack Tinker, in the *Daily Mail*, tried to put his finger on it:

What gives the performance its stranglehold on the audience – and stamps the play with a hard credulity despite its soft centre – is the aura of bleak isolation in which he wraps himself. Behind his level, watchful gaze there is that strange sense of separation which sets the successful criminal or gambler apart from his fellow man. The baleful watchfulness of a cat-like outsider.

Finney was already making the movie version of *Orphans* for Lorimar Productions when, in December 1986, he won the Olivier Award for best actor as Harold. Apart from obtaining a filmed record, the movie, produced and directed by Alan J Pakula, seemed a fairly pointless exercise. Kessler's additions and the attempts to 'open out' are perfunctory and the play's inherent theatrical danger – the Steppenwolf element, as it were – is inevitably diluted. That said, the performances are decent enough – Matthew Modine was the screen Treat – and the best lines are, happily, intact. Finney had some initial concern that Pakula's rather refined film-making style might tend to hone down the play's 'crudeness, its rough edges . . . a punk-drama quality.' It did, but Finney wasn't heard complaining too loudly.

Sporting closer-cropped hair and a trimmer waistline, Finney was a different kind of hostage in Ronald Harwood's play *J J Farr*, set in a Buckinghamshire half-way house for Catholic priests who've lost their faith. Just released from five months' captivity and torture in the

Middle East at the hands of Muslim fundamentalists, and
now set down in the Home Counties among five other
variously troubled colleagues, Farr must confront his once
severely dented faith. The twist is that Farr, who was, as
they say, lost, has now been found, which proves all too
much for Lowrie (played by Bob Peck), a macho atheist and
Farr-disciple, who thinks his hero's reconversion is psychotic.
Finney and Medwin were originally given the script by
producer Robert Fox as a possible co-production venture
for Memorial, and it was only with director Ronald Eyre's
prompting that Finney was finally offered the title role.
Harwood had been nervous about putting a possible strain
on their friendship, while Finney was surprised at how long
it had taken to offer him the part.

Two pieces of history came immediately to mind.
Twenty-five years before, at the same theatre, the Phoenix,
Finney had played another anguished cleric, Martin Luther.
More recently, Terry Waite, the Archbishop of Canter-
bury's envoy, had disappeared in the Lebanon, which
inevitably led to some comparisons with Harwood's
scenario. The playwright was quick to point out that the
piece had been finished long before Waite was kidnapped,
while Finney, talking to a journalist over lunch, spluttered:
'For a start, Terry Waite is not Catholic and he is not a
priest. He has nothing to do with the problems of J J Farr.
Let me put it another way. The similarities between the case
of Terry Waite and J J Farr are as strong as the physical
similarity I have to Mickey Mouse. OK?' End of argument.

Finney entered into the spirit of leading the *J J Farr*
company with the same gusto he had when at the National
a decade earlier. In Bath, during the play's pre-London run,
he organized a lavish Guy Fawkes party between the
matinée and evening performances and later, according to
Michael Billington, 'would take members of the company
out on a treat once a week – another show, the movies, a
meal, or whatever. He was very conscious he was head of
the company and that it was his responsibility to keep

morale high. And besides, he liked having a good time.'
This euphoria was as short-lived as the play – which made
the fact that he'd turned down a substantial film role as the
Mafia 'Don' in Michael Cimino's *The Sicilian* in order to
appear as Farr even more annoying. With some enthusiastic
exceptions, for most reviewers the play swung between 'short,
pompous and remarkably soporific' and plain 'soap opera'.
Comprising six short scenes set across a fortnight, the main
conflict was effectively centred between Farr and the cynical
Lowrie, very well played by Peck. Though Finney was never
less than solid, one couldn't help thinking that if they had
swapped roles, the play might have worked rather better.

Finney's next bout of Harwood, eighteen months on, was
altogether more successful. *Another Time*, like *The Dresser*
thinly veiled autobiography, gave Finney a double helping
of character. In the first act, set in a Cape Town flat during
the early 1950s, he was an ageing Jewish salesman with a
pianist prodigy for a son. For the second act, set thirty-five
years later in a London recording studio, he was the same,
though now middle-aged, son, debating whether he should
return to perform in South Africa. Billington thought that
the Finney performance was, like the play itself, a thing of
two distinct halves:

In the first act, he was the older man and did it through
impersonation, as it were.

I recall this strong centre parting, hair flattened to
the brow on either side, shoulders stiffly held; he
simulated an elderly man with extraordinary power. At
the end of the act, he also executed another of those
staggering death falls he's become so good at. In the
second half, he was playing something much nearer his
own age and, I thought, he got no marks; this time he
had no impersonation or disguise to hide behind, and
was simply agonizing about whether to return to South
Africa or not. He and the play became much less
interesting.

Finney had hoped to take *J J Farr* to Chicago as a sort of return fixture after his away success with Steppenwolf's *Orphans*. In fact, early in the spring of 1991 he took *Another Time*, which was staged in a production directed by Harwood, with members of the Chicago company supporting Finney in his dual roles.

Between Farr and the Windy City, Finney indulged, without really intending to, in one of his periodic spells of almost frenzied activity, with distinctly mixed results. The most forgettable was Bryan Forbes's interminable television adaptation of his own espionage novel *The Endless Game*, in which Finney played a world-weary British agent caught up in sub-Le Carré, pan-European spy shenanigans. As the perplexed Hillsden, he wore a permanently pained expression, which might have been explained by the fact that he contracted shingles on his face during the filming. Realizing that he was probably a bit run-down, Finney planned a recuperative break until the summer, when he was due to start rehearsing *Another Time*. But it was still grim English winter when, at three o'clock one morning, the phone went at his London home. An SOS from the Coen Brothers, Joel and Ethan, the producer-director-writer team of individualistic and offbeat American films like *Blood Simple* and *Raising Arizona*.

Trey Wilson, co-star of their new movie, *Miller's Crossing*, had suddenly died of a cerebral haemorrhage two days before shooting was due to begin in New Orleans. Could Finney take his place, they asked? Finney knew and admired their work, so he swiftly accepted. The result is one of his best pieces of work in one of the finest and most idiosyncratic films of the early 1990s. After a film noir and a madcap comedy, the Coens were anxious not to repeat themselves. They started from a genre, the gangster film, and an image: 'Big guys in overcoats in the woods – the incongruity of urban gangsters in a forest setting.' In fact, not so much gangster pictures as gangster novels, particularly the work of Dashiell Hammett and more specifically his *Red*

Harvest, with its 'dirty town' milieu.

Miller's Crossing is set in 1929 in an unnamed Eastern US city and revolves around the friendship of the city boss, Leo, and his right-hand man, Tom. When they fall in love with the same woman, the friendship is severed, and when it appears that Tom has also fallen in with Leo's enemy and political rival, Johnny Caspar, a bloody gang war erupts. All this would be quite conventional if it were not for the 'Coen twist', that factor which makes their work so unlike any other contemporary mainstream American film-maker's – a unique mixture of style and content, aided by regular collaborators like cinematographer, Barry Sonnenfeld, and composer, Carter Burwell. Unlike most other American film-makers, they are unafraid of dialogue; there are glorious torrents of it in *Miller's Crossing*, including genre language of their own invention. The role of Leo had been specifically written for Trey Wilson, who'd played the crusty but benign furniture tycoon, Nathan Arizona, in their previous film. The Irishman Gabriel Byrne was cast as Tom, but the role wasn't penned as first-generation Irish.

However, when Byrne read the script out loud to himself, it seemed to him that somebody from Dublin could have written it, so he suggested to the Coens that he play it with an accent. Sceptical at first, they eventually agreed. When Finney replaced Wilson, his character too acquired an Irish accent. The movie's belated 'Irishness' reaches its apogee in a fantastic sequence in which Leo nonchalantly dismisses the attempts of four would-be assassins to the sentimental tenor strains of 'Danny Boy' issuing from his Victrola. The night attack begins as Leo is stretched out on his bed, reading the newspaper and chewing a huge cigar. When he spots smoke coming through the floorboards, he calmly prepares for battle, stubs out the cigar and rolls under his double bed. When the gunmen burst into the bedroom, he shoots one twice with a revolver and grabs his Thompson sub-machine-gun before exiting quickly through his window to the street below. From there, he blasts the other gunman, who is conveniently framed by the light of the bedroom. This unfortunate performs a crazy dance of death as his own machine-gun riddles bullets all round him. Then, as casual as you please, still clad in robe and pyjamas, the cigar restored to his mouth, Leo walks down the street, peppering shots at the assailants' car, which eventually crashes into a tree and explodes.

Steven Levy described the filming of the scene in *Première* magazine:

> . . . even Finney got into the Thompson mania. Towards the end of the segment, as Leo walks down the street firing the gun at the speeding getaway car, Finney had to maintain a cool demeanour while controlling the powerful weapon. As an added challenge, the Coens set up a bucket behind him to see how many expelled cartridges he could land in it. 'He got a very high percentage,' says Ethan, as Joel collapses in laughter. 'Technically, he's a very good actor.'
>
> Finney's machine-gun virtuosity helps end the sequence with a flourish. But what really makes the scene is 'Danny Boy'. The Coens recruited Irish tenor Frank Patterson – he played the vocalist in John Huston's *The Dead* – to perform the song. After the scene was edited, Patterson went into the studio with an orchestra and watched the monitor so he could tailor the cadences of the song to the mounting body count. At the end, when Finney, cigar stub in his mouth, sighs in satisfaction as he watches his last assailants die in flames, the music swells in old-world mawkishness: '. . . and I will sleep in peace . . . until you come to . . . meeeee! . . .' – a deliciously droll commentary on the Thompson jitterbug that came before.

The sequence was shot over several weeks in various New Orleans locations and the sheer pyrotechnics were overwhelming. The death of the first gunman didn't prove vivid enough, so it had to be reshot while Finney, working with the notoriously inconsistent Thompson, needed much patience through endless retakes. Apparently, he became something of a neighbourhood favourite and would execute extravagant bows in his night attire as applause greeted the end of each take. With the *Sporting Life* sticking out of his back pocket and a baseball cap perched on his head, Finney was very much one of the lads, belying some initial concern felt by the American actors that he might be intimidating to work with. There was no 'Grand Act-or' about him at all, said Gabriel Byrne.

One of the many great strengths of *Miller's Crossing* had been the way the Finney–Byrne relationship sparked so beautifully. The actors and their roles seemed almost indivisible. The same was pretty much true in Finney's next film, *The Image*, a first-rate drama made for the cable channel Home Box Office. This saw his imaginative pairing with John Mahoney, a slight, grey-haired man who, suddenly in middle age, seemed to have arrived from nowhere to become one of America's most engaging and prolific character actors in films like *Moonstruck*, *Suspect* and *Tin Men*. The Mahoney–Finney link becomes even more intriguing when one realizes that not only did Mahoney create the role of Harold in *Orphans* for Steppenwolf but also, far from being the fully minted American he appears, he was born in Manchester.

   Mahoney's is one of those delightful fairy-tales of late fledging. He arrived in the States aged nineteen, toyed first with the army and journalism, and didn't begin taking acting lessons until he was thirty-five. Now he could pass for the quintessential Midwesterner. He and Finney, who quickly nicknamed him 'Baloney', worked a treat together in *The Image*, playing a top television newsteam. Finney was Jason Cromwell, a TV reporter-cum-anchorman, with Mahoney, as Irv Mickelson, his nuggety producer. The story itself wasn't hugely original. It was the old one about the media star – 'the man America really trusts' – who's bigger than any of the stories he reveals suddenly conscience-stricken when an unsubstantiated scoop turns sour. It almost goes without saying that his private life's a mess too. All that decently enough done, but it's the cut and thrust of the journo and his sidekick that gives the drama a solid core of credibility and sustained entertainment.

Finney was sent Brian Rehak's script for *The Image* while he was filming *Miller's Crossing*, and liked its exploration of how an anchorman might have to alter himself to be a success. He elaborated:

> I thought that it was interesting to examine what happens to those people. By the time they reach national eminence, have they polished their craft, and have they already formed their show personality or are they still in the process of doing so? And if they find certain aspects of themselves seem to be more successful than others – like certain sounds or a kind of inflection, a kind of rhythm of speech – do they then incorporate that and work on it? How acquired is that technique?

In other words, what is real and what just 'image'?

The idea for the film originated with Robert Cooper, a Canadian producer who'd once been a media ombudsman – not unlike the Cromwell character – before arriving in Los Angeles, where he set up a production company before becoming head of HBO. The project started life as *The Ombudsman* and was first supposed to star Robert Redford. The eventual director, Peter Werner, had known of the script for about a year before he became involved and found, to his pleasure, that Finney was also locked in to the central role.

Finney joined the HBO production for a week of rehearsals straight after finishing *Miller's Crossing*. During this time he and Werner met and gained some useful pointers from Peter Jennings, a long-time pillar of ABC News. As Werner recalled:

We didn't go into rehearsal with a script that any of us felt was properly finished; it was like a very coloured-in blueprint. After that week we began shooting and would have rehearsals of the following week's scenes each Saturday.

Albert said he felt that the making of our cable movie should try and be exactly like the way the people in our film made their cable TV show. When he said that, I guess that it was like giving me permission to be as improvisatory as possible, almost to wing it to try and get that excitement and energy. I think we captured that feeling. He also told everyone: 'Don't worry, let's have fun. We're all in this together.'

Finney and Mahoney quickly became firm friends and constantly rehearsed together to achieve what really smacks of a spontaneous double act – swapped gags, overlapping dialogue and so on. Typical, thought Werner, of their mutual understanding, was the manoeuvring of a scene which they began in New York, to be completed later in Los Angeles. As written, it was as though the Cromwell character had the same reaction in consecutive scenes. Finney suggested that he read Mahoney's part at that point and vice versa. They'd actually tried it quietly together in rehearsal and, said Werner, it made perfect sense: 'All we had to do was change the dialogue slightly to lead into it a bit better.'

Werner's one major concern about the film was the dialogue in the final sequence:

The producers wanted it made clear that Cromwell was leaving his mistress [played by Kathy Baker] and going back to his wife [Marsha Mason]. I just felt that to spell it out any more was insulting and too moralistic. We were into the last couple of days of production and everyone was pretty tired by then. So I basically said to Albert and Kathy that if they went along with the producers, then fine; but 'read the scene and see how you feel'. They read it and felt as strongly as me that it was terrible. However, the producers insisted. Then I managed to negotiate for two alternate endings.

At this point, Finney, doing their version, gave one of the most artistically controlled, masterful performances of a take that was so bad you could never use it, but there was also no way you could ever accuse him of doing it on purpose. It was magnificent. You simply couldn't say, 'He didn't try.' That persuaded them to let us have it our way.

The resulting film was, deservedly, the most award-nominated show to date in HBO's history.

Cromwell and Maurice Allington, the rubicund restaurateur in Kingsley Amis's *The Green Man*, are, like Finney's image at least, bigger than life. But there's also enough in the characters to suggest perhaps more than a hint of substance too: the clash between a public and a private life, the unrestrained sybarite, and so on. Certainly the sight of a heavily set (and thickening fast) middle-aged man, reddish-faced and baggy-eyed, disporting himself across prime time on Sunday nights must have dented a few fond memories, fuelled by occasional reruns of *Saturday Night and Sunday Morning* and *Tom Jones*. *The Green Man* marked Finney's return to the BBC for the first time in fifteen years (since the forgettable *Forget-Me-Not-Lane*). It was also Finney's return to a project with which he'd been first involved twenty years earlier, when he'd bought the rights to Amis's just published comic novel of sex and the supernatural. Then in his early thirties, he'd have been far too young to play the lecherous Allington, father of grown-up children, and the effects budget alone would have over-stretched Memorial's resources.

The year of Finney's last BBC foray was also the year he first encountered director Elijah Moshinsky, a bookish Australian who had given up Oxford for the arts, becoming

Peter Hall's assistant on the National's *Hamlet*. Much more recently, Moshinsky had directed Finney in *Another Time*. According to a guest at the 'reunion', Nicky Henson, who was playing a cuckolded husband in *The Green Man*, Finney 'took upon himself the same kind of responsibility for the whole unit as he had when leading the company at the National'. He described how:

> It was very interesting watching him work with Moshinsky, who had never directed on film before [apart from stage and opera, he'd done a number of taped Shakespeares]. Albert never came on too strongly but would just gently suggest stuff, and you knew that whenever he opened his mouth, he would be worth listening to. He's a powerful man, a powerful personality, and he doesn't want to waste his time. He won't mention something unless it's really important. As in my time at the National ten years before, Albert was particularly helpful to me, and in fact he's always been a bit of a guiding influence professionally to me. On *The Green Man*, I was doing a very difficult scene with him, just a two-hander, and about half-way through I was getting in quite a state about it. Nobody would have known apart from me. But Albert felt it. After about the third take, when I'd messed up again, Albert put a hand on my elbow, as if to say, 'Calm down, it's OK.' It was a sensitive thing to do and helped me a lot.

Moshinsky had described the serial as 'classy shlock – *Dallas* with real intellectual content'. The producer, David Snodin, stressed the £1.7 million adaptation's 'fidelity without servility'.

The Green Man proved a cheery enough romp. Certainly the sex was a deal more convincing than the much-vaunted supernatural special effects, which seemed cheesy in the extreme. Whether sniffing a claret, indulging in *al* fresco nookie or tipsily preparing for the 'showtime' of an evening's restaurant business, Finney was Allington incarnate. A poignant collision of life and art.

A Wednesday matinée in wintry Birmingham must surely be one of the less appetizing slices of bread-and-butter in an actor's lot. The Alexandra Theatre, less than 200 yards from the old Rep in Station Street, where more than thirty-five years earlier Finney set out on his professional career, was the first date after Darlington on a six-town tour – Bristol, Brighton, Manchester and Leeds still to come – before *Reflected Glory*, his latest collaboration with Ronald Harwood, would descend on London's West End in the spring. This is the time for a brand-new play to find its feet, its optimum length and its prime audience 'moments'. If necessary, this is when it will be cut best to fit.

The 'Alex' – which years earlier, during his Birmingham apprenticeship, Finney had condemned as 'middle-aged, musty and middle-class' – has, despite that youthful accusation, been a regular pit-stop on his and Harwood's previous journeys, and the locals rallied faithfully once again. Although the balcony was closed off for the afternoon, the rest of the theatre was veritably heaving, significantly more than half-full – 'very healthy for midweek', beamed the deputy manager – and as the bitter-sweet comedy unfolded, the audience, predominantly middle-aged and middle class though not noticeably musty, became noisily appreciative.

The play, about the attempted reconciliation of long-estranged brothers – one a cheerful Jewish restaurateur (Finney), the other an egocentric and manipulative writer-director (Stephen Moore) – has Harwood's usual mix of humour, pain, a little preaching and some anguish in his tale about art, the nature of siblings and family relationships – 'people who are bound to each other but don't necessarily have a great deal in common,' as Finney put it.

Reflected Glory struck particular chords with Finney,

who told local reporters, during the carefully orchestrated 'hype' surrounding a new opening:

> What can happen in one's middle-fifties is one can be bugged by something they [siblings] say that makes you react as if you are six. I was reminded of this a year ago when I was spending some time with one of my sisters. What she said and how she said it made me feel like a child. It may have been totally accidental on her part. That's the thing, it's hard to pull the wool over their eyes emotionally because they have seen you go through all sorts of things when you are growing up.

Many of the Birmingham audience would have seen Finney as a teenager. They warmed to him then and they warmed to him yet again, as, even though far from line-perfect, he beguiled them with a mixture of four-square bluster, a neatly choreographed song-and-dance routine of 'Me and My Shadow', some good jokes and no little pathos, as the outcome of play, like life itself, remained painfully unresolved. For his curtain-call, Finney was wreathed in smiles as he niftily executed a soft-shoe shuffle to front-of-stage. The 700 patrons had had their money's worth. Next stop, the Hippodrome, Bristol.

Almost as parochial had been Finney's recent trail up to the rehearsals for *Reflected Glory*, which would eventually go on to gather respectable reviews – rather better for Finney than for the play – in London. As it turned out, the engagement ended even more prematurely than the antici-pated closure following poor business when Finney sud-denly claimed he was owed money by the producers and decided to withdraw his labour. This, rather startlingly, pre-empted the inevitable closing notices. Earlier, in Charleston, South Carolina, amid the cobblestone streets, antebellum homes and attractive waterways, he was to be found playing a sort of older, more rumpled, version of *Shoot the*

Moon's George Dunlap, except that this time he was the abandoned party, in *Rich in Love*, from the same team – producers, director and screenwriter, anyway – that had been responsible for the Oscar-winning *Driving Miss Daisy*.

Unlike the more cosmopolitan population of Charleston, it is doubtful whether many of the good people in the tiny Irish borders village of Redhills, near Cavan, would have heard of him when, along with the paraphernalia of location film-making, he descended on them to co-star in *The Playboys*, a delightful 1950s romantic drama.

But for a film whose very title, not to mention subject matter, was redolent of Irishness, there was little at first glance to convince the folk of Redhills of that fact. Yes, it was co-written by an Irishmen (Shane Connaughton, who helped script *My Left Foot*), yet the principal stars, all playing Irishman, were American (Robin Wright and Aidan Quinn – who could, though, and regularly did, boast Emerald kinship) and English (Finney), the producers English, and the director Scots. All financed, naturally, with American money.

When Finney left Redhills a little over three weeks later, after completing his role as the dried-out, dried-up local policeman, Brendan Hegarty, who aches with unrequited love for Tara (Wright), a young single mother, he was probably the best-known and best-liked fellow in the peaceful little community. Though he was actually billeted some twenty minutes' drive away, in the middle of nowhere at the splendiferous Slieve Russell Hotel, there seem to have been few people who had not heard of, or even experienced personally, 'breakfast with Albert'.

Finney had first been offered the role of Freddie, the flamboyant leader of a band of travelling players who variously disrupt the lives of the village where television is still an unknown quantity. Perhaps fearing that the part was a little too reminiscent of 'Sir' in *The Dresser*, Finney turned it down (Milo O'Shea got the role), only for director Gillies MacKinnon and producer Simon Perry to suggest he might like to play Sergeant Hegarty, even though the actor was perhaps slightly older than the film-makers had originally considered the character to be. MacKinnon, making his first fully-fledged cinema feature after some acclaimed television dramas, found Finney a perfect ally as he tackled a movie which was both modestly budgeted and scheduled by a Hollywood yardstick.

The script was based on some elements of Connaughton's own father, who had also been a village policeman. According to MacKinnon:

Shane had described his father to me as a 'burning rock'. Now, I generally had little opportunity to rehearse, but there was one moment I recall when I had time to take Albert aside and explain that his character was 'this burning rock'. He looked at me amusedly and replied, 'And how the fuck do you act a burning rock?' That was rightly the end of the discussion.

He went on:

I actually found it fascinating to watch him in action. Whenever he came to the set to start a scene, he would ask our continuity girl, 'What time is it?' By this, he meant the time in the actual story. He very quickly had a nuts-and-bolts grasp of the part. I was under a lot of pressure and often had to settle for just one or two takes and he was always very cooperative.

On a rest-day during filming, Finney organized an outing for sixty of the unit to the races at Leopardstown, where they ate and drank at his expense in a private box overlooking the course. On his last day of filming, it was time for the favour to be returned – with a mischievous twist.

As he completed his final scene, still clad in sergeant's uniform, Finney was presented with a Cavan crystal goblet, filled for the occasion with wine. Playing to the crowd, he drank heartily from the cup. But even as he supped, sirens could be heard, and within a minute or so a police car had arrived and two real officers were busily reading Finney his rights, arresting him on a charge of impersonating a police officer. He was handcuffed and led away to the local 'nick'. The bluff went on for about a quarter of an hour before the slightly bemused actor was eventually released.

The film itself turned out to be a perfectly delightful blend of rural humour and melancholy, not unlike a Gaelic *Jean de Florette*, and early reviews suggested that it had the capacity to become deservedly a box-office 'sleeper' and award-winner.

'It's a pity,' says Lindsay Anderson, with typical bluntness, 'that he made so much money.' And so young, he might have added. For there is a fascinating case to be made for the view that after *Tom Jones* Finney never again exhibited the sort of artistic hunger that so often equates with extraordinary achievement (and nor, for that matter, did Tony Richardson or John Osborne).

The trouble about being handed the mantle of Olivier so early is that everything is subsequently measured against that awesome yardstick. Perhaps the great difference between Finney's generation of lower middle-class star actors and an earlier generation of top actors – like Olivier, Gielgud and Richardson – is that the latter were constantly driven by a kind of middle-class guilt, which dictated that they couldn't stop working. The fact that, in a notoriously volatile career like acting, Finney became independently so wealthy so soon removed at least one of the motors that kept someone like Olivier single-mindedly to the grindstone. Olivier was also motivated, arguably, by the desire to be not just a great actor but the greatest actor – up with and perhaps exceeding the likes of Kean and Irving. Also Olivier *needed* to act, not just for the cash to keep his ever extending family in comfort but because he actually knew no other way to exist.

What is quite clear from the pattern of Finney's life is

that he has enjoyed, and continues to enjoy, plenty of other things apart from acting. So money not only helped to remove the hunger of acting; it also created the delicious independence to indulge in hedonism. The years Finney spent away from the classical roles were the years in which Olivier would have been perfecting his art.

For Michael Billington, there remains something altogether more remarkable about the younger Finney compared with the older performer:

> He seemed to have the qualities of age in the body of a young man – that solidity, density and experience, seemingly, in the frame of a twenty-year-old. Most twenty-year-olds are willowy, gauche and uncertain of their bodies, their sexuality, and everything else for that matter. Yet with Finney, here was this muscular, packed and, above all, confident figure. But as he's got older, while he's retained his physical authority – he's the man you still look at as soon as he comes on stage – one has to wonder whether he has explored in any way yet the full range of his temperament and his acting prowess.

Bernard Hepton is also unconvinced that Finney has truly fulfilled his early promise:

> He used to watch quite a lot and was a great listener too. His technique? I don't think he's thought too much about that. The one thing on which I fault him very badly is his voice. I don't think he's got a pleasant voice and when I saw *Another Time* I was appalled. Couldn't hear what he was saying half the time. He's getting to sound more and more like Wilfred Lawson. No, he's never been able to free his voice.

Billington prefers to draw the comparison with Olivier, in the sense that he considers that Finney, like him, is deep down a vulgar character comedian. Many of the best performances I've seen him give in the last twenty or thirty years have used that talent. An obvious example would be the Feydeau farce, where he had an extraordinary physical dexterity, producing an amazing contrast between the moon-faced porter and the other bourgeois character. He'd be a natural for Archie Rice. There's a great deal of the pub entertainer about him, and I don't think that side of his talent has been sufficiently tapped in the way he's been cast.

Noting that he gets bored easily – and his dislike of routine in everything from school homework to long stage runs and lengthy romantic entanglements underscores that – Sheridan Morley also recognizes in Finney a lot of his own father's generation of actors: they 'didn't want to spend their lives talking to very intense, Cambridge-educated Shakespeare directors or be in permanent rehearsal at the Barbican . . . There's a world out there of racehorses, lunch, golf and travel, as well.'

Yet for Morley a Finney first night is still 'an event'. As he has said:

That partly has to do with its rarity value but also, like Laughton, whom he started with – and with whom he's rather akin, apart, of course, from a gay private life and the belief that he, Laughton, was going to have sand kicked in his face by a younger and better-looking actor – he shares that animal unpredictability. You don't know where he's going to come from next. Olivier had that too. It's also true that his career has often seemed becalmed. I've always thought of him as the natural leader of the profession. Actors will gather round him in a way that they're unwilling to gather round others. He commands the profession's respect, and he knows that somewhere inside him, he can always deliver the goods.

The reason he sometimes doesn't can be down to various alibis. He's not, for example, an actor who can survive a bad production – like the 1975 *Hamlet* – but he still has that ability to explode inside a bad play and give you a firework display of sheer theatricality.

If there has been a failure to fulfil expectations, then Morley believes this has really been

> a failure of the English theatre, of managements, directors and playwrights, who've been shamefully disorganized. Directors are nervous of him because he's so 'big'. They prefer those who'll shut up and do what they're told. He's noisy and starry and a lot of directors fight shy of that. As far as I can see, there has been no concerted attempt by the RSC or National to get him back, to give him a range of work. Directors have simply failed to programme him.

The dislike – maybe fear is not too strong a word – of routine has accounted not only for the quick changes in his career and lifestyle but also for the pattern of his emotional life. While he was probably too young and preoccupied to be affected unduly by the collapse of his first, short marriage, the collapse of his second, to Anouk, seemed to bruise him considerably. One feels he's not the sort of man who messes up his private life with the eagerness of an O'Toole or Richard Harris. He appears quite conservative and careful, by comparison. The numerous affairs – after Diana Quick, there have been, most publicly, Cathryn Harrison, Sarah Mason and Penne Delmarche – appear to have ended more in melancholy than tempest. He, for his part, dismisses any lack of continuity simply as gypsy spirit or the freelance instinct.

Do his critics, on the other hand, demand *too* much of Finney? Billington doesn't believe so, for with talent, he suggests, come obligations, and one of those obligations is an element of service:

If you come back to the inevitable comparison with Olivier, you see that with him he treated his talents not just as something you exercised, but as almost some kind of religious service. That you had a moral duty to make the most of your talent. I don't see that in Finney's career at all.

Given the momentousness of that talent at twenty, you ask where is it going now, in his mid-fifties? His career seems to have contained a lot of peaks, but also a lot of troughs, and moreover appears to have had no organic shape to it. That's why he often leaves critics and commentators with a sense more of frustration than actual disappointment.

Though he gives every impression of being a major international star, he is not, cinematically at least, in the league of Connery or Caine, who have worked tirelessly, often unashamedly, to big box-office bankability. Would Finney even want to be in that league?

Karel Reisz says that Finney doesn't want it enough:

I also think he lacks that feminine component, that wish to charm people, and when he has actually exercised it, he feels badly about it. It's similar in a way to Brando. For thirty years, Brando was contemptuous of the act of acting. He felt it wasn't a job for a man and, as a result, chose dreadful roles year after year. Albert is a mild example of that. I think he's certainly as naturally gifted as Connery, and while he was working in an uncomplicated way on things like *Saturday Night and Sunday Morning*, *Luther* and *Tom Jones*, he was an enormous star all over the world. And then he just didn't want it any more. Now, how consciously he didn't want it, I don't know. But I don't think it was ever a matter of actual laziness.

Billington picks up on Reisz's point about Finney's lack of feminine vulnerability:

That's extremely interesting, because it's true that the most incandescent actors have it. Olivier palpably did. Brando too. It's a constant thread throughout all acting – sexual ambiguity.

What we prize in Garbo is her masculinity and what we prize in Chaplin and Olivier is femininity. If it's there in Finney, he has suppressed it – even if he has played 'camp' quite amusingly from time to time. So, in the rarified atmosphere of great, great stars, he's not on that level. But I think that O'Toole hasn't utilized that side of his personality either, so Finney's in good company.

This, in effect, means that Finney can exhibit enormous charisma in his acting without too much accompanying charm – loyal friends will swear he has plentiful amounts of both in real life – and while that might also prevent him from entering the pantheon, it is quite clear – and Finney has stressed this often – that there is much potentially exciting work still in the offing. Morley thinks that Finney could come into his own in his late fifties and sixties, or even his seventies. Age isn't likely to wither him too rapidly. There is still a Lear or an Iago to be tackled, and then all of Ibsen and O'Neill, and much Chekhov, not to mention contemporary writers like Pinter, Hare, Shepard and even Ayckbourn, whom Finney hasn't yet begun to confront.

Olivier's mantle still remains unassigned as Finney, the most amiable of lurchers, defiantly remains ever his own man. That inscription on his father's old chalk board could as easily be interpreted as a neat summation to date of the son's own life and times: 'A Finney – Civility and Prompt Payment'.

The Credits

Theatre (in Britain and the US)

Julius Caesar (1956). Birmingham Repertory Theatre. Dir: Bernard Hepton. W: William Shakespeare. Cast: Alan Rowe (Julius Caesar), Kenneth Mackintosh (Marcus Brutus), Geoffrey Bayldon (Cassius), Geoffrey Taylor (Mark Antony), Ronald Hines (Casca), FINNEY (Decius Brutus).

Anne Boleyn (1956). Birmingham Repertory Theatre. Dir: Douglas Seale. W: Peter Albery. Cast: Charmian Eyre (Anne Boleyn), King Henry the Eighth (Ronald Hines), Bernard Hepton (Sir Thomas More), Geoffrey Taylor (Cardinal Wolsey), Colin George (Mark Smeaton), Geoffrey Bayldon (Thomas Cromwell), FINNEY (George Boleyn).

Caesar and Cleopatra (1956). Birmingham Repertory Theatre. Dir: Douglas Seale. W: George Bernard Shaw. Cast: Geoffrey Bayldon (Caesar), Doreen Aris (Cleopatra), Nancie Jackson (Ftatateeta), Alan Rowe (Apollodorus), Kenneth Mackintosh (Pothinus), FINNEY (Belzanor).

Henry V (1957). Birmingham Repertory Theatre. Dir: Douglas Seale. W: William Shakespeare. Cast: FINNEY

(Henry V), Michael Blakemore (Exeter), Bernard Hepton (Chorus), Geoffrey Bayldon (Pistol), Colin George (Fluellen), Sonia Fraser (Katherine), Kenneth Mackintosh (Charles VI), David Benson (Dauphin).

The Beaux' Stratagem (1957). Birmingham Repertory Theatre. Dir: Bernard Hepton. W: George Farquhar. Cast: FINNEY (Francis Archer), Colin George (Thomas Aimwell), Geoffrey Taylor (Squire Sullen), Elspeth Duxbury (Lady Bountiful), Paul Williamson (Boniface), Jacqueline Wilson (Cherry), Sonia Fraser (Dorinda), Nancie Jackson (Mrs Sullen).

The Lizard on the Rock (1957). Birmingham Repertory Theatre. Dir: Douglas Seale. W: John Hall. Cast: Kenneth Mackintosh (Robert Rockhart), Geoffrey Taylor (Roland), FINNEY (Malcolm), Colin George (David), Redmond Phillips (Arthur Canbery), Sonia Fraser (Ellen), Rosamunde Woodward (Arlow).

The Iron Harp (1957). Birmingham Repertory Theatre. Dir: Bernard Hepton. W: Joseph O'Conor. Cast: Colin George (Capt John Tregarthen), Sonia Fraser (Molly Kinsella), FINNEY (Michael O'Riordan), Geoffrey Taylor (Sean Kelly), Michael Blakemore (Peter Tolly), Arthur Pentelow (Shamus).

The Alchemist (1957). Birmingham Repertory Theatre. Dir: Bernard Hepton. W: Ben Jonson. Cast: FINNEY (Face), Kenneth Mackintosh (Subtle), Audrey Noble (Dol Common), Michael Blakemore (Lovewit), Paul Williamson (Pertinax Surly), Arthur Pentelow (Sir Epicure Mammon), Colin George (Ananias), Sonia Fraser (Dame Pliant).

Macbeth (1958). Birmingham Repertory Theatre. Dir: Bernard Hepton. W: William Shakespeare. Cast: FINNEY (Macbeth), June Brown (Lady Macbeth), John Carlin (Banquo), Paul Williamson (Macduff), Mark Kingston (Fleance), Peter Henchie (Duncan), Gary Hope (Malcolm), David Bell (Donalbain).

Other featured roles at Birmingham, 1956–8: *Happy As Larry* (Fourth Tailor), *The Lady's Not for Burning* (Richard), *Coriolanus* (Tullus Aufidius), *Dr Jekyll and Mr Hyde* (Police Inspector Newcomen), *The Emperor's New Clothes* (Tim Piggott), *The Slave of Truth* (An Officer), *Sganarelle* (Lélie), *Be Good, Sweet Maid* (Harry Hicks), *School* (servant, gamekeeper, cook, etc), *The Imperial Nightingale* (Bamboo).

The Party (1958). New Theatre. Dir: Charles Laughton. W: Jane Arden. Cast: Ann Lynn (Henriette Brough), Joyce Redman (Frances Brough), Charles Laughton (Richard Brough), FINNEY (Soya Marshall), Elsa Lanchester (Elsie Sharp), John Welsh (Harold Lingham).

King Lear (1959). Shakespeare Memorial Theatre. Dir: Glen Byam Shaw. W: William Shakespeare. Cast: Charles Laughton (Lear), Stephanie Bidmead (Goneril), Angela Baddeley (Regan), Zoe Caldwell (Cordelia), Robert Hardy (Edmund), Anthony Nicholls (Kent), Cyril Luckham (Gloucester), FINNEY (Edgar), Ian Holm (Fool).

Othello (1959). Shakespeare Memorial Theatre. Dir: Tony Richardson. W: William Shakespeare. Cast: Paul Robeson (Othello), Sam Wanamaker (Iago), Peter Woodthorpe (Roderigo), Paul Hardwick (Brabantio), Mary Ure (Desdemona), FINNEY (Cassio), Edward De Souza (Lodovico).

A Midsummer Night's Dream (1959). Shakespeare Memorial Theatre. Dir: Peter Hall. W: William Shakespeare. Cast: Anthony Nicholls (Theseus), Stephanie Bidmead (Hippolyta), Charles Laughton (Bottom), FINNEY (Lysander), Priscilla Morgan (Hermia), Vanessa Redgrave (Helena), Ian Holm (Puck), Robert Hardy (Oberon), Mary Ure (Titania).

Coriolanus (1959). Shakespeare Memorial Theatre. Dir: Peter Hall. W: William Shakespeare. Cast: Laurence Olivier (Coriolanus), Harry Andrews (Menenius), Edith Evans

(Volumnia), Vanessa Redgrave (Valeria), Mary Ure (Virgilia), Donald Eccles (Titus), Paul Hardwick (Cominius), Anthony Nicholls (Aufidius), FINNEY (First Roman Citizen).

The Lily White Boys (1960). Royal Court. Dir: Lindsay Anderson. W: Harry Cookson. Music: Bill Le Sage, Tony Kinsey. FINNEY (Ted), Monty Landis (Razzo), Philip Locke (Musclebound), Georgia Brown (Jeannie), Shirley Anne Field (Eth), Ann Lynn (Liz).

Billy Liar (1960). Oscar Lewenstein Plays Ltd (Cambridge Theatre). Dir: Lindsay Anderson. W: Keith Waterhouse and Willis Hall, from Waterhouse's novel. Cast: Mona Washbourne (Alice Fisher), George A. Cooper (Geoffrey Fisher), FINNEY (Billy Fisher), Trevor Bannister (Arthur Crabtree), Ethel Griffies (Florence Boothroyd), Ann Beach (Barbara), Juliet Cooke (Rita), Jennifer Jayne (Liz).

Luther (1961). Théâtre des Nations/English Stage Company (Royal Court, then Phoenix). Dir: Tony Richardson. W: John Osborne. Cast: FINNEY (Martin Luther), Bill Owen (Hans), George Devine (Staupitz), John Moffatt (Cajetan), Peter Bull (Tetzel), Charles Kay (Leo).

Twelfth Night (1962). Royal Court. Dir: George Devine. W: William Shakespeare. Cast: Julian Glover (Orsino), Corin Redgrave (Sebastian), Morris Perry (Antonio), Robert Lang (Sir Toby Belch), Charles Kay (Sir Andrew Aguecheek), Nicol Williamson (Malvolio), FINNEY (Feste), Samantha Eggar (Olivia), Lynn Redgrave (Viola).

The Birthday Party (1963). Glasgow Citizens' Theatre. Dir: FINNEY. W: Harold Pinter. Cast: Alex McCrindle (Petey), Sylvia Coleridge (Meg), Graham Crowden (Stanley), Anne Kristen (Lulu), Martin Miller (Goldberg), John Croft (McCann).

School for Scandal (1963). Glasgow Citizens' Theatre. Dir: FINNEY. W: R B Sheridan. Cast: Sylvia Coleridge (Lady Sneerwell), Robert James (Joseph Surface), Graham Crowden (Crabtree), Roddy MacMillan (Sir Oliver Surface), Anne Kristen (Lady Teazle), Eric Jones (Sir Benjamin Backbite), James Cairncross (Sir Peter Teazle).

Henry IV (1963). Glasgow Citizens' Theatre. Dir: Piers Haggard. W: Luigi Pirandello, translated by John Wardle. Cast: FINNEY (Henry IV), Eric Jones (Lolo), Peter John (Pino), Glyn Worsnip (Momo), Jon Croft (Franco), Lillias Walker (Donna Matilda), Kay Gallie (Frida), Alex McCrindle (Giovanni).

Luther (1963). St James's Theater (New York). Dir: Tony Richardson. W: John Osborne. Cast: FINNEY (Martin), Kenneth J Warren (Hans), Frank Shelly (Staupitz), Peter Bull (Tetzel), John Moffatt (Cajetan), Michael Egan (Leo).

Much Ado About Nothing (1965). National Theatre (Old Vic). Dir: Franco Zeffirelli. W: William Shakespeare. Cast: FINNEY (Don Pedro), Derek Jacobi (Don John), Ian McKellen (Claudio), Robert Stephens (Benedick), Maggie Smith (Beatrice), Lynn Redgrave (Margaret), Frank Finlay (Dogberry).

Armstrong's Last Goodnight (1965). National Theatre (Chichester Festival, then Old Vic, 1966). Dir: John Dexter, William Gaskill. W: John Arden. Cast: FINNEY (John Armstrong), Caroline John (His Wife), Ronald Pickup (King James the Fifth), Robert Stephens (Sir David Lindsay), Frank Wylie (Alexander McGlass), Geraldine McEwan (A Lady), Graham Crowden (Willie Armstrong), John Hallam (Tam Armstrong), Michael York (Archie Armstrong).

Love for Love (1965). National Theatre (Old Vic). Dir: Peter Wood. W: William Congreve. Cast: Anthony Nicholls (Sir Sampson Legend), John Stride (Valentine), FINNEY (Ben), Laurence Olivier (Tattle), Robert Lang (Scandal), Miles Malleson (Foresight), Geraldine McEwan (Angelica), Joyce Redman (Mrs Frail), Lynn Redgrave (Miss Prue).

Miss Julie/Black Comedy (1965). National Theatre

(Chichester Festival, then Old Vic, 1966). Dir: Michael Elliott, John Dexter. W: August Strindberg/Peter Shaffer. Cast for *Miss Julie*: FINNEY (Jean), Maggie Smith (Miss Julie), Jeanne Watts (Christine); for *Black Comedy*: Derek Jacobi (Brindsley Miller), Louise Purnell (Carol Melkett), Doris Hare (Miss Furnival), Graham Crowden (Colonel Melkett), FINNEY (Harold Gorringe), Paul Curran (Schuppanzigh), Maggie Smith (Clea), Ronald Pickup (George Bamberger).

A Flea in Her Ear (1966). National Theatre (Old Vic). Dir: Jacques Charon. W: Georges Feydeau, translated by John Mortimer. Cast: FINNEY (Chandebise/Poche), Robert Lang (Etienne Plucheux), Geraldine McEwan (Raymonde Chandebise), Edward Hardwicke (Edward Chandebise), John Stride (Romain Tournel), Sheila Reid (Antoinette Plucheux).

A Day in the Death of Joe Egg (1968). Brooks Atkinson Theater (New York). Dir: Michael Blakemore. W: Peter Nichols. Cast: FINNEY (Bri), Zena Walker (Sheila), Susan Alpern (Joe), Elizabeth Hubbard (Pam), John Carson (Freddie), Joan Hickson (Grace).

Alpha Beta (1972). Royal Court. Dir: Anthony Page. W: E A Whitehead. Cast: FINNEY (Mr Elliot), Rachel Roberts (Mrs Elliot).

Krapp's Last Tape (1973). Royal Court. Dir: Anthony Page. W: Samuel Beckett. Cast: FINNEY (Krapp).

The Freedom of the City (1973). Royal Court. Dir: FINNEY. W: Brian Friel. Cast: Carmel McSharry (Elizabeth Doherty), Stephen Rea (Fitzgerald), Raymond Campbell (Hegarty), Basil Dignam (The Judge), Matthew Guinness (Professor Cupley), Alex McCrindle (Dr Winbourne).

Cromwell (1973). Royal Court. Dir: Anthony Page. W: David Storey. Cast: FINNEY (O'Halloran), Alun Armstrong (Morgan), Brian Cox (Proctor), Frances Tomelty (Joan),

Colin Douglas (Chamberlain), John Barrett (Moore), Mark McManus (Matthew).

Chez Nous (1974). Memorial Enterprises (Globe Theatre). Dir: Robert Chetwyn. W: Peter Nichols. Cast: FINNEY (Phil), Denholm Elliott (Dick), Geraldine McEwan (Diana), Pat Heywood (Liz).

Loot (1975). Royal Court. Dir: FINNEY. W: Joe Orton. Cast: Arthur O'Sullivan (McLeavy), Jill Bennett (Fay), David Troughton (Hal), James Aubrey (Dennis), Philip Stone (Truscott), Michael O'Hagan (Meadows).

Hamlet (1975). National Theatre (Old Vic, then Lyttleton). Dir: Peter Hall. W: William Shakespeare. Cast: FINNEY (Hamlet), Angela Lansbury (Gertrude), Denis Quilley (Claudius), Susan Fleetwood (Ophelia), Roland Culver (Polonius), Simon Ward (Laertes), Philip Locke (Horatio).

Tamburlaine the Great (1976). National Theatre (Olivier). Dir: Peter Hall. W: Christopher Marlowe. Cast: FINNEY (Tamburlaine), Susan Fleetwood (Zenocrate), Barbara Jefford (Zabina), Denis Quilley (Bajazeth), Brian Cox (Theridamas), Oliver Cotton (Techelles), Gawn Grainger (Usumcasane).

Uncle Vanya (1977). Royal Exchange, Manchester. Dir: Michael Elliott. W: Anton Chekhov. Cast: Leo McKern (Vanya), FINNEY (Astrov), Alfred Burke (Serebryakov), Eleanor Bron (Elena), Joanna David (Sonia), Peggy Thorpe-Bates (Maria), Michael Feast (Telegin), Susan Richards (Marina).

Present Laughter (1977). Royal Exchange, Manchester. Dir: James Maxwell. W: Noël Coward. Cast: FINNEY (Gary Essendine), Diana Quick (Joanna), Lindsay Duncan (Daphne Stillington), Rosalind Knight (Miss Erikson), Eleanor Bron (Monica), Polly James (Liz Essendine).

The Passion (1977). National Theatre (Cottesloe). Dir: Bill Bryden. W: Tony Harrison, from the York Mystery Plays.

Cast: Mark McManus (Jesus), Michael Gough (John Baptist), Keith Skinner (Angel), Kenneth Cranham (Peter), Brian Glover (Cayphas), FINNEY (Annas/The Blind Man), Richard Johnson (Pontius Pilate), Edna Doré (Mary Mother), Brenda Blethyn (Mary Magdalene), Oliver Cotton (Judas).

The Country Wife (1977). National Theatre (Olivier). Dir: Peter Hall, with Stewart Trotter. W: William Wycherley. Cast: FINNEY (Mr Horner), Robin Bailey (Sir Jasper Fidget), Elizabeth Spriggs (Lady Fidget), Kenneth Cranham (Mr Harcourt), Gawn Grainger (Mr Dorilant), Ben Kingsley (Mr Sparkish), Richard Johnson (Mr Pinchwife), Susan Littler (Margery Pinchwife).

The Cherry Orchard (1978). National Theatre (Olivier). Dir: Peter Hall, with Stewart Trotter. W: Anton Chekhov, translated by Michael Frayn. Cast: FINNEY (Lopakhin), Susan Littler (Dunyasha), Ralph Richardson (Firs), Nicky Henson (Yepikhodov), Susan Fleetwood (Varya), Robert Stephens (Gayev), Patience Collier (Charlotta Ivanovna).

Macbeth (1978). National Theatre (Olivier). Dir: Peter Hall, with John Russell Brown. W: William Shakespeare. Cast: FINNEY (Macbeth), Dorothy Tutin (Lady Macbeth), Daniel Massey (Macduff), Nicholas Selby (Duncan), Nicky Henson (Malcolm), Robin Bailey (Banquo), Michael Beint (Angus).

Has 'Washington' Legs? (1978). National Theatre (Cottesloe). Dir: Geoffrey Reeve. W: Charles Wood. Cast: FINNEY (John Bean), Robert Stephens (Sir Flute Parsons), Bob Hoskins (Joe Veriato), Gawn Grainger (Wesley), Niall Toibin (Carl Dorf), Tel Stevens (Mary Jane Pendejo).

The Biko Inquest (1984). United British Artists (Riverside Studios). Dir: FINNEY. W: Jon Blair and Norman Fenton, from inquest material. Cast: FINNEY (Sydney Kentridge), Mark Dignam (Martinus Prins), John Standing (Van Rensburg), Nigel Davenport (Colonel Goosen), Michael

Gough (Professor Loubser), Edward Hardwicke (Professor Proctor), Stafford Gordon (Major Snyman).

Serjeant Musgrave's Dance (1984). United British Artists/ Triumph Apollo (Old Vic). Dir: FINNEY. W: John Arden. Cast: FINNEY (Musgrave), Max Wall (Bludgeon), Cathryn Harrison (Annie), Mark Jefferis (Private Sparky), Alun Armstrong (Private Hurst), Allan Surtees (Private Attercliffe).

Orphans (1986). Steppenwolf (Hampstead Theatre). Dir: Gary Sinise. W: Lyle Kessler. Cast: FINNEY (Harold), Kevin Anderson (Philip), Jeff Fahey (Treat).

J J Farr (1987). Robert Fox/Memorial (Phoenix). Dir: Ronald Eyre. W: Ronald Harwood. Cast: FINNEY (J J Farr), Dudley Sutton (Oliver Bude), Bob Peck (Kenneth Lowrie), Trevor Peacock (Andy Anderson), Hugh Paddick (Austin Purvis), Bernard Lloyd (Dennis Mulley).

Another Time (1989). Triumph Theatre Productions (Wyndham's). Dir: Elijah Moshinsky. W: Ronald Harwood. Cast: FINNEY (Ike Lands/Leonard Lands), Janet Suzman (Belle Lands), Sara Kestelman (Rose Salt), David de Keyser (Professor Zadok Salt), Christien Anholt (Jeremy Lands). In April/May 1991 at Steppenwolf Theater, Chicago: Dir: Ronald Harwood. Cast: FINNEY and members of Steppenwolf Theatre Company.

Reflected Glory (1992). Mark Furness Ltd (Vaudeville Theatre). Dir: Elijah Moshinsky. W: Ronald Harwood. Cast: FINNEY (Alfred Manx), Stephen Moore (Michael Manx), Nicky Henson (Derek Tewby), Stephen Greif (Robert Jaffey), Holly Wilson (Susan Davis), Katherine O'Toole (Regina Melnick), Mark Tandy (James Wiley).

Films (year of release in the UK)

The Entertainer (1960). Dist/Prod Co: British Lion/ Bryanston, Woodfall, Holly. P: Harry Saltzman. Dir: Tony

Richardson. W: John Osborne, Nigel Kneale, from Osborne's play. Cast: Laurence Olivier (Archie Rice), Brenda de Banzie (Phoebe Rice), Roger Livesey (Billy Rice), Joan Plowright (Jean Rice), Alan Bates (Frank Rice), FINNEY (Mick Rice). 96 mins.

Saturday Night and Sunday Morning (1960). Dist/Prod Co: Bryanston/Woodfall. P: Harry Saltzman, Tony Richardson. Dir: Karel Reisz. W: Alan Sillitoe, from his own novel. Cast: FINNEY (Arthur Seaton), Shirley Anne Field (Dorcas Gretton), Rachel Roberts (Brenda), Hylda Baker (Aunt Ada), Norman Rossington (Bert). 89 mins.

The Wild and the Willing (1962). Dist/Prod Co: Rank/Box-Thomas. P: Betty E Box. Dir: Ralph Thomas. W: Nicholas Phipps, Mordecai Richler, from Laurence Dobie's play *The Tinker*. Cast: Virginia Maskell (Virginia Chown), Paul Rogers (Professor Chown), Ian McShane (Harry Brown), Samantha Eggar (Josie), John Hurt (Phil), Catherine Woodville (Sarah), FINNEY (uncredited). 112 mins.

Tom Jones (1963). Dist/Prod Co: United Artists/Woodfall. P-Dir: Tony Richardson. W: John Osborne, from Henry Fielding's novel. Cast: FINNEY (Tom Jones), Susannah York (Sophie Western), Hugh Griffith (Squire Western), Edith Evans (Miss Western), Joan Greenwood (Lady Bellaston), Diane Cilento (Molly Seagrim), George Devine (Squire Allworthy), Micheal Mac Liammoir (Narrator). 128 mins.

The Victors (1963). Dist/Prod Co: Columbia/Open Road, Highroad. P-Dir-W: Carl Foreman. Cast: Vincent Edwards (Baker), FINNEY (Russian Soldier), George Hamilton (Trower), Melina Mercouri (Magda), Jeanne Moreau (French Woman), George Peppard (Chase). 175 mins.

Night Must Fall (1964). Dist/Prod Co: MGM British. P: Lawrence P Bachmann, FINNEY, Karel Reisz. Dir: Karel Reisz. W: Clive Exton, from Emlyn Williams's play. Cast: FINNEY (Danny), Susan Hampshire (Olivia Bramson),

Mona Washbourne (Mrs Bramson), Sheila Hancock (Dora), Michael Medwin (Derek). 105 mins.

Two for the Road (1967). Dist/Prod Co: Twentieth Century Fox/Stanley Donen. P-Dir: Stanley Donen. W: Frederic Raphael. Cast: Audrey Hepburn (Joanna Wallace), FINNEY (Mark Wallace), Eleanor Bron (Cathy Manchester), William Daniels (Howard Manchester), Claude Dauphin (Maurice Dalbret), Nadia Gray (Francoise Dalbret). 111 mins.

Charlie Bubbles (1967). Dist/Prod Co: Universal/Memorial Enterprises. P: Michael Medwin, George Pitcher. Dir: FINNEY. W: Shelagh Delaney. Cast: FINNEY (Charlie Bubbles), Billie Whitelaw (Lottie), Colin Blakely (Smokey Pickles), Liza Minnelli (Eliza), Richard Pearson (Account-ant). 89 mins.

The Picasso Summer (1969). Dist/Prod Co: Warner-Seven Arts/Silver Cosby Corp. P: Bruce Campbell, Wes Herschen-son. Dir: Robert S. Sallin, Serge Bourguignon. W: Ray Bradbury. Cast: FINNEY, Yvette Mimieux, Luis Miguel Dominguin, Theo Marcuse, Tutti Lemkow, Graham Stark. Unreleased theatrically; eventually shown on CBS television in 1973. 90 mins.

Scrooge (1970). Dist/Prod Co: Twentieth Century Fox/ Waterbury, Cinecenter. P: Leslie Bricusse, Robert Solo. Dir: Ronald Neame. W: Leslie Bricusse, from Dickens's novel. Cast: FINNEY (Ebenezer Scrooge), Alec Guinness (Jacob Marley), Edith Evans (Christmas Past), Kenneth More (Christmas Present), Laurence Naismith (Fezziwig), David Collings (Bob Crachit). 118 mins.

Gumshoe (1971). Dist/Prod Co: Columbia/Memorial Enter-prises. P: Michael Medwin. Dir: Stephen Frears. W: Neville Smith. Cast: FINNEY (Eddie Ginley), Billie Whitelaw (Ellen), Frank Finlay (William), Janice Rule (Mrs Blankerscoon), Carolyn Seymour (Alison Wyatt), Fulton Mackay (John Straker). 84 mins.

Murder on the Orient Express (1974). Dist/Prod Co: EMI/ GW Films. P: John Brabourne, Richard Goodwin. Dir: Sidney Lumet. W: Paul Dehn, from Agatha Christie's novel. Cast: FINNEY (Hercule Poirot), Lauren Bacall (Mrs Hubbard), Martin Balsam (Bianchi), Ingrid Bergman (Greta Ohlsson), Jacqueline Bisset (Countess Andrenyi), Jean-Pierre Cassel (Pierre Paul Michel), Sean Connery (Col Arbuthnot), John Gielgud (Beddoes), Wendy Hiller (Princess Dragomiroff), Anthony Perkins (Hector McQueen), Vanessa Redgrave (Mary Debenham), Rachel Roberts (Hildegarde Schmidt), Richard Widmark (Ratchett), Michael York (Count Andrenyi), Colin Blakely (Hardman). 131 mins.

The Adventure of Sherlock Holmes' Smarter Brother (1976). Dist/Prod Co: Twentieth Century Fox/Jouer. P: Richard Roth. Dir-W: Gene Wilder. Cast: Gene Wilder (Sigerson Holmes), Madeline Kahn (Jenny Hill), Marty Feldman (Sgt Orville Sacker), Dom DeLuise (Gambetti), Leo McKern (Professor Moriarty), FINNEY (uncredited). 91 mins.

Finney, who was visiting the set at the invitation of his chum Gene Wilder, was invited to play a member of an opera audience and speak one immortally prescient line (in view of the dire nature of the movie): 'Is this rotten or wonderfully brave?'

The Duellists (1977). Dist/Prod Co: CIC/Scott Free, Enigma. P: David Puttnam. Dir: Ridley Scott. W: Gerald Vaughan-Hughes, from Joseph Conrad's novel. Cast: Keith Carradine (Armand d'Hubert), Harvey Keitel (Gabriel Feraud), FINNEY (Fouché), Edward Fox (Colonel), Christina Raines (Adele), Diana Quick (Laura). 101 mins.

Loophole (1981). Dist/Prod Co: Brent Walker. P: Julian Holloway, David Korda. Dir: John Quested. W: Jonathan Hales, from Robert Pollock's novel. Cast: FINNEY (Mike Daniels), Martin Sheen (Stephen Booker), Susannah York

(Dinah Booker), Colin Blakely (Gardner), Jonathan Pryce (Taylor), Robert Morley (Godfrey). 105 mins.

Wolfen (1981). Dist/Prod Co: Warner/Orion, King-Hitzig. P: Rupert Hitzig. Dir: Michael Wadleigh. W: David Eyre, Michael Wadleigh, from Whitley Strieber's novel. Cast: FINNEY (Dewey Wilson), Diane Venora (Rebecca Neff), Gregory Hines (Whittington), Edward James Olmos (Eddie Holt), Tom Noonan (Ferguson), Dick O'Neill (Warren). 115 mins.

Looker (1981). Dist/Prod Co: Warner/The Ladd Company. P: Howard Jeffrey. Dir: Michael Crichton. W: Michael Crichton. Cast: FINNEY (Dr Larry Roberts), James Coburn (John Reston), Susan Dey (Cindy), Leigh Taylor-Young (Jennifer Lang), Dorian Harewood (Lt Masters), Tim Rossovich (The Moustache Man), Darryl Hickman (Dr Belfield). 94 mins.

Shoot the Moon (1982). Dist/Prod Co: MGM. P: Alan Marshall. Dir: Alan Parker. W: Bo Goldman. Cast: FINNEY (George Dunlap), Diane Keaton (Faith Dunlap), Peter Weller (Frank Henderson), Karen Allen (Sandy), Dana Hill (Sherry Dunlap), Viveka Davis (Jill Dunlap), Tracey Gold (Marianne Dunlap), Tina Yothers (Molly Dunlap). 123 mins.

Annie (1982). Dist/Prod Co: Columbia/Rastar. P: Joe Layton. Dir: John Huston. W: Carol Sobieski, from the stage play (book, Thomas Meehan, lyrics, Martin Charnin, music, Charles Strouse). Cast: FINNEY (Oliver 'Daddy' Warbucks), Carol Burnett (Miss Hannigan), Aileen Quinn (Little Orphan Annie), Ann Reinking (Grace Farrell), Bernadette Peters (Lily St Regis), Tim Curry (Rooster), Geoffrey Holder (Punjab), Edward Herrmann (FDR). 128 mins.

The Dresser (1984). Dist/Prod Co: Columbia/Dresser, Goldcrest, World Film Services. P-Dir: Peter Yates. W:

Ronald Harwood, from his own play. Cast: FINNEY (Sir), Tom Courtenay (Norman), Edward Fox (Oxenby), Zena Walker (Her Ladyship), Eileen Atkins (Madge), Michael Gough (Frank Carrington), Cathryn Harrison (Irene). 118 mins.

Under the Volcano (1984). Dist/Prod Co: Twentieth Century Fox/Ithaca, Conacine. P: Moritz Borman, Wieland Schulz-Keil. Dir: John Huston. W: Guy Gallo, from Malcolm Lowry's novel. Cast: FINNEY (Geoffrey Firmin), Jacqueline Bisset (Yvonne Firmin), Anthony Andrews (Hugh Firmin), Ignacio Lopez Tarzo (Dr Vigil), Katy Jurado (Señora Gregoria), James Villiers (Brit). 111 mins.

Orphans (1988). Dist/Prod Co: Twentieth Century Fox/ Lorimar. P-Dir: Alan J Pakula. W: Lyle Kessler, from his own play. Cast: FINNEY (Harold), Matthew Modine (Treat), Kevin Anderson (Phillip). 115 mins.

Miller's Crossing (1991). Dist/Prod Co: Twentieth Century Fox/Circle Films. P: Ethan Coen. Dir: Joel Coen. W: Joel and Ethan Coen. Cast: FINNEY (Leo), Gabriel Byrne (Tom), Marcia Gay Harden (Verna), John Turturro (Bernie), Jon Polito (Johnny Caspar), J E Freeman (The Dane). 115 mins.

The Playboys (1992). Dist/Prod Co: The Samuel Goldwyn Company/Green Umbrella Films. P: Simon Perry. Dir: Gillies Mackinnon. W: Shane Connaughton, Kerry Crabbe. Cast: FINNEY (Hegarty), Aidan Quinn (Tom), Robin Wright (Tara), Milo O'Shea (Freddie), Niamh Cusack (Brigid), Ian McElhinney (Cassidy). 105 mins.

Rich in Love (1992). Dist/Prod Co: MGM/The Zanuck Company. P: Richard Zanuck, Lili Fini Zanuck. Dir: Bruce Beresford. W: Alfred Uhry, from Josephine Humphrey's novel. Cast: FINNEY (Warren Odom), Jill Clayburgh (Helen Odom), Kathryn Erbe (Lucille Odom), Piper Laurie (Vera Oxendine), Kyle McLachlan (Billy McQueen), Suzy Amis (Rae Odom McQueen), Ethan Hawke (Wayne Frobiness).

Television (date of transmission)

She Stoops to Conquer (6 Jan 1956). Dist/Prod Co: BBC/
RADA. Dir: Edward Burnham. Dir. for TV: Dennis
Monger. W: Oliver Goldsmith. Cast: Susan Fuller (Mrs
Hardcastle), FINNEY (Mr Hardcastle), Roy Kinnear (Tony
Lumpkin), Patricia Burness (Kate Hardcastle), Geraldine
Hagan (Constance Neville). 120 mins.

The Miser (19 July 1956). Dist/Prod Co: BBC/Birmingham
Rep. Dir: Bernard Hepton. Dir. for TV: Barrie Edgar. W:
Molière, adapted by Miles Malleson. Cast: Kenneth
Mackintosh (Harpagon), Ronald Hines (Valère), Charmian
Eyre (Elise), FINNEY (Cléante), Eric Jones (La Flèche),
Doreen Aris (Mariane). 90 mins.

The Claverdon Road Job (27 Aug 1957). Dist/Prod Co:
BBC. Dir: Peter Dews. W: Willis Hall. Cast: Leslie Sands
(Police Sergeant Cargill), FINNEY (PC George Grayson),
Margaret Anderson (Mary Grayson), Joby Blanshard (PC
Sam Thompson), Alan Rothwell (Ernest Armitage), Nancie
Jackson (Mrs Armitage). 45 mins.

'. . . View Friendship and Marriage' (29 June 1958). Dist/
Prod Co: BBC. Dir: Michael Elliott. W: Evelyn Frazer.
Cast: Bessie Love (Mrs Dudley-Brown), Ralph Michael
(Capt Skinner), Newton Blick (Fred), Lally Bowers (Madame
Arlotti), Avril Elgar (Louise), FINNEY (Arnold). 90 mins.

Emergency Ward 10 (four episodes, Jan/Feb 1959). Dist/
Prod Co: ATV. Dir: Hugh Rennie. W: Rachel Grieve. Cast:
Charles Tingwell (Alan Dawson), Barbara Clegg (Jo
Buckley), FINNEY (Tom Fletcher), Diane Aubrey (Elizabeth
Fletcher), Desmond Carrington (Chris Anderson), John
Carson (Donald Latimer). 30 mins.

A Midsummer Night's Dream (1960). Dist/Prod Co: NBC.
Dir: Fletcher Markle, from Peter Hall's Stratford Centenary

production. Cast and credits as listed under Theatre. 90 mins.

Alpha Beta (1974). Dist/Prod Co: Memorial Enterprises. P: Timothy Burrill. Dir: Anthony Page. W: E A Whitehead, from his own play. Cast: FINNEY (Mr Elliot), Rachel Roberts (Mrs Elliot). 65 mins.

Forget-Me-Not-Lane (5 Nov 1975). Dist/Prod Co: BBC. P: Graeme McDonald. Dir: Alan Bridges. W: Peter Nichols. Cast: FINNEY (Frank), Gemma Jones (Ursula), Bill Fraser (Charles), Joan Newell (Amy), Robin Davies (Young Frank), Leonie Palette (Miss 1940). 110 mins.

Pope John Paul II (1984). Dist/Prod Co: Taft/Cooperman-De Paul. P: Burt Nodella. Dir: Herbert Wise. W: Christopher Knopf. Cast: FINNEY (John Paul II), Michael Crompton (young Karol Wojtyla), Alfred Burke (Wojtyla Sr), Nigel Hawthorne (Cardinal Wyszynski), Jonathan Newth (Adam Sapieha). 142 mins.

The Biko Inquest (1985). Dist/Prod Co: UBA/Embassy Communications/Transvideo. P: Cecil Clarke. Dir: FINNEY. Dir. for TV: Graham Evans. Cast and credits as listed under Theatre. 102 mins.

The Endless Game (1989). Dist/Prod Co: TVS Films/Reteitalia/Pixit. P: Fernando Ghia. Dir: Bryan Forbes. W: Bryan Forbes, from his own novel. Cast: FINNEY (Hillsden), George Segal (Miller), Kristin Scott Thomas (Caroline), Ian Holm (Control), Sir Anthony Quayle (Glanville), Derek De Lint (Arbamov). Two × 90 mins.

The Image (1990). Dist/Prod Co: HBO/Citadel Entertainment. P: Ron Roth. Dir: Peter Werner. W: Brian Rehak. Cast: FINNEY (Jason Cromwell), John Mahoney (Irv Mickelson), Kathy Baker (Marcie Guilford), Swoosie Kurtz (Joanne Winslow-Darvish), Spalding Gray (Frank Goodrich), Marsha Mason (Jean Cromwell). 102 mins.

The Green Man (1990). Dist/Prod Co: BBC. P: David Snodin. Dir: Elijah Moshinsky. W: Malcolm Bradbury, from Kingsley Amis's novel. Cast: FINNEY (Maurice Allington), Michael Hordern (Gramps), Linda Marlowe (Joyce), Sarah Berger (Diana), Nicky Henson (Jack), Josie Lawrence (Lucy). Three × 50 mins.

Select Bibliography

Sally Beauman, *The Royal Shakespeare Company: A History of Ten Decades*, Oxford University Press, 1982

Ivan Butler, *The Making of Feature Films: A Guide*, Pelican, 1971

— *Cinema in Britain: An Illustrated Guide*, Barnes-Tantivy, 1973

Simon Callow, *Charles Laughton: A Difficult Actor*, Methuen, 1987

Michael Coveney, *The Citz: 21 Years of the Glasgow Citizens' Theatre*, Nick Hern Books, 1990

Brian Cox, *Salem to Moscow: An Actor's Odyssey*, Methuen, 1991

Jake Eberts and Terry Ilott, *My Indecision Is Final: The Rise and Fall of Goldcrest Films*, Faber, 1990

John Elsom, *Post-War British Theatre*, Routledge & Kegan Paul, 1976

Face to Face with John Freeman, BBC, 1989

Boris Ford (ed.), *The New Pelican Guide to English Literature: Vol. 8*, Pelican, 1983

Tony Flynn, *Hanky Park*, Neil Richardson, 1990

John Goodwin (ed.), *Peter Hall's Diaries: The Story of a Dramatic Battle*, Hamish Hamilton, 1983

Lew Grade, *Still Dancing*, Collins, 1987

Trevor R Griffiths and Carole Woddis, *Theatre Guide*, Bloomsbury, 1988

Lawrence Grobel, *The Hustons*, Scribners, 1989

Otis L Guernsey, *Curtain Times: The New York Theater 1965–1987*, Applause, 1988

Alec Guinness, *Blessings in Disguise*, Fontana, 1985

Peter Haining, *Agatha Christie: Murder in Four Acts*, Virgin, 1990

Charles Higham, *Charles Laughton*, W H Allen, 1976

Pauline Kael, *Going Steady*, Temple Smith, 1971

— *5001 Nights at the Movies*, Elm Tree Books, 1982

— *State of the Art: Film Writings 1983–85*, Arena, 1987

Stanley Kauffmann, *A World on Film*, Delta, 1966

Walter Lassally, *Itinerant Cameraman*, John Murray, 1987

T E Lawrence, *Seven Pillars of Wisdom*, Jonathan Cape, 1926

Jonathan Moor, *Diane Keaton*, Robson Books, 1990

Peter Nichols, *Feeling You're Behind*, Weidenfeld & Nicolson, 1984

Laurence Olivier, *Confessions of an Actor*, Sceptre, 1982

Shakespeare Memorial Theatre 1957–59, Reinhardt, 1959

Stephen M Silverman, *David Lean*, André Deutsch, 1989

Andrew Sinclair, *Spiegel: The Man Behind the Pictures*, Weidenfeld & Nicolson, 1987

John Trevelyan, *What the Censor Saw*, Michael Joseph, 1973

J C Trewin, *The Birmingham Repertory Theatre: 1913–1963*, Barrie & Rockliff, 1963

Kathleen Tynan, *The Life of Kenneth Tynan*, Methuen, 1987

Kenneth Tynan, *Curtains: A Critic's View of Plays, Players and Theatrical Events 1950–1960*, Longmans, 1961

— *Tynan Right and Left*, Atheneum, 1967

Alexander Walker, *National Heroes: British Cinema in the Seventies and Eighties*, Harrap, 1985

Nicholas Wapshott, *Peter O'Toole*, New English Library, 1983

Ian Woodward, *Audrey Hepburn*, W H Allen, 1984

Index

Stage productions are indicated by the inclusion of the playwright's name in brackets after the name of the work